Tina Turner

Tina Turner

BREAK EVERY RULE

MARK BEGO

Taylor Trade publishing
ocm52387963
Lanham   New York   Toronto   Oxford

Published by Taylor Trade Publishing
An imprint of The Rowman & Littlefield Publishing Group, Inc.
4501 Forbes Boulevard, Suite 200
Lanham, Maryland 20706

Distributed by National Book Network

Library of Congress Cataloging-in-Publication Data
Bego, Mark.
    Tina Turner : break every rule / Mark Bego.— 1st Taylor Trade
Pub.ed.
        p.   cm.
    Includes bibliographical references (p. 254) and index.
    ISBN 1-58979-020-0 (alk. paper)
    1. Turner, Tina. 2. Rock musicians—United States—Biography.
I.Title.
    ML420.T95 B44 2003
    782.42166'092—dc21

                                                    2003012643

♾ The paper used in this publication meets the minimum requirements of American
National Standard for Information Sciences—Permanence of Paper for Printed
Library Materials, ANSI/NISO Z39.48–1992.

Manufactured in the United States of America.

books by mark bego

The Captain & Tennille (1977)

Barry Manilow (1977)

The Doobie Brothers (1980)

Michael! [Jackson] (1984)

On The Road with Michael! [Jackson] (1984)

Madonna! (1985)

Rock Hudson Public & Private (1986)

Sade! (1986)

Julian Lennon! (1986)

The Best of "Modern Screen" (1986)

Whitney! [Houston] (1986)

Cher! (1986)

Bette Midler: Outrageously Divine (1987)

The Linda Gray Story (1988)

TV Rock (1988)

Between the Lines [with Debbie Gibson] (1990)

Linda Ronstadt: It's So Easy (1990)

Ice Ice Ice: The Extraordinary Vanilla Ice Story (1991)

One Is the Loneliest Number [with Jimmy Greenspoon of
Three Dog Night] (1991)

Madonna: Blonde Ambition (1992)

contents

To Isiah James,
Thank you for introducing me to the Buddhist way of
focusing and finding mental serenity.
"Nam-myoho-renge-kyo."

acknowledgments

The author would like to thank the following people for their help and encouragement with this book:

Anne Bego
Robert and Mary Bego
Angela Bowie
Rick Colarelli
Hector DeJean
Michael Dorr
Jan Kalajian
John Klinger
Charles Moniz
Ross Plotkin
Tony Seidl
Barbara Shelley
Andy Skurow
Beth Wernick

prologue

THE QUEEN OF ROCK & ROLL

Sometimes you just have to wonder about life: what's *luck* got to do with it?

Occasionally it plays a big part. During the 1980s, how lucky I was to have lived in an apartment on East 11th Street and Broadway in New York City. At that time, the nightclub known as The Ritz was just down the street, a block and a half from me. It was literally my neighborhood rock club! I even worked there once, as a publicist when The Who presented a huge satellite concert special, and threw a viewing party from the club.

I remember how thrilled I was to find that the incomparable Tina Turner was to headline The Ritz in 1983. She had just scored a huge hit in England with the song "Let's Stay Together," and New York radio station WBLS was playing it constantly. I loved the song so much that I specifically went on a quest to buy the twelve-inch vinyl import single of the British hit. It was a great song, and I especially loved the photo of Tina and her sexy dancers on it. I had been in love with her 1975 *Acid Queen* album, and her hot versions of songs by The Rolling

Stones, The Who, and Led Zeppelin. I remember thinking even then, "Tina Turner was born to sing rock & roll."

I immediately made plans to catch Tina's new club act at The Ritz. That night, there was such anticipation in the crowd. How would Tina look? Would she sound fabulous—like she did on this new import single? At The Ritz, there was no reserved seating, so once the lights dimmed for the show to start, everyone was sure to jam their way up to the stage. Knowing this, I got myself a cocktail and immediately went to a place about six feet from the edge of the stage, unwilling to relinquish my ideal spot on the floor.

I remember distinctly—as the sound of the music started and a gasp of delight came from the crowd—the moment Tina made her entrance. She was energetically breathtaking in her black leather miniskirt, and she looked genuinely thrilled by the crowd that had assembled for her big New York City return. I will never forget seeing Tina and her dancers moving to the song "Let's Stay Together" that night, and the thrill I got from her high-wattage performance.

Then, in 2000, I found myself living in Los Angeles and working for a publishing company. It was again sheer luck that a day before Tina's December 6 appearance at Arrowhead Pond in Anaheim, California, I ended up with a ticket for the show. I had attended one of Tina Turner's comeback shows at The Ritz in the 1980s, and now I was going to be present for the final show of her sold-out "farewell" *Twenty Four Seven* concert. It was another unforgettable night!

When the opportunity came along for me to write this book, I immediately agreed. So much more had happened to Tina since her own book and since the release of her subsequent biographical film. Again I felt lucky to have the chance to tell her entire seven-decade story.

Tina not only is a fabulous singer, dancer, actress, and performer—she is also an incredible inspiration. I am fortunate to have been present for two of the most important concert appearances in her career, and I have been happy, lucky, and excited to have had the opportunity to tell her story—all of it—in this book. Tina Turner is someone who has never given up on her dreams. She truly is the Queen of Rock & Roll!

introduction

SHE'S GOT LEGS

It is Wednesday, December 6, 2000, in Anaheim, California. Tonight, the massive indoor arena, Arrowhead Pond, is filled to capacity with 18,000 cheering fans of all ages. It is the last night of what is being billed as the final stadium tour of the legendary Tina Turner. The worldwide concert tour, like her latest album, is named *Twenty Four Seven*. It is aptly entitled, as Tina Turner is someone who succeeds at being one of the sexiest women on the planet—*twenty-four* hours a day, *seven* days a week.

Another rock & roll legend, Joe Cocker, has just finished his own blistering warm-up set of rock & roll hits. However, the crowd has come here tonight to witness, experience, and pay homage to the one person who is acknowledged as "the hardest working woman in rock & roll"—the one and only Tina Turner!

David Bowie once stated that whenever Tina is on stage it is "the hottest place in the universe." And tonight she is about to prove that 100 percent accurate.

Finally the intermission between acts comes to a close and the stadium lights begin to dim. Resounding screams of delight and anticipation emit from the crowd as the houselights fade to black and the music begins to play. As the stadium plunges into darkness, the resonant and distinctive voice of James Earl Jones is heard over the loudspeakers announcing, "Work like you don't need a thing. Love like you've never been hurt. Dance like no one is watching. Ladies and gentlemen: Tina Turner."

The curtains part to reveal a three-tiered stage setup of rampways and staircases. On the second level of the stage stands Tina Turner—looking larger than life—surrounded by her sleek troupe of five dancing girls. The red-hot touring band she has, led by rocker John Miles, explodes into the opening notes of the song "I Want to Take You Higher." There is the diva herself—twenty feet above the stage floor, repeating the word "higher!" as though that is the stratosphere she is about to take all 18,000 awe-struck spectators that night.

Dressed in skin-tight pantsuit of knickers and a bustier in black vinyl and steel chains, she is immaculate. Her shoulderless top reveals her perfect café au lait skin and her trim and toned body. As she launches into the song, she looks like she has the body of a thirty-five-year-old—yet she has just turned sixty-one the week before. She is wearing her trademark black high heels, shoes in which she smoothly struts back and forth across the stage with skilled agility.

As she launches into the verses of the party anthem of a song, which she recorded in the 1970s, she is in her element. A broad smile beams across her face as the crowd lets out an excited gasp in unison. Throughout the evening she makes the most of the multilevel labyrinth of platforms and staircases on stage. The action doesn't cease for the next two hours. Dancing her way down to the main stage floor, she never misses a step of the intricate choreography that takes her five female dancers through their paces.

From her first minutes on stage, there is no question that

Tina Turner is the star of the night. All eyes are on her, and she radiates a genuine warmth and excitement every minute that she is in the spotlight. Tonight's songbook is a time-warping cavalcade of Tina's past and present—including "A Fool in Love" and "Proud Mary" from her days as half of Ike & Tina Turner. It features her hits from her movie career "Acid Queen" and "We Don't Need Another Hero." It salutes her phenomenal mid-1980s comeback with "Private Dancer" and "What's Love Got to Do With It." And it highlights songs from her latest album, including "Absolutely Nothing's Changed" and "Twenty Four Seven."

More than just a concert, tonight's show is a thrilling rock & roll circus of exciting staging, flashy lighting effects, stunning song performances, and several staged surprises. One of the most dramatic numbers comes on Tina's interpretation of the Motown classic "I Heard It through the Grapevine." The huge stage set of platforms splits apart to reveal a simulated wall of flames on huge projection screens. Out prances Tina and her dancers, all clad in studded black vinyl like a gang of tough biker chicks on the prowl. And it's the feisty Ms. Turner who is the leader of the pack.

At the end of "We Don't Need Another Hero," the platform she is standing on suddenly breaks loose from the second story of the set, and she descends to the stage floor on a contraption suspended in mid-air. As she reaches the stage floor, the pyrotechnics blaze in an explosively dramatic flourish of flames and light.

While singing "Nutbush City Limits" in a sexy white fringe-covered pantsuit, Tina dances down a walkway to what looks like a little cage of waist-high railing. All of a sudden the entire fifty-foot walkway swings outward to extend over the heads of the first three-dozen rows of audience members. Now she isn't just the life of the party, she is hovering twenty feet above it!

The crowd roars with excitement. While continuing to sing the song, she dances her way down the neck of the gang-plank toward the stage, without a railing, in dangerously high-heeled pumps! This stunt isn't for divas who are afraid of heights. But then, Tina Turner is someone who has lived much of her life at dangerous elevations. The woman is simply invincible! Rock stars a quarter of her age can't compete with her.

It isn't just about singing sizzling rocking songs with passion, or the amount energy expelled on dance numbers, or all of the exhilarating lighting effects. There is something much more that comes from this rock & roll diva on stage. She exudes heart, spirit, and sincerity. Tina Turner never, ever does things nice and easy. She does them nice and rough, and that's the way her fans love it—and they love her for it. For six decades she has been astounding audiences around the world. This is a night that no one present wants to see come to an end. Tonight isn't just the end of a concert, it is the end of an era in rock spectaculars.

There is no one in the world of show business quite like Tina Turner. Yes, there have been other women in the music world whose careers have had great longevity. But few have matched the wattage, the vitality, and sheer excitement that Tina creates.

There have been other women with public careers who have overcome adversity and tragedy in their lives. Yet, somehow Tina has walked away from her oppressive and degrading life with Ike Turner with such dignity and spirituality that she has become an inspiration for others.

In the 1960s and 1970s Tina Turner, along with her then-husband Ike, had become rhythm & blues and rock & roll legends. Their string of hits included "It's Gonna Work Out Fine," "River Deep-Mountain High," and "I Idolize You." They were famous in music circles because of their extensive club tours across the globe. They were also elevated to rock superstardom, largely due to their extensive touring as the opening act for The Rolling Stones. It was acknowledged that Tina was the dynamic star of the show, and that it was Ike who was the genius behind the act. It was also highly publicized that they were happily married and loved each other deeply.

If you were to believe Tina's 1970s song repertoire like Ike's composition "Contact High," or if you were to see Tina as the substance abuse guru "Acid Queen" in the film *Tommy*, and take it at face value, you might think that she was a drug use proponent or that she was a wild party girl.

If you were to hear her convincingly singing the songs "Fool for You," "Poor Fool," and "It's Gonna Work Out Fine," you would believe that these were odes of love from Tina to her devoted husband, Ike. If you were to catch Ike & Tina Turner's act in the early 1970s, while they were performing the song "I've Been Loving You Too Long," in which Tina mimicked fellatio on her phallic-shaped microphone, you might have the impression that she was some sort of uninhibited sex goddess.

On stage every night she whirled, twirled, and performed fast-paced kinetic dance steps that made audience members' heads spin. She expelled so much energy, she appeared to be the epitome of a woman who was totally liberated and in the throes of a joyful life of stardom and excitement.

However, nothing could be further from the truth. None of these images were based in reality. According to her, "Tina Turner—that woman who went out on stage—she was somebody else. I was like a shadow" (1). By 1976, the real Tina was trapped in a marriage that made her life a living hell. Her life onstage was an act, and her life offstage had become torture.

The drugs and the partying? That was Ike's life. Tina never

did recreational drugs of any sort, and wanted nothing to do with them.

As far as her marriage was concerned, it was a sham. Ike was never faithful to her. On more than one occasion, she had walked into her own living room only to find a woman on her knees performing oral sex on him.

Her happy and joyful life? Nothing could be further from the existence in which she found herself trapped. Not only did Ike treat her like his hired hand, expected to come whenever called, when she displeased him or complained, Ike would beat her mercilessly. As time went on, and Ike's rampant drug use escalated, so did his physical tirades. No one—except those closest to them—knew that, in reality, Ike controlled Tina with intimidation and fear.

Tina had become an expert at applying pancake makeup to her blackened eyes. She regularly performed to cheering crowds with split lips, bruises, and even broken bones. She felt so alone and trapped that even her desperate attempt at suicide failed her.

Then a friend introduced her to something that gave her inner strength and encouraged her to stand up for herself: Buddhism. Awakened to the spirituality and life-force within her, she was able to chant and to look within her own soul to surmount the courage to leave Ike.

When she finally made up her mind to leave Ike in 1976, there was no turning back. It wasn't an easy fight. At first it was a physical battle, then a legal battle. She soon learned that she was not alone, that she did have friends to help her. Cher encouraged her by telling her how she had reclaimed her own life by leaving her then-husband, Sonny Bono. Ann-Margret—her co-star in the film *Tommy*—helped her mount her own post-Ike solo act. And through Olivia Newton-John, she met the manager who would help her break through to superstardom and realize her own career dreams.

Her road to resurrection was not an easy one, but she relished the climb and the freedom. After a brief incarnation as a glitzy Las Vegas creation, she gravitated toward the music that she truly loved: rock & roll. In 1984, when she released her incredible watershed album and the head-turning hit "What's Love Got to Do With It," audiences around the world delighted to the sassy self-confidence Tina's voice exuded. Every song on her *Private Dancer* album seemed to reshape her image. "I Might Have Been Queen" glorified her strong beliefs about faith, destiny, and reincarnation. "Show Some Respect" and "Better Be Good to Me," were musical testimonies to her strength and determination. And, her version of David Bowie's "1984" staked her claim to that very year. It was that year that she was acknowledged as the rock world's reigning diva.

At the height of Tina's "What's Love Got to Do With It" comeback, she looked twenty years in the future and said in her forties, "There is no way a sixty-year-old woman can look the way I look." (2) Now, in her sixties, she looks exactly the same as she did in her forties. On stage and in person, she is still equally as sexy and as energetic as she was back in the 1960s when she wowed audiences on TV shows like *American Bandstand*, *Top of the Pops*, and *Shindig*. In 2000, when she headlined a global rock concert tour at the age of sixty, it was ranked as the top-grossing concert attraction of the entire year, taking in more than $80 million!

Once her solo star rose, Tina sang only songs of strength and empowerment. And what songs she has chosen to bring to life—"Break Every Rule," "The Best," "Steamy Windows," "Look Me in the Heart," "We Don't Need Another Hero," "Whatever You Need," and "Absolutely Nothing's Changed," to name a few.

In the mid-1980s, fans still didn't grasp why she left Ike. Tired of being asked to talk about him in interviews, she penned her 1986 autobiography, *I, Tina*, just to set the record straight. In 1993 the book became the basis of an Academy Award–nominated hit film, *What's Love Got to Do With It?*

Although her revealing book and the film about her life took Tina's fascinating story up to her 1984 comeback, so much has happened in Tina's life since then. She elevated herself from a nightclub attraction to an incredible stadium-filling international superstar. She swept the Grammy Awards in 1985 and has gone on to release several hit solo singles and albums. She has continued to pursue her acting career, was inducted into the Rock & Roll Hall of Fame, has sold millions of records, found true love, moved to Europe, and she now lives a truly glamorous and harmonious life in the south of France with the man of her dreams. Even though she billed her *Twenty Four Seven* concert tour as her final stadium style show, her adoring public realizes that there is still much more to come.

With all that the general public knows about Tina's fascinating life—through her music, her book, and the film about her life—her real story is really so much deeper and more complicated than a two-hour movie could possibly depict.

Looking back it is hard to believe that she grew up feeling like she never truly belonged anywhere. Few people realize that her life is much more complex than just being trapped in a dysfunctional marriage, finding freedom, and suddenly becoming a rock legend.

A strong believer in psychics and astrology, she was once told that she was destined to become amongst the biggest stars in show business, while Ike's career would wither and fall. At the height of her newfound fame, Ike was arrested and put in prison. After serving time behind bars, in 1999 Ike Turner attempted to clear his reputation in his own autobiography,

Takin' Back My Name. The plan backfired. Not only did he not deny that he relentlessly beat Tina, he tried to make it sound like it was her fault for driving him to it.

Soothsayers also told her something that she had suspected all of her life—that she was born unwanted by her mother. Confronting her mother, Zelma Bullock, toward the end of Zelma's life confirmed that fact to Tina once and for all. What she lacked in receiving maternal love, she has made up for both in her personal and professional life. Today, in the twenty-first century, she is one of the most beloved women in show business.

Tina's life continues to be an amazing saga of strength and survival. She laughs at her own legacy, "Nobody had a life like mine—not even Joan Collins!" (1)

With all that she has lived through and all that she has triumphantly survived, there are still several illusions about her. One of the main ones is that she is a tall and imposing woman. In reality, she stands only five feet, four inches tall, and weighs 125 pounds. And, what a remarkable body it is—acknowledged as belonging to one of the most beautiful and admired women on the planet.

With all of the Platinum records, sold-out shows, and accolades, Tina Turner still looks at herself as a work-in-progress. "People all over the world keep asking me when I'm going to slow down, but I'm just getting started!" (1)

What makes Tina Turner tick? How has she escaped from a life that would have consumed most people? What role did Mick Jagger, David Bowie, Keith Richards, and Rod Stewart play in her triumphant resurrection? How often did Ike Turner actually physically beat her, and what is their relationship like to this day? And, in her life, what *does* love—or the lack of it—really have to do with it? These are all questions that her public longs to hear. When Tina sings in the song that she "never,

ever" does anything "nice and easy," she means it. She took the hard road and, in the end, went from "victim" to "victor."

Hers is a life in which she broke every rule—and ultimately carved out a spot in the world that is uniquely all her own. She is the one and the only Tina Turner. To fully understand this legend, one has to go way back. Back to a tiny town of Nutbush, Tennessee. That's where the legend all began.

I

NUTBUSH CITY LIMITS

About fifty miles northeast of Memphis, Tennessee, and about twenty miles from the Mississippi River, on the Arkansas border, is a small town on Highway I-19. It's located in the middle of the cotton fields. There's a little dry goods store there called Gause's, which has a gasoline pump out front to attract motorists—and not much else. As Tina Turner was later to immortalize the tiny town in her song "Nutbush City Limits," there wasn't much more there than a church house, a gin house, a schoolhouse, and an outhouse. It was the land of cotton gins and whiskey stills. It hardly seems like the worthy birthplace of a rock & roll legend, but it is where Tina Turner came from. To say she put Nutbush on the map is a bit of a stretch, since you practically have to take a magnifying glass to find it on a roadmap.

Humble as it is, that's where Tina grew up. Her debut to the world took place on November 26, 1939, in the basement of Haywood Hospital—ten miles away from Nutbush—in the nearby town of Brownsville.

Her father, Floyd Richard Bullock, whom everyone called "Richard," was a deacon at the Woodlawn Baptist Church. He lived with his wife and their three-year-old daughter Alline, in a four room wooden "shotgun" house. Also in the household was four-year-old Evelyn, his wife Zelma's other daughter, by a former boyfriend. Richard worked as an "overseer" on the Poindexter farm, upon whose land their little house sat. He would supervise the workers for the white owners of the farm.

Tina's mother, Zelma Bullock, was part black and part Native American. Zelma's father was three-quarters Navajo, although that particular area of Tennessee was predominantly Cherokee land. Zelma's mother was three-quarters Cherokee. They were both only one-quarter black.

By all reports, Zelma was less than excited when she discovered she was expecting another child. She was a frustrated young woman who was not at all happy at the prospect of having another mouth to feed.

The baby, who would grow up to be known the world over as "Tina Turner," was born Anna Mae Bullock. Anna Mae grew up in a world with lots of other children and family members around her. Nearby were her grandparents on her mother's side, Josephus and Georgiana, from whom she got her unmistakable American Indian features.

Richard's parents, Alex and Roxanna Bullock, lived off of Highway 19 with Anna's uncle, Gill. He was the only one of the Bullock's seven children who still remained at home. Also in the household were two of their grandchildren, Margaret and Joe Melvin Currie. Their father, Richard's brother, Joe Sam, was recently widowed and could not raise them on his own. Margaret was to become Anna's favorite cousin, as well as a cherished friend.

The Bullock's tiny house was not far from the brick house of their white employers, Ruby and Vollye Poindexter. The Poindexters were quite friendly with the Bullocks. Ruby loved Zelma's egg custard pies, and they felt more like relatives than having an employer/employee relationship. Anna Mae recalls the "easy" affection that the Poindexters seemed to have toward each other. She was also mystified at the warmth and obvious love that existed between the inhabitants of both of her grandparents' houses. It was something that was somehow missing in her home. Instead, the prevailing tone at the home of her parents was that of disharmony, arguing, and emotional coldness. At an early age, Anna Mae learned to look within herself for peace. The sense of feeling alone in one's own home was a part of Anna's existence for much of her early life.

Did Zelma love her youngest daughter, Anna? According to grown-up Tina, "She didn't. I wasn't wanted. When she was pregnant with me, she was leaving my father. She was a very young woman who didn't want another kid" (3).

Were they ever close at any time in her life? "Never," claims Tina. "Even when I was a girl I knew she didn't love me. When I was very young, I wondered why we weren't close, but I was always a loner, and then I became independent and didn't care anymore" (3). Still, Anna loved her and hoped that one day Zelma would grow to love her back. "My mother wasn't mean to me, but she wasn't warm, she wasn't close" (4).

As she explains it, "My mother was not a woman who wanted children. She wasn't a *mother* mother. She was a woman who bore children" (5). Still, as a child, Anna did find things in life to make herself happy. She spent much time alone and found ways to pass time by wandering through the fields of Tennessee.

Likewise, she never felt love from her father either. She could tell that he didn't want her around. Little Anna was a painful reminder to him that he was in a marriage that was very unhappy. She distinctly remembers her mother and father fighting with each other. There were also whispers in the community that Anna was not really Richard's child. Prior to Anna's birth, Richard's sister, Martha Mae, and her husband lived with Richard and Zelma. Apparently, Martha Mae was carrying on with another man while residing there. Because of this, there were those who believed that it was actually Zelma who was having an extramarital affair, and that Anna was the by-product of it. True or not, these rumors did not help matters.

The love she did receive within the house came from her sister Alline, whom Anna always loved. As long as Alline was around, she was happy to be in her company. However, Anna felt that Alline was "slow" and "quiet," while Anna loved to run through the fields and play with the farm animals.

In spite of the relatively loveless household, by local standards, the Bullock family had much to be thankful for. Tina recalls seeing the homes of some of the other local black families' houses full of children, with dirty and worn-out mattresses to sleep on, and the smell of filth. "I knew we weren't poor," she was to later remember about life in her parents' home (1).

The Bullock's house was clean and organized, and she grew up knowing what it was like to have your surroundings harmonious and in order. According to her, "We always had nice furniture, and our house was always nice. We had our own separate bedroom and a dining room, and we had pigs and animals. I knew the people who didn't, so I knew the difference, and we weren't poor" (6).

Living on a farm, Tina fondly remembers the hearty farmer's diet she grew up eating. Lots of pork and fresh vegetables were part of every meal. Breakfast would consist of salted pork with biscuits and syrup. The personal garden of the Bullock family yielded onions, tomatoes, turnips, sweet potatoes, cabbages, and watermelons. There were plenty of chickens for eggs, and fresh milk came from their own cows. There were also local ponds where perch were caught in the spring, summer, and fall. In the winter there wouldn't be any fresh pork, but there were plenty of pork sausages that had been made and stored in the autumn.

In 1942, Richard and Zelma began to get restless to leave the farm. There were jobs to be found hundreds of miles away in the big city of Knoxville, Tennessee. There were construction jobs for Richard, and Zelma could make good money cleaning people's houses. It was decided that Anna and Alline were to go live with their grandparents. Alline got to live with Grandma Georgie, and Anna was assigned to live with Grandma Roxanna and Grandpa Alex, who had a major drinking problem. Anna was jealous because she too wanted to live with Grandma Georgie and her two cousins, Margaret and Joe Melvin.

Tina remembers her first childhood musical exposure. Grandma Roxanna would drag her off to church every Sunday morning. Once there, she heard the music of the gospel choir. She also heard fabulous gospel singers on the radio. When asked who her first musical influences were, she replies, "Well, it was a church person in the early days, Mahalia Jackson. And Rosette Tharpe. These spiritual, very strong voices. I only knew that they were figures in the black race, recognizable and respected. But I must admit, I've always covered the songs of males. I haven't followed up on women or listened to that much women's music" (7).

Tina recalls being brought up as "a country girl" (1). For a child who wanted to lose herself in her surroundings, life on a farm in Nutbush had its advantages. "Listen, roaming the pastures of Tennessee, it was green and beautiful. You could never find me. I was always out there. I was in the universe, you know. It was wonderful. I would sit there and eat tomatoes off the vine and burst open a watermelon and eat it. I know what things are supposed to taste like. The life wasn't so bad. I was taken care of, but there was a hand, and eye, watching over me" (8).

Growing up, she had a very strong negative impression of what her own body was like: tall, gangly, and awkward. According to Tina, "I hated my body. I had a short neck and torso, and all legs" (9).

Little did she know at the time that one day this "ugly" duckling would grow up to be a beautiful and admired swan of a woman. "My body is an unusual one," she proclaims. "It's a very strong body. A body that I at one time didn't like. . . . I looked like a little pony when I was a girl. These long legs— nothing worked together" (8).

During this same era, Anna's Uncle Gill got in trouble with the law. It seems that there was some kind of dispute over a woman, and Gill took a shotgun and killed the other man in this love triangle. He was hauled off to prison, and it was a local scandal in Nutbush.

The second summer that Richard and Zelma were in Knoxville, Anna and Alline came to live with them. Anna was absolutely fascinated with the big city of Knoxville. The streets were paved, the houses were brick, and there was so much excitement. Occasionally, when Zelma took Anna shopping, Anna would sing songs for the sales ladies. To reward her for her singing, the ladies gave Anna pennies or nickels to show their appreciation. Little did those women know at the time, but they were being treated to the very first Tina Turner concert performances!

According to her, "I remember singing some of the McGuire Sisters' songs. I had a little bank that I collected all these shiny coins in, and it was taken from me, and I was really broken-hearted. That makes me remember how long I have really been singing. But I had no voice training" (10).

While Richard and Zelma were at work during the day, Anna and Alline were left in the care of Mrs. Blake, the woman the Bullocks boarded with in Knoxville. Anna remembers going to the Pentecostal church with Mrs. Blake and hearing for the first time the vibrantly "sanctified" services at the church, the jubilant singing, hand clapping, and dancing in the aisles that happened when people felt the word of God. One time little Anna danced so hard at church, her underpants fell down to her ankles.

Anna wasn't quite certain why these people were jumping around and dancing like there was no tomorrow, but she liked it. She recalls, "It was wild. I didn't know what it was about. I just thought, they must be really happy!" (1)

Before long, the summer came to an end, and Anna and Alline went back to Nutbush, living with their respective grandparents. Eventually, Richard and Zelma also returned to the Nutbush area because their jobs in Knoxville had been phased out, when the nation's attention was suddenly turned toward the U.S. entry into World War II.

Reunited, the Bullock family settled in Flagg Grove, not far from Nutbush. Anna didn't see her cherished cousins Margaret and Joe Melvin as much as she used to when they lived closer. However, she got to see them on the weekends. That was when the Curries and the Bullocks would join their friends in nearby Ripley, in an area fondly referred to as "The Hole." In actuality, "The Hole" was a strip of rib restaurants and taverns down a cobblestone alley off of Washington Street. Anna and Alline and her cousins would be given money to go to the movies while the adults played.

Anna found the atmosphere in "The Hole" fascinating. She recalls that, "It always seemed to me that there was sex in the air down there in 'The Hole.' It wasn't far from the theater we went to" (4).

Around 10 P.M. the movie would be over, and the kids would go back to retrieve the adults. Their parents however, were never quite ready to end their evening. Tina remembers being in "The Hole" when she was about nine years old. She would be dressed in her flat shoes and her little cotton dress. Although it was predominantly a black area of town, there would also be white people there, looking on in fascination at all the fun and the revelry that would be going on. Occasionally she would witness fights in the street or in the juke joints where her parents were.

Anna Mae was fascinated by all of the women who would be dressed up for a Saturday night on the town. They wore exotic two-toned high-heeled shoes, tight skirts, and tailored suits. She would also see into the steamy windows of parked cars, where adults were clearly up to something sexual. She found "The Hole" to be both dangerous and wonderfully fascinating at the same time.

She also looked forward to going to the movies. Even as a child in Tennessee, young Anna dreamed of one day growing up to have a show business career. Seeing films at the local theaters instilled her with a new set of daydreams. "When I was small, I wanted to act. I would go to the movies and come home and act them out for my parents," she remembers (11).

Zelma was later to recall of her daughter Anna that she would leave the movies singing the songs she had heard performed on the screen. According to her mother, Anna had a strong and clear singing voice even at that early age.

Anna was asked to join the local church choir once word got around that she could really sing. Here was this skinny little girl with a strong and distinctive voice. She loved singing the songs, and whenever there was a really upbeat song, she occasionally sang the lead vocal part. At the age of nine or ten, she was already a headliner!

As a child, she would also be called upon to help out in the fields at harvest time. The local farmers would hire all the children to pick cotton and strawberries when each of these crops were in season. Picking strawberries was a lot of fun, and you could eat them right off the plant. However, cotton was another story. According to Tina, "I hated the cotton because I didn't like the spiders and the worms in it. I was very afraid of the— the insects. And I couldn't ever really pack my sack like everybody else's. I couldn't get that much in it, so I wasn't happy with my performance, actually, and I was really happy when it was over with. But there were other things that I did like, like picking strawberries and, like, the orchards" (12).

Tina still remembers community picnics in the summer months, where there would be freshly baked fruit pies, hot barbecue, and lemonade. Often the music would be provided by local musical legends like Bootsy Whitelaw, who was a noted trombone player in the area.

There were all kinds of things for a child to explore and to witness back then. It wasn't long before Anna and Alline got quite a sex education by peeking through the slats of one of the sheds on the farm where they lived. They knew they were witnessing something excitingly taboo when they watched a teenage couple go at it one day. Anna wasn't quite certain what they were doing, but it sure looked fascinating.

In 1950, when Anna was just ten years old, something devastating happened. Her mother, fed up with her marriage, packed her things one day and left without saying goodbye. Richard came home one evening and Zelma simply wasn't there any longer. She had moved to St. Louis, and she wasn't coming back.

Little Anna didn't realize that she had loved her mother as much as she did until she was suddenly gone. She cried and cried after Zelma left the family. Anna was torn with mixed emotions. She loved her mother deeply, but at the same time she resented and hated her for leaving. Her feelings about her mother would be perpetually conflicted from this point forward. "I was so hurt. I cried and cried, but it didn't do any good. It never does, you know," says Tina (1). She cried for so long, and then finally one day she said to herself, "Damn you, mother" (4). No matter who came or went in her life, and no matter what they did, nothing could hurt as much as this. Already Anna knew deep in her heart that she was a true survivor.

2

TEENAGE ANN

Determined to maintain his family of three daughters, Richard Bullock proceeded to get involved with a series of women whom he moved into their small house in Spring Hill. One of the first ones was a divorced woman from nearby Ripley named Essie Mae—whom he married. Her own daughter, Nettie Mae, accompanied her.

Anna and Alline, and their half sister, Evelyn, almost instantly disliked the pair. In fact, they nicknamed Essie Mae "Frog," and referred to Nettie Mae as "Pig." Tina remembers "Frog's" full hips and her mouthful of gold-capped teeth. She also recalls being green with envy at "Pig's" extensive wardrobe.

Upon "Frog's" insistence, the family moved to nearby Scott's Hill. They settled into a house next to the local cemetery. However, harmony in the Bullock household did not last. Richard and Essie Mae began to fight. On more than one occasion, they would physically get into it. One of their most dramatic battles ended with Essie Mae stabbing Richard Bullock in the groin with a knife.

It wasn't long before "Frog" and "Pig" packed up their things and left for good. At this point, Richard quit taking his daughters to church. This led to a series of babysitters and housekeepers. Among the women who cared for Anna and her sisters during this time were Miss Jonelle and Ella Vera, who was one of Richard's brother's mothers-in-law.

Either people would come in and stay with Anna, Alline, and Evelyn, or they would go to the homes of these caregivers. At one point Miss Jonelle lived in the girls' room with them. However, it wasn't long before the fights and the arguments started between Richard and Miss Jonelle. Soon, Miss Jonelle also packed her bags and left.

Her life was anything but happy. Still, Anna was able to maintain her own identity in this revolving cavalcade of care-givers and her father's women. "If anyone took care of me, it was my sister," she recalls (1).

When she was thirteen years old, something embarrassing happened to Anna. Somehow, cousin Ella Vera got wind of the fact that Anna had not yet had her first menstrual period. Ella Vera was concerned that there was something wrong, and she went and told Richard. He then took Anna to a doctor to have an examination. Anna was horrified to be examined by the doctor, and not long afterwards, her first period did come. That was even more horrific to Anna. In her own teenage mind she blamed him for making this monthly nuisance a regular part of her life.

However, that was nothing compared to what came next. Her father suddenly deserted the family and moved north to Detroit. Only three years after her mother had left, Anna, Evelyn, and Alline were made orphans—by desertion.

"I couldn't believe it," Tina recalls. "There I was, thirteen years old, with no mother. And now my father was gone too" (1).

They were shuffled off to live with cousin Ella Vera. Although Ella Vera was nice to them, Anna was not too thrilled with this new living situation. They were also looked after by a local woman named Florence Wright. Florence had been a beautician whom Richard had found to do Anna and Alline's hair—prior to his leaving the family. Tina recalls of this phase of her life, "I was always shifted. I was always going from one relative to another. So I didn't have any stability" (5).

For a while, Richard sent some regular support money to cousin Ella Vera, but, before long, that stopped coming. Anna was very frustrated with her awkward life and the painful fact that she had been abandoned by both of her parents.

To earn money, Anna landed a job of her own working for a white married couple named the Hendersons. This job brought a sense of belonging and continuity into her confused life. She also learned a lot of life lessons from working for Guy and Connie Henderson in their house. According to Tina, "I went to work for a white family as a maid. A lot of my training in being a woman—except for cooking—was from the Hendersons, because I was like their younger daughter. I learned how to take care of their baby, so, when I had mine, I knew everything" (11).

Guy Henderson was the owner of a Chevrolet dealership franchise in Ripley, Tennessee, and his wife, Connie, had been a teacher prior to getting married and retiring. Their baby, David, was to become Anna's charge while she worked for them. While she was in their employment, she learned how to clean and organize a house and every aspect of looking after a baby. From changing diapers to doing household laundry, Anna felt like a valuable member of their household, and they treated her as such. For the time being, she felt that she belonged somewhere.

While living with the Hendersons, she also witnessed what

a real family unit was like. It was a household where there were no physical fights, there were no threats of either of them having outside affairs, and there was a lot of outward love and affection that Guy and Connie expressed for each other. By just being themselves and caring about Anna, they opened up her eyes to the possibility of a whole different way of life. They showed her what a marriage could be like—an example completely different than what she had come to accept as normality. It made her long for a harmonious home life like the one they had. Living with the Hendersons gave Anna a sense of security and of being cared about.

Still, living in the area that they grew up in, Anna, Evelyn, and Alline were in close proximity to their relatives, so even though they had been deserted by their own mother and father, a sense of family remained. By 1954 there were many new changes in fourteen-year-old Anna's world. Papa Alex had died, leaving Mama Roxanna a widow. And Uncle Gill had been released from jail—having served his sentence for shooting and killing his rival. Mama Roxanna now lived with Uncle Gill, who had since married.

Anna's half sister, Evelyn, found herself pregnant by a local well-to-do high school boy. When he proposed that they get married, Evelyn turned him down. She was in love with another boy and wanted nothing to do with the father of her child. Instead, she had her baby, whom she named Dianne Curry, and she and the baby lived with Mama Georgie and Uncle Gill.

Evelyn and cousin Margaret had become very close friends. In fact, Mama Georgie made certain that the two girls were constantly in each other's company, so they wouldn't get into too much trouble. Anna would see them every Saturday in Ripley, and she looked forward to their visits.

Being a a few years older than the other girls, Evelyn was a bit cool and aloof toward Anna. She gave off the air that she would rather hang out with young adults than be with the younger girls. But Margaret always gladly accompanied her, and Anna just loved her cousin. In fact, she would spend the whole week looking forward to her time with Margaret.

In many ways, Margaret became like a surrogate mother to Anna. She would talk to her young cousin about life and the world. In fact, it was from Margaret that Anna learned the facts about love and about sex. Margaret would tell her about boys and kissing and who was sleeping with whom. Anna delighted in Margaret's stories about their relatives and hearing all of the local gossip.

That very year, Margaret too became pregnant by one of the local boys. She was very upset about this dilemma and was doing what she could to get her body to reject the baby that was growing inside her.

Anna was the only person whom Margaret told about her dilemma. To this day, she remembers the last time she saw Margaret alive. It was this same visit in which she announced her pregnancy. Margaret had heard that drinking black pepper and hot water would cause the baby to abort itself, so she was consuming this awful concoction in a desperate attempt to reverse fate.

After that visit, something very tragic happened to Margaret and Evelyn. Together with another cousin, Vela Evans, the girls had gotten a ride to a local basketball game with a man in his car. Unfortunately, the man had been drinking heavily, and his judgment behind the wheel was seriously impaired. When he changed lanes to pass a slow vehicle, he ran straight into an oncoming diesel truck. Both Margaret and Evelyn were instantly killed that night.

Anna was at the Henderson's house when the telephone rang with the awful news. When she heard the news she fainted. Until that moment, she had lived under the illusion that only white people were capable of fainting at the announcement of horrible things. She thought that black people just accepted tragedy and somehow soldiered through any hardships. That night she found out that anyone's body could collapse with shock. When Anna heard that Margaret was dead, she could feel her legs just collapse from under her.

Anna had been to Papa Alex's funeral. She had seen him lying in his casket so peacefully, like he had gone off to some sort of deep and rewarding sleep. However, Margaret and Evelyn's funeral presented a different, colder, and more horrific view of death. There was beloved cousin Margaret lying in her coffin, her head flattened by the accident, with a huge cut running down her face. There had been little attempt to cosmetically disguise the reality of the accident, and it was a heartbreakingly awful sight to behold.

Looking at their young and lifeless bodies, Anna cried out "Margaret! Evelyn!" But there was never to be a reply. Again, Anna had learned a valuable lesson about life and how temporary it all could be. Now her half sister, Evelyn, was gone, and so was cousin Margaret. She had died with the secret of her pregnancy intact; only Anna knew of the fact.

Anna felt a hurt and hollowness deep inside her. She thought that the pain of being deserted by her mother, and then her father, had been tragic. However, this was much worse and far more painful—it was a deep and aching kind of hurt that would not subside.

The year 1954 was one of many changes in Anna's young life. Some of the changes came to her via the radio. There was always a radio in the house, and Anna was exposed to a different world out there on the other side of the airwaves. She and Alline used to listen to the dramatic series that were broadcast. She remembers hearing the mystery program *Inner Sanctum* and the crime series *The Fat Man*. She and Alline would cook a plain sweet potato on top of the stove, or pop some popcorn in a skillet, and they would sit and listen to the programs. There were no sodas or cookies, just a glass of water and a sweet potato and some popcorn. Listening to the radio, their imaginations would entertain them for hours. Her grandparents would often listen to country & western music on the radio as well, so Anna was exposed to different kinds of current music.

During this era, the world of popular music was changing and growing. The "big band" swing sound of the 1940s had evolved into new forms of music. Jazz and blues had given way to rhythm & blues and a new, upbeat kind of guitar-driven music that would eventually be categorized as "rock & roll." Anna remembered hearing LaVern Baker gleefully sing the song "Tweedle Dee," and Faye Adams singing "Shake a Hand." There was also the sound of B. B. King and his guitar, which he had named "Lucille." Anna learned all the words to "Tweedle Dee," and she would sing it out loud.

In the fall of 1954, fourteen-year-old Anna started classes at the Lauderdale High School in Ripley, Tennessee. It was a different world. She looked around and saw the girls older than she was who had nice clothes to wear and shapely bodies to fill them out. It only made her feel more and more out of place. In her mind, she was like a stranger in a strange new land.

She took a good hard look at her own body and felt even more awkward. According to her, "I was very skinny when I was growing up. Long, long legs and nothing like what black people really like. I must say that black people in the class where I was at the time liked heavier women" (5).

The girls she went to high school with had curves, full hips, and shapely legs. When Anna looked at her own reflection in the mirror, she found that she had none of those attributes. "It wasn't so good in the early days when I was very young," she recalls, "because I—I saw myself as very skinny. Everything was in the wrong place" (12).

However, a new world seemed to open up for Anna at Lauderdale High. Eager to try new things, Anna found all kinds of fun activities in which to become involved. Since her high school had the number one basketball team in the area, there was a lot of excitement surrounding the basketball games. Anna tried out for the cheerleading squad and became one of the school's cheerleaders.

It was while she was a cheerleader that she recalls meeting her first real true love. He was a basketball player for one of Lauderdale's rival schools, Carver High School in Brownsville. She spotted him on the basketball court when Lauderdale played Carver. It was a case of love at first sight. He was so handsome in Anna's eyes. He had great teeth, an athletic body, and smooth dark skin. He was the opposing team's number nine player.

Determined to find out who he was, Anna went over to one of the Carver High School coaches and asked who number nine was. The coach simply walked over to number nine and came back to where Anna was, with him in tow. Anna surprised even herself with her openly assertive behavior.

Number nine turned out to be the captain of Carver's basketball team. His name was Harry Taylor. According to her, it was love at first sight. However, their first encounter was brief. Harry recalls that at a break during the game, he went over to where the opposing team was situated, in hopes of talking to Anna. But when he did so, she was gone.

Unfortunately, Anna wasn't the only cheerleader on the squad who had caught Harry's eye. Anna's prime rival was on the same cheerleading team, and her name was Rosalyn. Anna had known Rosalyn in school for quite some time. In fact, they had both gone to the Johnson Grade School Annex together.

Anna was horrified to find out that Rosalyn had given Harry her phone number. Anna, who didn't even have a telephone at home, started feeling worse about herself.

Yet, as fate would have it, some sort of divine intervention took place. During this time, her father, Richard Bullock, had been sending cousin Ella Vera some support money for Anna and Alline. The money stopped coming suddenly, and Anna and Alline had to move back to the Nutbush area, where they moved in with Grandma Roxanna and Uncle Gill.

This move took them out of Lauderdale County and put them back in Haywood County, and a totally different school district. Suddenly, Anna found herself a student at Carver High—where Harry went to school! How perfect was that?

Being transplanted to Carver High signaled several positive changes in Anna's young life. First of all, there was a principal there who took a liking to Anna. His name was Roy Bond. One day, Anna got into some sort of minor misbehavior at school, and she was sent to the principal's office. Mr. Bond took one look at Anna Mae Bullock and told her that he expected "better" of her. He told her that such unbecoming behavior in school was something he would have expected from one of the other students—but not from her. This statement made Anna take a good hard look at herself. In her visit to Mr. Bond's office, he gave told her that he realized she wasn't like the other students—that he spotted something special in her. Maybe being different wasn't such a bad thing.

Instead of feeling that the principal had just punished her, she actually felt enlightened. She had always felt that she was awkward and didn't fit in everywhere. Maybe that was actually a good thing, like having a special quality that others could see.

It was common knowledge amongst the teaching staff that Anna was without parents at home. One by one, Anna sensed her teachers somehow looking out for her and giving her guidance along the way. One day, the school librarian saw Anna walk by and stopped her. She told Anna that no young lady should go around with such bad posture, as to stick her stomach out. She informed her that she needed to hold her stomach in, and not to let people—especially boys—see her stomach protruding out. From that time on, Anna was always conscious of her posture and how she carried herself.

Transplanted to Carver High School, Anna soon got involved in other activities as well. She not only joined the cheerleading team, she also played girls' basketball for the varsity team. She was so involved in her after-school activities that occasionally, instead of riding the bus home to Grandma Roxanna's house, she would stay in town and sleep over at the home of one of the other cheerleaders—Carolyn Bond (no direct relation of Mr. Bond—the principal). Anna also got involved in the school's track team, where she was a fast and competitive runner. Anna might have lamented that her legs were so thin, but they were sure strong, and she was good on her feet.

Carolyn Bond later recalled how energetic and well-liked Anna was in high school at Carver. She got involved in the school plays and all of the talent shows. At halftime during the basketball games, Anna would come out on the court as an entertainer and dance and sing along with recorded music.

Anna and Carolyn were also in the school choir together. Tina loved to sing, and all of her classmates were startled to find what a great voice she possessed—even then. There weren't many places for young black teenagers to hang out in those days. To give the students something organized to do, the school would host Saturday afternoon dance parties. Anna loved to attend these too.

On the nights when Anna would come to stay with Carolyn, she noticed that Anna never had any clothes to change into after the events they would attend. Often Carolyn would loan Anna her own clothes. Anna was particularly in love with a certain pair of Carolyn's jeans—because when she wore them she felt that they made her legs and hips look bigger.

It was the weekend before school was about to start its next session when Anna and Alline went into Brownsville to walk around and check things out. They weren't going to see or do anything special, so Anna wore one of her dresses, which she never particularly liked. According to her, the black guys in Brownsville would wear white shirts, skin-tight blue jeans, and the black girls they hung out with wore skirts and blouses, in the popular sort of 1950s' rock & roll fashion.

Sure enough, that was the night she ran straight into the man of her dreams—Harry Taylor. He was hanging out in downtown Brownsville with a bunch of his friends—in an area that was also nicknamed "The Hole." Anna was overcome by a sense of shyness, and she just hung out for a while, hoping that she would catch his eye. Sure enough, he spotted her, came over to her, and started up a conversation. Sparks flew, and that was the beginning of Anna's first love affair.

When school went back into session, Anna and Harry became quite an item. With Anna's arrival on the scene, Harry stopped seeing his former girlfriend, Antonia Stubbs. Skinny little Anna Mae had won his heart.

On Wednesday nights, Harry would come over to the house with a friend of his named John Thankster. Harry and John would "officially" be coming over to pick up Anna and Alline to take them to the movies. That would appease Grandma Roxanna. However, more times than not, they never had any intention of going to the movies at all. John and Alline would often go off to a local juke joint—a one-room club that served liquor and had a jukebox. Since neither of them was into drinking and smoking, Anna and Harry would stay in the car.

On one of their late nights in John's car, Anna and Harry made love in the backseat. Like her 1980s hit song, "Steamy Windows," Anna Mae lost her virginity in a steamed up automobile, with Harry.

As she was later to recount, "It hurt so bad, I think my earlobes were hurting. I was just dying, God. And, he wanted to do it two or three times! It was like poking an open wound. I could hardly walk afterwards." (4)

The dress that Anna wore that night in the backseat of the car was a mess. She thought she was being clever when she wadded it up and stuck it at the bottom of a trunk that was under her bed. It was just her luck that Grandma Roxanna decided it was time to do some spring cleaning the very next day. She confronted Anna with the dress, and Anna tried to tell her that she had just gotten her period, and that was what stained the garment. Grandma was far too wise for that tale. She told her granddaughter that if she wanted to get pregnant, that was her affair, since she had no mother or father to watch out for her. That was the last time for quite a while that Harry was allowed to come over and pick up Anna for a trip to "the movies."

Anna soon found out that Harry was not that interested in her, now that she had become one of his sexual conquests. He was a very popular young man in school, and not long afterwards, he began dating Anna's friend Carolyn. However, that did not last long either. Soon, Harry graduated and joined the Air Force. Anna would still see him from time to time. One day she got on the school bus, and a friend informed her that Harry had suddenly been married. When he had gotten one of his other girlfriends, Theresa, pregnant, Theresa had pressured him into marrying her.

Anna was heartbroken to hear this news. She had harbored the idea in her heart that she and Harry were going to end up together. However, it was not to be. Her entire life seemed to be falling apart around her. Her mother left her. Her father left her. Evelyn and cousin Margaret had been killed in a car crash. Alline was about to graduate from high school and she had plans to move up to Detroit to be with their father. Soon she would be gone too. Anna was sick of living with her grandmother, and now Harry was suddenly gone from her life. What was she going to do? She felt deserted and alone.

Suddenly, she had an idea. She did have another grandmother who lived nearby. Anna would simply move in with her. As she recalls, she went over to Grandma Georgie's, on the Poindexter farmland. Grandma Georgie already had her hands full, as she was raising the little girl that Evelyn had left behind after the car accident that killed her and Margaret. However, with resignation, she allowed Anna move into her house.

Anna found that her old friends, the Poindexters, weren't too happy about her living on their property and not working for them in some capacity. To elevate this problem, Anna went back to work for Connie and Guy Poindexter as a housekeeper and babysitter.

In the summer of 1956, the Poindexters were going on a little vacation to Dallas, Texas. They took Anna along with them to take care of their child. While Anna was in Texas, Grandma Georgie suddenly died. When Anna went home for the funeral, she saw someone whom she hadn't seen in ages—her mother.

Recently, Zelma Bullock had been sending a little support money and clothing to her daughter. Slowly, the hurt and resentment that Anna felt toward her mother was subsiding. When she arrived at her grandmother's funeral, she was startled at what she saw.

There was Zelma, looking smart and sophisticated in a white suit with stylish shoulder pads and a pair of two-toned brown and white high heels. Zelma and her daughter had a long talk at Grandma Georgie's funeral. Zelma told her that she wanted Anna to move to St. Louis with her.

By this time, Alline had gone to Detroit to live with their father and hadn't been happy with that situation. So, Alline was currently living in St. Louis with her Zelma. To Anna, moving to St. Louis to live with her mother and sister seemed like the perfect solution.

Looking back at these times, Tina was later to recall, "I always wanted to leave the fields. Tennessee was fine. I loved sitting under a tree at the end of the day. But I knew there was more. That's why I joined my mother in St. Louis. To me, that was the big city" (1).

With that, Anna Mae Bullock packed her few belongings and off to St. Louis she went. It was "goodbye" to Nutbush, Henderson, and western Tennessee all together. She left there and never looked back.

3

ENTER IKE TURNER

In 1956, sixteen-year-old Anna Mae Bullock arrived in St. Louis, Missouri. This truly was the biggest city she had ever lived in. St. Louis back then was a pretty sedate place, situated on the Mississippi River. However, across the river and the state line, lies East St. Louis, Illinois. East St. Louis had a wild reputation for raucous clubs and nightlife.

After living all of her life in a rural area, the move to St. Louis really opened up Anna's eyes about a whole different way of life, where the music and the party seemed to never stop. According to Tina, she liked the Midwestern sophistication of St. Louis, but East St. Louis was rougher territory and reminded her of the South.

Anna's mother, Zelma, didn't live all that wild a life in St. Louis. She worked as a maid, and she was living with a man named Alex Jupiter, who was a truck driver. Alline had landed a job working for a well-to-do black nightclub owner by the name of Leroy Tyus. She was making good money at his club, The Tail of the Cock.

Alline would work during the week, and after work, she would often go out on dates with the men she met. However, on the weekends after work, Alline would go out with her girl-friends—nightclub hopping.

Anna enrolled in Sumner High School in St. Louis. It was an all-black school, but her classmates were a different class of people than she was used to being with. They were the sons and daughters of doctors and other professional black people. She felt conspicuously lower class than them, like a backwoods country cousin who suddenly arrived in the big city.

Little Anna was amazed at the transformation that had occurred in Alline since she had last seen her. Her older sister now dressed in a classy and stylish fashion. She wore high heels and nylons, and Tina recalls one particular wool coat with velvet stripes down it that Alline owned. Alline didn't so much *wear* the coat—she draped it over shoulders, so that she could make sweeping entrances wherever she went.

One particular Saturday night, Alline invited Anna to accompany she and her girlfriends on one of their club-hopping excursions. Zelma consented, even though it was kind of doubtful as to whether or not sixteen-year-old Anna could successfully masquerade as a twenty-one-year-old woman to even be admitted to the clubs.

Anna dressed up in some of Alline's clothes and applied lip-stick and make-up to her young face, in an attempt to look more womanly. Alline announced to Anna that on that particular evening, they were going to go see a popular local band that had a reputation for creating the hottest sound in all of St. Louis. The band was called Ike Turner & The Kings of Rhythm. In Anna's mind, it sounded like an exciting evening, whatever was on the agenda.

The Kings of Rhythm were so successful in the area, in fact, that they would play at Club D'Lisa in St. Louis, Missouri, until that place closed for the evening, and then they would go across the river to East St. Louis, and from 2 A.M. they would play at the Club Manhattan—late into the night.

Alline announced to her little sister Anna that this particular evening, the plan was to head straight across the Mississippi River to Club Manhattan. It sounded exciting, and slightly taboo. Well, as planned, Anna's make-up job, and Alline's more womanly clothes on her, made her look old enough to be admitted to the nightclub.

The Club Manhattan was every bit the hot spot it was reputed to be, and it reminded Anna of some of the clubs she had seen in "The Hole" areas of Ripley or Brownsville. The club seated about 250 people, and the performing stage was in the center of the room surrounded by tables and chairs. Tina remembers, on one wall of the club was a painting of Ike Turner & the Kings of Rhythm.

Anna wasn't all that impressed so far. The Kings of Rhythm were already on stage, playing a warm-up set before the celebrity bandleader made his entrance. She quietly sat with Alline and her friends and waited for something to happen. And, happen it did. In walked the popular Ike Turner, and there seemed to be instant waves of excitement throughout the club.

"Hey, Ike," someone in the crowd would call out to him. He would shake several hands and take another few steps. "Ike, how you doing?" someone else would holler out. Anna was witnessing for the first time what it was like when a celebrity enters the room. Somehow, all eyes seemed to be on Ike Turner.

Anna also noted that the audience was filled with women who obviously came to see this local "sex symbol." Right then and there, Anna recalls noting to herself that although she found Ike interesting to watch, he was decidedly not the kind of man she was attracted to—in the least.

She later recounted, "What an immaculate-looking black man. He wasn't my type, though—not at all. His teeth seemed wrong, and his hairstyle, too—a process thing with waves that lay right down on his forehead. It looked like a wig that had been glued on. When he came closer, I thought, 'God, he's ugly'" (4).

However, once he hit the stage and started playing his guitar, he somehow turned on the charisma. Suddenly the whole club seemed to be on its feet, dancing and swaying and partying along to the music. Tina recalls that she nearly went into a trance listening to the music that night. Although she didn't like him physically, there was something about the way he moved on stage and the energy he exuded that was mesmerizing.

Ike Turner was someone who had been working on his music and his sexual charisma for a long time. He had scored some minor successes in the record business, but he was having trouble keeping featured singers in his band. It seemed that every time he had a hit recording on the market, the singer would up and leave with dreams of solo stardom. Up to this point, his biggest hit was a song called "Rocket 88," but the song was released under the name of Jackie Brenston & The Delta Cats. However, Ike Turner had his eye on the big time. One of these days he was going to find a singer to stick with the band and the chemistry would click. However, for the time being, he was a huge star on the St. Louis nightclub circuit.

Born Izear Luster Turner Jr. on November 5, 1931, in Clarksdale, Mississippi, his father was a Baptist minister, and his mother, Beatrice, was a seamstress. Beatrice nicknamed him "Sonny," and it was a name that she called him all of his life. His only sibling was his sister, Lee Ethel, who was ten years older than him.

When he was a young boy, Ike too was left fatherless. Unlike

Anna's father, who just up and moved away, Ike's dad died following a severe beating. It seemed that Ike Sr. had been doing more than "ministering" to the wife of a local white resident. Ike still recalls the day an angry gang of white men—led by the woman's husband—came to the Turner house and dragged Ike Sr. out of his house in front of his wife and children. Hours later he was dumped back onto his property, beaten and full of holes. When a local white hospital would not admit him to their facility, he was treated in a special tent that was put up in the Turner front yard. Although his father lived another three years, he never left the bed on which he was treated.

Ike Turner started his musical career at an early age. He started his sex life even earlier. According to him, "I started [having] sex when I was six years old. Yes, I did. The woman was forty-five or fifty years old; her name was Miss Boozie. She used to put me on top of her and show me how to move. . . . Well, today they call it 'child molesting.' To me, I was just having fun" (13).

His first job was in the Alcazar Hotel, in downtown Clarksdale. He went from operating the elevator in the hotel to working at radio station WROX, which was located in that same building. Ike recalls, "I got a job driving the elevator in the Alcazar, and the radio station was on the second floor. It was very exciting to me, a radio station. I'd run up to the second floor and look through the window at the guy spinning records. He saw me and told me to come in and showed me how to 'hold a record.' I'd sit there and hold it until the one playing stopped, then I'd turn a knob and the one I was holding would play. Next thing I know, he was going across the street for coffee and leaving me in there alone. I was only eight. That was the beginning of my thing with music" (14).

As a kid, he was able to hang out in one of the local nightspots because the mother of his friend Raymond Hill owned it. Regular entertainers at the club included guitarist Robert Nighthawk and harmonica player Sonny Boy Williamson.

Ike's love affair with music continued when he suddenly became fascinated with the idea of learning to play the piano. "When you're a kid, seeing a piano in church, you don't notice it. I didn't," says Ike. "Then one day I was on my way home out of school, and we passed by [childhood friend] Ernest Lane's daddy's house. I heard this music! Pinetop Perkins was banging the heck out of a piano! Me and Lane started looking through the window at him, and next thing you know, we're inside the house at the end of the piano looking at him. I ran home and told my mama 'Mama, I want a piano!' She told me, 'Pass the third grade and bring me a good report card—I'll get you one.' When I came home from school with that report card, there was that *durn* piano" (14).

Ike loved to hang out in pool halls, even as a boy. He would go there with his friend Ernest. That's where he first heard Joe Willie "Pinetop" Perkins play the boogie-woogie piano. It didn't take much to convince Ike that playing some hot jazz music was sure a lot more fun than playing the classical piano pieces that he had been taught by his teacher. Recalls Ike, "Pinetop taught both me and Ernest to play" (14).

Soon Ike joined his first band, The High Hatters. The star of the show was a trombone-playing dentist named Dr. E. G. Mason. They would play in bars, at juke joints, parties, and local dances. Around 1948, when The High Hatters split up, the musicians who were more professional and could actually read music formed their own group called The Dukes of Swing. The less sophisticated, but younger and more aggressive guys formed their own group, which they named The Kings of Rhythm.

Ike recalls the long and extensive gigs they would land. "We played juke joints," he says. "We'd start playing at 8 P.M. and wouldn't get off till 8 A.M.—no intermission, no breaks. If you had to go to the restroom, well, that's how I learned to play drums and guitar! When one had to go, someone had to take his place" (14).

Ike had big dreams of stardom. Playing these nightspots, he would see all kinds of people come to hear the music. According to him, "I would see white guys pull up with their little white girls in their father's car with the mink stole, and I'd say, 'Oh boy, one of these days I'm going to be like that'" (5).

One night, The Kings of Rhythm went into a blues club in Chambers, Mississippi, where the headliner was B. B. King. Six years older than Ike, King too was a local star, and he had quite a following due to the fact that he had records out. After King had played the set, the club invited Ike and The Kings of Rhythm to play a set of their music. When they were finished, B. B. King told Ike that he had a hot band and that he should start recording.

It wasn't long before they did just that. Ike went to Memphis and paid the founder of Sun Records, Sam Phillips, to record his group. Three years later, a young truck driver named Elvis Presley also came to Phillips to record a song for his mother's birthday—and so began one of the biggest success stories in all of music history. But that's a whole different story.

The song that Ike's band recorded that day was "Rocket 88," which Turner wrote with the man who was then singing with the group—a man named Jackie Brenston. Originally, Ike tried to do the lead vocal but had less than successful results.

Sam Phillips recalls, "I listened to Ike sing in the studio, and I told him in no uncertain terms that I just didn't hear him as a singer. The inflections weren't there, the phrasing, none of it. But he was a whale of a damn musician—one of the best piano players that I had heard up to that time. So, he told me that

Jackie could sing, and that's when we cut 'Rocket 88'" (4).

Ike was later to complain, "Sam Phillips put Jackie Brenston's name on there, but not mine, with the excuse that he was going to record me, and he didn't want to put two records out with Ike Turner's name on it" (15).

When "Rocket 88" came out in 1951 on Chess Records by "Jackie Brenston & The Dixie Cats," it became a No. 1 hit on the nation's rhythm & blues music charts. In fact, it is often credited as being the first true rock & roll record.

Trying to explain the sound of the song, in his own rough style, Ike says, "I didn't go in there to try to cut nothin' different. To me, 'Rocket 88' is rhythm & blues and boogie-woogie combined" (15).

Jackie Brenston was convinced that he was now a big singing star, and he promptly quit The Kings of Rhythm. Through a chance meeting at a B. B. King recording session, Ike was introduced to a man named Joe Bahari, who was the owner of Modern/RPM Records. Soon Turner was working for Bahari, scouting out new blues talent for Bahari's label to record.

While all of this was going on, Ike continued to play with The Kings of Rhythm. Setting the blueprint for the act that was eventually known as "The Ike & Tina Turner Revue," in 1952 Turner released a single called "My Heart Belongs to You" backed with "Looking for My Baby." It was accredited to "Bonnie & Ike Turner" on vocals.

The following year, four more tracks were recorded under the name of "Ike & Bonnie Turner." The recordings went nowhere. It seemed that Ike was a great musician, but no one really liked his singing.

Indeed, Ike's singing voice, as heard on some of the later Ike & Tina albums, is not at all distinctive or pleasant to hear. It is flat, thin, and lacks any resonance. He wrote and played great music, but he could not sing.

In 1953, the latest incarnation of the group featured a pianist named Bonnie Mae Wilson and a singer named Johnny O'Neal. In a pattern that he would later repeat, he married Bonnie, and they continued to play music together. Before long, Bonnie retired from the stage and worked in the business end of Ike's budding musical operation. However, Ike's marriage to Bonnie ended not long afterward.

Over the next three years, Ike and his Kings of Rhythm were quite busy, appearing on dozens of singles for Sun, Modern, RPM, and Federal Records.

By 1956, Ike had a singer named Billy Gayle in the band as its featured singer, and they recorded a hit for Federal Records called "I'm Tore Up." Again, as soon as the record was a hit, Gayle also left the band. There seemed to be quite a pattern of events already set. Ike desperately longed to find a singer who would stay with him.

The night that Anna Mae Bullock came to see Ike, she was transfixed by what she saw and heard on stage. Ike had a stage routine where he would invite pretty women in the audience to sing with the band. A microphone on a long cord was passed around, and—naturally—some women had great voices, while others couldn't sing a note. Watching the show that night, Anna knew that she could out-sing all of the women she heard on the microphone, and she longed for the opportunity to demonstrate her vocal skill.

Tina recalls, "I heard Ike Turner for the first time; I saw Ike Turner for the first time. And I really wanted to sing with him for a very long time, but I didn't look the part" (16).

Not only did Ike Turner have a reputation as a great musician and an accomplished talent scout, but he also had a track record for notorious violence and a short-fused temper. "He had a bad reputation. He was known as 'pistol-whipping Ike Turner,'" says Tina (5).

But she was undeterred. "I was a fan. Well, I became a fan after seeing his show, and great musicians—they really rocked the houses. It was incredible," she proclaims (16).

Watching these amateur would-be-singers having their sing-along moment of fame in the spotlight made Anna long for a chance to show Ike Turner what kind of singer she really was. "I wanted to get up there with those guys," she vividly remembers. "They had people on their feet. That place was rocking! I needed to get up there with that energy" (5).

Anna was an instant fan of Ike Turner & The Rhythm Kings, and she and Alline and their girlfriends would spend nearly every Saturday night club-hopping from Club D'Lisa to Club Manhattan. They went to so many shows that the two Bullock sisters became friendly with a couple of the members of the band. In fact, Alline eventually started dating the band's drummer, Gene Armstrong.

Then, one fateful night, Anna Mae Bullock got her chance at the microphone. According to her, "It was the story of Ike discovering a talent. I had wanted to get on-stage with him before—was just *dying* to get up there, because of the musical attraction, you know. But I was always this kind of very skinny girl, and I didn't look the part, so I was never called. And then, finally, my sister was dating the drummer, and he was teasing her 'cause he knew that she couldn't sing. He gave her the microphone, and she passed it on to me, and I started to sing. . . . I did a song of B. B. King's. And that was how Ike recognized me" (7).

The song she sang was B. B.'s recent recording "You Know I Love You." Ike Turner was completely blown away after he heard Anna's voice. He was so startled that he stopped playing the organ, got off the stage, came over to Anna, and picked her up in the air.

As Tina recounts, "Everyone came running in to see who

the girl was that was singing. Then Ike came down. He was real shy. He said, 'I didn't know you could *really* sing!'" (6). He then asked her what other songs she knew.

Anna told him that she knew all of the songs by Willie John and several other songs currently being played on the radio. Ike took Anna up on the stage and had her sing song after song for him, and for the audience.

"And I got onstage with Ike, and I was, of course, very excited. Very competent, because I've been a singer all my life," recalls Tina (7).

When Ike asked her to tell him her name, she told him, "Anna." She was so young and skinny that he called her "Little Ann." After the show, Ike told Anna all about his band and his problems with singers leaving him as soon as their records become hits. "My problem, Little Ann, is people always took my songs" he claimed. He was so impressed with Anna's singing voice that he asked her to start singing semi-regularly with his band. She was elated. As she explains of her trajectory up onto the stage, "When I got there, Ike was shocked, and never let go" (5).

On that particular night, why was it Anna that so eagerly took the microphone, and Alline gladly passed it up? Why didn't Alline sing? As sisters, they surely must have had similar voices. According to Tina, she always had this fire inside of her, and Alline simply did not. "Some people have it naturally and don't have to really work on it, but I did, and I'm happy I did. My sister and I were totally different. She was very slow and I was always very fast" (12). Anna's own talent was something that was deep inside of her, and it was unique. "Then I started singing regularly on weekends. I was still in high school," says Tina (7).

However, it wasn't as easy as all that. Anna naturally accepted his offer, but she knew that her mother would have a fit if she found out that her daughter was singing with the most notorious womanizer of a musician in East St. Louis. For a short while, Anna was able to keep it all a secret from her mother.

Then, one afternoon, a big Cadillac pulled up in front of the house where Anna lived, and out stepped a woman named Annie Mae Wilson. She knocked on the door, and Zelma answered it. Annie asked where Anna was, because she was late for her rehearsal. Well, the cat was out of the bag now. When Anna Mae returned to the house from swimming with a friend, her mother confronted her about singing with Ike Turner's band. She slapped her across the face with the back of her hand and asked if she had been singing at nightclubs. After all, she was only seventeen years old. Anna admitted that it was true.

Her mother then told her that she thought Anna was going to become a nurse, not a nightclub singer—with Ike Turner no less. Anna told Zelma that she would much rather be a singer. Her mother's reply to her was, "No more singing—don't even ask" (1).

For a while that edict stood as law. But before long, Ike Turner himself showed up at the house to talk to Zelma. It seemed that he was in a jam again and he really needed a singer for his band. Dressed up smartly in a sharp Ban-Lon shirt and gabardine pants, he had totally charmed Anna's mother by the time he was finished. He promised that he would personally take care of Little Ann and make sure that nothing happened to her. With that, Zelma relented and Anna Mae started singing with The Kings of Rhythm on a regular basis.

Without a doubt, Anna Mae Bullock had a wonderful and very different voice, even back then. According to her, "When I started to sing with Ike, I was basically patterning myself after most of the male singers that I was around, like Ray Charles and Sam Cooke. When I started singing, there were more male singers than female. I think my voice is heavy because my mother's voice is quite low, as is my sister's. I think the raspiness in my voice is the natural sound. But the style really came from mimicking and copying my surroundings. Mine is not a pretty voice. Actually, it sounds ugly sometimes. I don't like to sing 'sing' that much. The pretty way of singing is not my style. I don't enjoy singing pretty songs. I like them rough, rocky, and rock & roll because it suits my type of voice" (10).

For a while, Anna Mae felt that she was suddenly Cinderella. It was all too exhilarating to find herself suddenly in the spotlight. "I became like a star. I felt real special. Ike went out and bought me stage clothes—a fur, gloves up to here, costume jewelry and bareback pumps, the glittery ones; long earrings and fancy form-fitting dresses. And I was wearing a padded bra. I thought I was so sharp. And riding in this Cadillac Ike had then—a pink Fleetwood with the fish fins. I swear, I felt like I was rich! And it felt good" (6).

Ike began to mold Anna into the kind of star he knew she could be. He paid for her to go to the dentist to fix her long-neglected teeth. He even bought her a gold tooth, which made her instantly feel like somebody special. "I was having a dental problem, and my mother didn't have money at that point for dental work. He corrected all that. And then I was a little star around him. I was loyal to this man. He was good to me," says Tina (5).

She remembers, "There were three dresses, the gloves, the bare-back shoes and the stockings with the seam in the back. That was, you know, really grown-up clothes. And I was very excited, riding in a pink Cadillac. I've always been crazy about movie stars. I felt like I was Bette Davis or somebody. I had my chin up and all of that. But I outgrew that pretty quickly" (7).

It seemed like a dream come true to be working for Ike and the band. "Ike had some kind of innate quality about him that you really loved him. And if he liked you, he would take the clothes from his back, so to speak. I was there because I wanted to be. Ike Turner was allowing me the chance to sing. I was a little country girl from Tennessee. This man had a big house in St. Louis, and he had a Cadillac, money, diamonds, shoes—all of the stuff that a different class of blacks would look up to" (5).

And Ike was completely knocked out by Anna's talent. "I could sing his songs the way he heard them in his head," she claims (1). "I was a singer; Ike was not. I—I felt his pain, because he had—he wanted so badly to be a star, you know?" (12). However, she also got a good look at what his personal life was like.

She knew, right up front, that Ike was every inch the womanizer his reputation had fostered. According to her, "Oh, God, I remember some nights when he would have maybe six girlfriends in the house, and he would stay up there and call his wife to come to the club that night—it was the only way they could save him" (6).

Anna harbored no desires to have Ike Turner as her man. She was not interested in him in that way. After all, he was still legally married, was heavily involved with one woman, and had a string of girlfriends on the side. Anna didn't want to get entangled in all of that. She was a singer, he was the bandleader, and they were great friends. He was able to confide in her like a buddy or a sister. She was happy to have their relationship remain this way.

As she saw it, "Ike was very good to me when I first started my career. I was in high school and started to sing weekends with him, and we were close friends. We had a very fun life in some kind of way" (16).

Often Ike would complain to Anna how he felt that everyone deserted him right before he was about to make it really big. Anna knew a lot about being deserted. She could totally empathize with him. "He was brokenhearted because every time he got a hit record on somebody, of course they got to be the star," she recalls. "The man was very nice and very generous to me. Way before our relationship started, I promised him that I wouldn't leave him" (8).

In the 1960s she was to go on and record such Ike Turner compositions as "Tina's Prayer" and "A Letter from Tina." Her first year with Ike and The Kings of Rhythm could have been another such song, which could have been entitled "Tina's Promise." It was a promise she fully intended to keep—a vow of non-desertion. It was a vow that no one else in her young life had ever made to her. And it was promise that was to haunt her for years to come.

But for now, Anna Mae Bullock from Nutbush, Tennessee, was a singing star. And she was still in high school! Finally, for the first time in her life, she felt like she was somebody. She had a place to belong, people in her life who cared about her as a friend, and a job that she had only fantasized about one day having. Suddenly, her life had gone from horrible to wonderful. For the moment—at the age of seventeen—she was living "Little Ann's Dream."

4

SEXY ANN

Anna Mae Bullock was not in love with Ike Turner at the beginning of their relationship. She loved him as a friend, and she loved singing on stage with his band, but it was never intended to be a love affair. The first year that she was the featured singer with The Kings of Rhythm, she felt for the first time in her life that her dreams and goals could actually come true. In her mind, Ike Turner was the man who had rescued her from a dismal and unhappy life. He was her friend, and she trusted him implicitly. Yet she knew full well the rumors about him. She saw with her own eyes how unfaithful he was to the women in his life with whom he was romantically linked. He didn't have a love life so much as he had a harem of transfixed women.

Anna didn't care—after all, she wasn't involved with him in that way. "I happen to have been a 'friend' of Ike Turner's in those early days. I stepped in as a high-school girl just coming from Tennessee," she recalls. (8)

What she felt was gratitude. "Since he had been so good to

me, I thought, 'Well, I will—I will give that—that favor back.' So that's what all the singing was, in spite of the fact that he felt that it was—that a relationship was needed, actually, to keep me. But our friendship could have done it, actually" (12).

Still a senior in high school, the man that Anna Mae Bullock was in love with at the time was one of the men she had met through Ike. He was Raymond Hill, whose mother had owned a nightclub when he was growing up. At that time, Raymond was playing in Ike's band. Anna liked Raymond a lot. His skin was light, or "yellow," as she was to later describe him. Raymond was kind of quiet, compared to the other more rowdy musicians in The Kings of Rhythm.

Anna Mae's high school classmates noted the change in her appearance and the way she carried herself. The shy little country girl they met when she first came to St. Louis had been replaced with a more self-confident young woman. In fact she had a new nickname—they called her "Sexy Ann."

The next thing she knew, further changes came—in a big way—when she discovered that she was pregnant with Raymond's baby. Anna assumed that since she was carrying his child, she and Raymond would eventually be getting married. However, that was not going to happen as Anna had hoped that it would.

Every night after the shows, the band and the girls they were hanging out with would go back to Ike's house in East St. Louis. There would be all-night parties and all sorts of drinking and horsing around. Tina confesses that she was a bit naïve back then, "I guess they were parties, and I guess the girls went to bed with the guys, but I didn't really know" (6). Since she was part of the entourage, eventually Anna moved into the house as well. It made sense, since she had no way of getting back to her mother's late at night after shows.

One night, in the bathroom of one of the clubs that the band was performing at, Raymond and one of the other band members—Carlson Oliver—got involved in a wrestling match, and 260-pound Carlson fell on Raymond's ankle. They heard it crack, and they both hoped that it was only a sprain. Raymond wrapped the ankle in a tight bandage and went on stage and performed that night. However, the ankle seemed to be going from bad to worse. Several days later, Raymond had to go the hospital, where doctors confirmed that it was indeed a break.

That was the end of Raymond being in The Kings of Rhythm. He packed his bags and returned to Clarksville. That was also the end of Anna Mae Bullock seeing Raymond Hill, the man whose baby she was carrying.

Meanwhile, Ike Turner's current girlfriend was a woman by the name of Lorraine Taylor. Lorraine's father was a local sausage manufacturer. However, while Ike was dating and living with Lorraine, he was also sleeping with several other women. Lorraine was known to become insanely jealous of any woman who got close to Ike in any way. At the time, Lorraine was carrying Ike's baby.

Anna Mae was no threat to Lorraine as long as Raymond Hill was still in the picture. However, when Raymond left for home, there was "Little Ann," living right there under the same roof—in Turner's spacious house.

Now that Anna Mae was pregnant, Lorraine's instinctive radar made her suspect that perhaps it was actually Ike's child that Anna was carrying.

Late one night, drunken and distraught, Lorraine burst into Anna's room, brandishing Ike's loaded .38 pistol and an iron poker from the stove. With the gun to Anna's head, Lorraine demanded to know whether or not Anna was sleeping with "Sonny." Horrified, and innocent of these charges, Anna swore there was nothing going on between she and Ike.

Disgusted by Anna's presence, and only half believing her,

Lorraine conceded out loud that Anna was so insignificant to her that she wasn't "worth the bullet" (4). Still distraught, Lorraine went into the bathroom and locked herself inside. Suddenly the sound of the gun being shot shattered the silence from within the bathroom. Frightened, Anna went screaming for help. Lorraine had aimed the gun for her own chest. She ended up firing the bullet through both of her lungs. An ambulance was called, and a seriously bleeding Lorraine was taken away in a stretcher. Fortunately, Lorraine survived her gunshot wound. However, this was only the beginning of trouble at the house of Ike Turner.

After that event, Anna moved back in with her mother, Zelma. She was less than thrilled that her teenage daughter had returned home, pregnant and unwed. In the spring of 1958, Anna graduated from high school. On August 20 of that same year, she gave birth to her son, Raymond Craig.

On October 3, Lorraine too gave birth. Her baby, a son, was christened Ike Turner Jr.

At this point, Anna Mae Bullock was no longer just a "featured" singer who would sing three or four songs with The Kings of Rhythm; she was the lead singer of the whole group. Ike was paying her fifteen dollars a week to perform with the band. To make more cash, Anna worked during the days in the maternity ward of the local Barnes Hospital. This gave her enough money to afford to rent her own tiny apartment, which she and infant Craig moved into. It also gave her enough money to afford a babysitter for Craig.

Although the apartment that she rented near the Hoderman Tracks was surrounded by whorehouses and rib shacks, Barnes Hospital was in a nice section of town. In fact, it was a Jewish hospital, and its clientele was very wealthy.

Working at Barnes really opened up Anna's eyes to a whole new world. She was amazed to see women who had come there to have their babies, who lounged in their beds in satin night-gowns with fur collars. One day Anna walked into the ladies room, where she saw one of the women looking at her image in the mirror and applying flawless makeup. According to her, the woman looked beautiful and she was very happy about the birth of her baby.

Anna found the woman fascinating. As they chatted, she showed Anna what she was doing with her mascara and her eyebrow pencil, demonstrating the latest technique. That very weekend, Anna purchased her first Maybelline pencil and mascara.

Although she was no longer fascinated with the idea of being a nurse, Anna did enjoy her job at Barnes. She liked washing and taking care of the babies. However, after a while, the grind of holding a day job and then working all night as a singer with Ike's band started to wear on her.

Ike had a habit of always arguing with his musicians. If a musician was late, or missed a note, Ike would fine him, eliminating money from his paycheck. He needed someone to keep track of who had what infractions subtracted from their pay. Since Tina was good with numbers, she began keeping track of Ike's books for him.

When Ike raised her salary to twenty-five dollars a week, she and her baby, Craig, moved out of the apartment near the Hoderman Tracks and back into Ike Turner's house. Tina recalls that's how her personal relationship with Ike slowly began.

Once Lorraine came back to the house with her baby, whatever jealousy she felt toward Anna had subsided. Since the atmosphere at Ike's house was just like a big house party, often Anna would fall asleep on Ike and Lorraine's bed, while all three of them were in it.

During this period of time, Ike was still going into the recording studio, trying to recapture the success that he had with "Rocket 88" years before. However, he never quite found the right formula. Often, he and The Kings of Rhythm would be accompanying other lead singers, including Jackie Brenston ("You Keep on Worrying Me"), Tommy Hodge ("I'm Gonna Forget about You"), and Betty Everett ("Tell Me Darling"). On one such record, a song credited to Ike Turner's Kings of Rhythm, featuring Ike and Carl and entitled "Box Top," Anna provided background vocals. This was to go down in history as her first recording experience.

On some occasions, Ike would take Anna out with him when he was checking out new singers or other bands at the local clubs. He would talk to her about all of the blues music that he liked. Anna learned all about Big Mama Thornton and Howlin' Wolf. In this way, Anna began to feel like Ike was her musical mentor.

Tina would later recall that she felt like her relationship with Ike was that of "brother and sister." Ike was still in a relationship with Lorraine, and there was another girlfriend of his in town named Pat, with whom he also had another child. Sometime around 1959, Lorraine and Ike broke up, and Ike was without a main lady in his life. This was when his roving eye landed on Anna Mae. According to Tina, the first time that he attempted to touch her sexually was in his car, on their way back from a club date. She remembers how wrong it felt to allow him to have his hands on her, but Ike was her Svengali, her mentor, so she just let it progress from there.

One night, one of the musicians in the band threatened to come to Anna's bed and have sex with her. She had no interest in this, so she went to Ike's bed, wanting to sleep there for protection. When she woke up in the morning, Ike started fooling around with her in a sexual way, and one thing led to another. Since she thought of Ike as her older brother, this really felt wrong and taboo, but she let it happen. And that was the beginning of her sexual relationship with Ike Turner.

What was it about Ike Turner that made all of these women interested in him? He certainly was not the most handsome guy. And his reputation for violence sure should have repelled most women. Still, he seemed to have a harem of girlfriends having sex with him and having babies out of wedlock with him. It seemed like none of the women in East St. Louis in the 1950s owned a box of condoms.

Did the secret to Ike's attraction lie in his pants? According to Tina, "I really didn't like Ike's body. I don't give a damn how big his 'member' was. I think that must have been attractive to a lot of white women. I swear, the first time I saw Ike's body, I though he had the body of a horse. It hung without an erection, it hung with an erection. He really was blessed, I must say, in that area. . . . Was he a good lover? What can you do except go up and down, or sideways, or whatever it is that you do with sex?" (5). Well, Ike Turner was certainly up to something in bed that women couldn't seem to get enough of—and now Anna was caught up in it as well.

As their newly established sexual relationship progressed, Anna started to fall in love with Ike. As she did, Lorraine came back in the picture. The next thing she knew, both she and Lorraine were pregnant—by Ike. Depressed, confused, and "addicted" to her relationship with Ike, Anna moved out of his house on Virginia Place.

Expecting her second child, Anna and baby Craig moved into a small house in St. Louis. She found a woman nearby to take care of her baby while she worked.

In addition to all of the St. Louis and East St. Louis club dates that The Kings of Rhythm were playing, Ike and Anna and the band were also performing at several college dances and fraternity parties.

Anna was torn about her relationship with Ike during this

period—circa 1959. Could she ever be more than just one of his many women? And did she actually want her relationship with him to be anything more than that? She could always quit the band and go back to work for the hospital. She began to weigh out her options. And there was also the fact that she was now carrying his baby.

She was stuck between a rock and a hard place. "The mistake was when in some kind of way it became personal and [it] wasn't my doing. . . . Had it not become personal, we would have possibly still been together today," she claimed in 1997 (16).

The longer she sang with the band and spent time with Ike, the more deeply entrenched in his world she became. "He was giving me money for singing. He went out and bought me clothes. . . . Something was going on—maybe the feeling he could protect me. That's the kind of girl I am. If I go to bed with you, then you're my boyfriend. It wasn't love in the beginning; it was someone else who I found to give love to," she claims (5).

And how could she ever hope to successfully leave him and strike out on her own? She knew nothing about the music business: "I didn't know anything else—or anybody else. And I wanted to sing" (1).

Was there something *so* seductive and addicting about being on stage and feeling like a star? Explains Tina, "In the beginning, yes, *very* exciting in the beginning because to sing on stage, actually, to—the feeling to get on stage and sing, which is I think what every[one wants to do]—well, a lot of people want to do—to have that feeling. And that's what it was in the beginning—it was fantastic!" (16).

According to Tina, the relationship she was having with Ike both cemented their association with each other and simultaneously doomed it from the start. "We were very close friends, and then what ruined it, actually, was when our relationship became a reality, so to speak," she recalls (12).

As 1959 was coming to an end, and the 1960s were about to dawn, "Little Ann" was pregnant and emotionally torn. However, she also felt like a star when she was onstage singing for a cheering crowd. Although she described her affair with Ike Turner as an "addiction," the real drug wasn't "love" for Turner, it was love of performing. It was in her blood now, and there was no turning back.

5

JUST A FOOL IN LOVE

Ike Turner and The Kings of Rhythm, along with "Little Ann," were busy touring around the St. Louis area. They were very popular—as a local bar band. However, this wasn't exactly mainstream success by any means. What the group really needed was a gimmick to set it apart from other bands. They also needed that elusive and all-important commodity—a hit record.

The record that started it all was a song called "A Fool in Love." However, it was not written for "Little Ann," it was written for a singer by the name of Art Lassiter. While Ike wrote the song, and while he rehearsed it with Lassiter, Anna was right there by his side. So by the time the recording date approached, she knew the song backward and forward.

Ike recalls lending Lassiter eighty dollars to purchase new tires for his car. Ike then booked Technosonic Recording Studio to record "A Fool in Love," with Art singing the lead vocal. The studio time began, and there was no Art Lassiter. Apparently,

Art took the eighty dollars, got the tires, and drove in the opposite direction with his brand new free wheels.

Meanwhile in the recording studio, there sat Ike, the band, and Anna. The studio time was booked and paid for, so they had to do something. Ike decided to record the song, putting Anna's voice on one track and the band on the other track. That way when Lassiter showed up, Anna's voice could be taken off, and he could record the song as originally planned.

Art never showed up, and Ike started taking the finished recording around to see if he could get a label to release it. He played it for a local St. Louis radio station disk jockey, and the D.J. in turn sent copies of the song out to several record labels. He got a very positive response and ultimately landed Ike a "singles" deal with New York–based Sue Records.

Paranoid that "Little Ann" was going to leave him, he decided that he would make up a new stage name that could be put on the record. Of receiving her new name, Tina said, "Black women were very heavy in those days, with big hips and things. And I was very small, so I was 'Little Ann.' When my career started, Ike thought we had to get a name with a sound for the stage. He had a thing for the women in movies who swing on the vines—the jungle queens" (2). Ike chose the name "Tina" for "Little Ann," because it rhymed with *SHEENA, Queen of the Jungle,* one of his favorite fictional heroines. And, from that point forward, the former Anna Mae Bullock was always to be known as "Tina Turner."

In the summer of 1960, the song "A Fool in Love" by Ike & Tina Turner was released by Sue Records and began its climb up the record charts. It made it to No. 2 on the rhythm & blues chart and No. 27 on the pop chart in *Billboard* magazine in the United States.

The sound of Tina's distinctive "whoooooaaaaaoooo" yelp

that kicked off "A Fool in Love," is one of the most distinctive on-record debuts from any rhythm & blues or rock & roll performer before or after. Since the song was originally in a key more suited for a male voice, Tina's leap into a gruff, masculine kind of delivery was to become her audible identity. Her voice is raspy and growling on this classic song, which became a star-making turn for both Ike and Tina.

That was the end of Anna Mae Bullock's singing career, and the beginning of Tina Turner's. Since Tina was carrying Ike's baby, and they now performed as "Ike & Tina Turner," the public assumed that this was a husband-and-wife team. To simplify matters, from this point forward, they just pretended they were married. That was also the end of The Kings of Rhythm, as they were now christened "The Ike & Tina Turner Revue."

As the song was starting to make noise on the radio and on the American music charts, Tina was suddenly sidelined with health problems. She had taken Craig to the doctor because he had a cold or some other sort of childhood ailment, but the doctor took one look at Tina and informed her that it wasn't Craig who was sick—it was she. He told her that she was yellow with jaundice and had a severe fever. The doctor refused to let her leave the hospital. She was diagnosed with hepatitis, and she was very infectious. She ended up being hospitalized for six weeks, and the doctors still did not want her to leave their care.

While all of this was going on, "A Fool in Love" was getting bigger and bigger, and the demand for performances by The Ike & Tina Turner Revue was mounting. Finally, tired of turning down gigs, Ike sent one of his buddies to bust Tina out of the hospital. The next day the group had a booking in Cincinnati, Ohio, on a bill with Jackie Wilson. This was the first show where they officially performed together as "Ike & Tina Turner." No matter what Ike had to do, Tina was going to be there. He wasn't about to miss this gig. He didn't want to hear about her health problems.

Tina rode to Cincinnati with Ike in his big pink Cadillac. The band rode in a station wagon. On the way to the gig, there was an accident, and the band rolled the station wagon on the road. No one was fatally injured, but they arrived a bit bumped and bruised.

To disguise her pregnancy on stage, Tina wore a sack dress, which she covered with waves of chiffon to hide her stomach. It is kind of an amusing idea to think of unwed Tina performing "A Fool in Love," while several months pregnant. Yet, without knowing it, that's what Cincinnati got that night.

To round out the show, Ike added a singing and dancing background trio of girls; he called them "The Ikettes." The initial set of The Ikettes included Robbie Montgomery, Jesse Smith, and Vanetta Fields. They were the first of what was to become an ever-changing lineup of girls throughout the years.

"A Fool in Love" peaked on the charts in August of 1960. That's the same month that "The Ike & Tina Turner Revue" made their debut at the famed Apollo Theater in Harlem. Tina was eight months pregnant at the time.

At the Apollo that night, Ike and Tina shared the bill with Hank Ballard and the Midnighters ("Finger Poppin' Time"), Ernie K-Doe ("Mother-In-Law"), Joe Jones ("You Talk Too Much"), Lee Dorsey ("Workin' in a Coal Mine"), and a young comedian by the name of Flip Wilson.

On October 3, 1960, Ike & Tina Turner made their American national television appearance on Dick Clark's *American Bandstand*. They were seen performing their first big hit, "A Fool in Love."

As if all this wasn't exciting enough, the next major gig they had was in Las Vegas. They arrived in Vegas, checked into their hotel, and performed their first show there as planned. That night after the show, Tina undressed in the room they were sharing. Ike took one look at her stomach, and asked her when it was that she was supposed to have the baby. She told him that she had no idea, as her mother was with her when she had Craig.

Frightened that she was going to give birth right then and there in a Las Vegas hotel room, Ike canceled the rest of the gig, and the entire entourage immediately got on the road for Los Angeles. Ike knew that he could find more work out there, while Tina gave birth and recuperated. They arrived in Los Angeles at seven in the evening and ordered some food. That's when the labor pains started, and Tina knew that she was going to give birth any moment.

On the morning of October 27, 1960, Tina Turner gave birth to her second son, Ronald Renelle. When he was born, both Ike and Tina lied to Lorraine as to who the father of the child actually was. And so, the vast marital complications in the Turner household continued to mount and intertangle.

Ike had always dreamed of one day moving to Los Angeles, and this seemed like as good a time as any to put down some roots there. This was the beginning of their long and rocky West Coast life together.

There were times when Lorraine would come out on tour with the band, and Tina recalls that she felt very ashamed of the situation that she was in at the time. Lorraine would be in the backseat of the car with Ike, and Tina would be in the front seat of the car, feeling very much like the girlfriend with the illegitimate baby. She also suspected that Ike was simultaneously sleeping with one of The Ikettes.

Only days after the birth of Ronnie, Ike insisted that Tina get out of the hospital—against doctor's orders—to perform at a gig in Oakland, California. This time, she had to comply with the doctors. However, she was later to find out that to make money and capitalize on the hit record, Ike hired another singer who masqueraded as "Tina Turner." Tina was furious over this. To make matters worse, the woman turned out to be a hooker and apparently turned several tricks also using the name "Tina Turner." According to the real Tina, because of this event a false rumor that she was a prostitute followed her for years. Welcome to the complicated world of Ike Turner.

During this time, Ike was called back to St. Louis, as he was embroiled in a legal case. It seemed that he had somehow procured several thousands of dollars of bank money, which he needed to buy the band new outfits. He claimed that he had no involvement in any shady deals, but Tina was always convinced that he was quite guilty of something illegal.

One of the next key dates for The Ike & Tina Turner Revue was the Howard Theater in Washington, D.C. Prior to the show there, Tina decided to get her hair bleached blonde. The hairdresser made a big mistake when she left the heat cap on for too long, and all of Tina's hair fell out! Tina had nothing left but stubble—she was horrified! This chance occurrence became a precedent-setting event, as it marked the beginning of Tina wearing long wigs on stage. She had little choice in this decision, as she wasn't about to set foot on stage without hair!

That night, Tina fell in love with her new hairstyle. She adored the way it moved when she danced on stage, and it became part of her trademark look during this era.

In December of 1960, the group's next single, "I Idolize You" peaked at No. 5 on the R&B chart and No. 82 on the Pop chart in *Billboard* in America.

In 1961 Sue Records released the debut album by the group, entitled *The Soul of Ike & Tina Turner*. It included the Tina Turner classics "It's Gonna Work Out Fine," "Poor Fool," and "You Shoulda Treated Me Right." In September of 1961, Ike &

Tina scored their highest charting single of this era, "It's Gonna Work Out Fine." It hit No. 14 on the Pop chart, and No. 2 on the R&B chart in America.

Tina was later to recount that she would have loved to have left Ike Turner at this point. "I was caught in his web," she claimed with resignation (5).

As their hit records began making them stars, Tina knew that this was going to change her life as well. Of her complicated existence with Ike, she explains, "I was his vehicle to get him to being a star. That's why I had no say. He was being a star through me. I even saw it then" (5).

As early as this point in her relationship with Ike, she began to envision leaving him. "I was helping him," she recalls. "And one year into our relationship, I said, 'After I help you get where you want to, I'm not going to stay.' Because we weren't each other's type" (8).

Describing his sexual relationship with Tina, Ike was later to recount, "Out on the road, though, I started to have sex with Tina again. As far as that side of our relationship was concerned, I've always felt that Tina was attractive, but not really sensuous in bed. She felt more like my sister, not my wife. To be honest I felt that having sex with her was almost a duty" (17).

The glamorous life of stardom was turning out to be quite disillusioning. Tina was either on the road, going from one gig to the next, or she and The Ikettes were rehearsing, recording, or performing. Besides, Tina had two babies to take care of as well. She recalls this as being the beginning of the truly unhappy times for her. She was trapped in a nightmare not of her own design.

Even before he was to actually marry Tina, the physical abuse had begun. Describing Ike during this period, Tina recounts, "When he was fun he was fun, but he just had a real mean streak. I can only tell you there was genuine love there, but it wasn't a passion, a husband-and-wife love" (18).

The mean streak seemed to come from out of nowhere. According to Tina, she would be sitting across a table from Ike, and suddenly he would get this look in his eyes, he would begin emitting an odd sort of hum, start tapping his fingernails on the table, and the next thing she knew, his fist was coming at her face. With tears in her eyes, Tina would ask what she had done, and he would again sock his fist into her face.

Before long she would become a professional makeup artist, due to having to devise new ways to disguise a blackened eye or a swollen and split lip. He would start fights with her for no apparent reason. One time on the road, Ike came back from the grocery store with a pound cake. When he presented it to Tina, she asked why he had purchased it. He told her that one of the band members had told him she wanted it, and he made her sit and eat the entire cake. She did as she was told for fear that he would beat her up again.

In 1962, the Ike & Tina Turner song "Poor Fool" made it to No. 38 on the Pop chart, and No. 4 on the R&B chart in the United States. In an interesting move, Ike was able to record a song, "I'm Blue (The Gong Gong Song)" by The Ikettes (with Tina singing in the background), and sell it to a different record label than the one to which Ike & Tina were signed. "I'm Blue" peaked at No. 19 on the Pop chart. Meanwhile, the Ike & Tina single, "Tra la la la La," peaked at No. 50, and "You Shoulda Treated Me Right" only made it to No. 89.

There was suddenly a new pressure on Ike to produce more hits. According to Tina, this only made him more irritable. More often than not, he would become frustrated, and his violence would be unleashed upon Tina. She had made Ike Turner a star, only to be used as his own personal punching bag. Recalling the beatings that became a regular event, Tina says, "I went home, put on an ice pack, found a way to sing the next few days. Just kept going" (8).

Tina later recounted with horror how Ike would beat her with his fists, with his shoes, and even with his wooden shoe trees. He was like a ticking bomb, but she never knew when she was going to get hit, or with what.

What was the best thing that Tina could have hoped for at this time? Was the prospect of becoming Mrs. Ike Turner such a big prize? According to her, "I had gotten to the stage where I started to think that I didn't want to be Ike's wife, and I didn't care about the money. I was thinking the whole time, 'How could I fulfill my promise and get out of it all right?'" (5).

Marriage to Ike Turner was only useful in legal circumstances. Describing his personal life during the 1940s and 1950s, he was later to recount, "The first woman I married was Edna Dean Stewart from Ruleville, Mississippi. I was fifteen or sixteen. . . . Edna and I stayed together a while, but she didn't want to stay up in Clarksdale, so she ran away. . . . After her I met Thelma Dishman, who at that time was a pretty girl. Thelma was pregnant, not by me, but I liked her. . . . When I moved to West Memphis I married Rosa Lee Sane. Her mind flipped on her. . . . Then I started going with 'Snow'—her real name was Etta Mae Menfield. But I never married her. . . . The next time I married, I married Alice. . . . After I married Alice, the next Mrs. Turner was a girl named Anna Mae Wilson" (17).

And, this doesn't even take into account all of the girlfriends and the one-night-stands. Ike's trail of wives and women and children is more complicated than that of any three characters on *Dynasty* or *Dallas*!

There came a time in the early 1960s when marriage again became a useful solution to one of Ike's problems. It seemed that his last legal wife, Anna Mae Wilson, showed up to demand her percentage of his belongings. According to Tina, "This woman was asking for money, so Ike felt he'd better marry me so she couldn't get [community] property" (5).

Ike took Tina down to Tijuana for a quickie Mexican marriage. She had wanted to be Ike Turner's number one woman, and instead—by marrying him—she was being used as an excuse to save him money.

All that Tina remembers about the wedding she had once dreamed of is that somebody pushed a piece of paper across a table, and she signed it. She took a look around the tacky room she was in, and thought to herself, "THIS is my wedding?" (1). The next day, Tina called her mother in St. Louis and told her the news. Zelma said she was very happy, as she assumed that Tina was happy as well. Tina wanted to tell her the truth, but couldn't. She wanted to tell her mother to keep her congratulatory words, for what was being passed off as a marriage was a sham designed to keep money in Ike Turner's pockets. Now she was really stuck because now she was truly Mrs. Ike Turner.

According to Ike, he never took the marriage seriously, since he had never divorced his former wife. It seemed like some sort of sad masquerade from the very start. Tina was later to state with disgust, "As far as I'm concerned, I've never been married" (5).

Furthermore, Ike never had any intention of being faithful to Tina. According to him, "I was not a great believer in monogamy anyway. I wanted my cake and wanted to eat it, too. I want my home woman and other women outside to run with—that's the dog in a man" (17).

Yet, somehow—knowing all of this—Tina chose to stay with him. "Still—I kept my word. I promised that I would be there for him," she recalls (12). Was Tina Turner just a fool in love, hopelessly devoted to Ike Turner? In many ways she was. But she didn't know where to go if she left him. Ike was not only the man who was tormenting her and beating her physically, he was also the man who was making her a singing star. So she stayed, as she became more and more entrenched in his web of lies, deception, and abuse. From this point forward, she knew that one day she would leave him—if she survived long enough.

6

RIVER DEEP-MOUNTAIN HIGH

Based on the first few hit singles that they had, Ike recorded three very similar "Ike & Tina" albums for Sue Records in 1963. They were *Dynamite* (including "It's Gonna Work Out Fine," "A Fool in Love," "Poor Fool," "I Idolize You," and "Letter from Tina"), *Don't Play Me Cheap* (with "Love Letters" and "Don't Play Me Cheap"), and *It's Gonna Work Out Fine* (featuring "It's Gonna Work Out Fine," "Poor Fool," and "Foolish"). The albums began to overlap with regard to the material that was on them.

What was quite ironic is the fact that the songs Ike Turner wrote for Tina to sing during this era were all songs in which she confessed her undying and irrational devotion toward her man. This must have been the ultimate ego trip for Ike—who considered himself the quite a ladies' man. "I Idolize You," finds Tina worshipping at the feet of Ike. In "Letter from Tina," she sings about how her man controls her every movement of her life, and how she gladly surrenders all will to him. In "It's Gonna Work Out Fine," she describes what bliss would come from marrying him. Nothing could be further from the truth. Marriage to Ike was more like a prison sentence than a love connection!

Many performers talk about their preparations before going on stage. Some people meditate or pray for a good performance. Others quietly, mentally, center themselves right before the curtain's rise. Tina Turner's life, however, had a completely different tone. She found herself living in perpetual fear of what Ike was going to do to her, before or after a show. Her time spent on stage was the only hours in which she knew she was truly safe.

In reality, before the shows, Ike would often beat Tina up, and then expect her to sing that evening like nothing was wrong. Well, one might rationalize that it must have at least been a high-paying gig for Tina, and that she must have been making lots of money for herself. One would surely think that was the case—and that she could simply save her money and eventually buy her freedom. However, the reality of it was that Tina never saw any of the money. She was expected to wait on Ike hand and foot, have sex with him, get beaten up by him whenever he saw fit, and still be the glamorous and energetic star of the show as if nothing was wrong. Yet she had not a cent of cash to show for her work or her mental anguish. Ike controlled everything about her life and her environment. She wasn't even allowed to have any of her own friends. In this way, he made it impossible for her to escape. He saw to it that she had nowhere to go, and no one to whom she could turn.

When their initial recording contract with Sue Records was over, Ike began throwing out albums right and left, taking advances from several different record companies for single albums. In 1964 they released an album called *Get It* for Cenco Records, which was also released as *Her Man, His Woman* on

Capitol Records. Then came a whole series of "one shot" albums, recorded live. There was *The Ike and Tina Turner Revue, Live* on Kent Records, *The Ike and Tina Turner Show, Live, Volume 2* on LOMA Records—both in 1964—and a totally different album called *The Ike and Tina Turner Show, Live* on Warner Brothers Records in 1965, which made it up to No. 126 in *Billboard* in the United States.

No one could tell Ike Turner how to run his business. He insisted on being the road manager, the stage manager, the songwriter, the booking agent, and the band leader. He was talented enough to have gotten the group this far, but he was unable to take their success to the next level.

Since Ike was doing all of the booking, and since he insisted on being paid in cash, the places that the revue played were often very rough and downscale. Often fights would break out during the shows. Yet, somehow in spite of Ike's gross mismanagement and short-sighted judgment, the revue kept on working.

In 1964, Juggy Murray, the head of Sue Records, paid Ike $40,000 to sign a new recording contract. Ike immediately took the money and purchased something that he had longed for—a house in the Hollywood Hills. The house he purchased was a one-story ranch style home with three bedrooms. It was located just off of La Brea, in an area called View Park Hills. At the time, the neighborhood was mainly white. However, both Nancy Wilson and Ray Charles had homes in that area as well.

Now that they had a whole house, they sent for their children. Up until this time, Lorraine had been back in St. Louis, taking care of her two children by Ike. And relatives back in Tennessee were caring for Tina's two boys. With their cumulative family all in Los Angeles now, Tina and various housekeepers would take care of the four young boys.

Also in 1964, Ike signed a singles deal with Kent Records. They released only one single on Kent, a song called "I Can't Believe What You Say," which only made it to No. 95 in *Billboard*. During the Christmas season of that year, they recorded the holiday song "Merry Christmas Baby" for Warner Brothers Records. "Merry Christmas Baby" is still a treat to hear, and it often shows up on holiday compilation CDs, including *The Best of Cool Yule* (Rhino Records). In 1965, as part of the new contract, Sue Records released *Ike & Tina Turner Greatest Hits*. With all of the competing albums that they had on the marketplace, it failed to reach the charts. Although their act was still popular in clubs, their recording career was quickly sinking.

It was also in 1965 that Ike recorded several songs with The Ikettes alone. A couple of the tracks became bigger hits than the ones Ike & Tina were releasing. The Ikettes' "Peaches & Cream" made it up to No. 36, and "I'm So Thankful" peaked at No. 74 on the Pop chart. Due to the popularity of these two songs, The Ikettes were asked to perform on their own, so Ike simply cast a new trio of Ikettes and sent them out on the road, while another three ladies were The Ikettes in The Ike & Tina Turner Revue. When the recording Ikettes found out that three different women had been hired by Ike to sing their hit song and impersonate them, all three of them promptly quit. One of the original Ikettes, Vanetta Fields, went on to become one of the most in-demand background singers in the 1970s, appearing on Barbra Streisand's *Stony End* and *Barbra Joan Streisand* albums.

With the original trio gone, Ike had another excuse to look for new women, and The Ikettes became a revolving door for his sexual appetite. At one point in their ever-changing lineup, none of the replacement Ikettes could sing on key, even though they looked great on stage. To make it through a show, the band had to sing the back-up vocal parts while The Ikettes danced.

On several occasions, new girls landed jobs as Ikettes simply so Ike could seduce them.

Once, and only once, there was a white Ikette—and she later became a full-fledged rock star as well. Bonnie Sheridan is more commonly known by her later married name, Bonnie Bramlett. In the late 1960s Bonnie married Delaney Bramlett, and they formed their own group, Delaney & Bonnie & Friends. Among the "friends" on their albums were such rock luminaries as Eric Clapton, Dave Mason, Leon Russell, and Rita Coolidge. Bonnie was a regular cast member of the highly rated *Rosanne* TV show for several seasons. In the 1990s Bonnie and Delaney's daughter, Bekka Bramlett, filled in for Stevie Nicks in Fleetwood Mac.

Even in the early 1960s Bonnie had an incredible and soulful voice—especially for a white blues singer. She was a big fan of R&B music, she had a great voice, and she loved to sing. As a young girl, she would follow The Kings of Rhythm from one club to the next in the St. Louis days. At the time, she was performing under the name she was born with, Bonnie Lynn O'Farrell.

When one of the Ikettes suddenly dropped out of the group, Bonnie was hired at the last minute. Unfortunately, her tenure as an Ikette was very short. During this era, The Ike & Tina Turner Revue was playing a lot of one-nighters in the Deep South, where—in the 1960s—Jim Crow laws of segregation were still taken very seriously. If they played in a white club, drunken patrons would shout things at her onstage. For one gig in Kentucky, blonde-haired Bonnie put Man-Tan skin bronzer all over her face and arms to look darker. Even with a wig on, she just looked like a very orange white woman. The final incident came on the highway, when a car full of drunken white supremists tried to run Ike's Cadillac off the road, amidst shouts aimed at Bonnie calling her a "nigger lover." After that, it was mutually decided that she shouldn't be part of the act. However, Bonnie now has the distinction of being the first, and only, white Ikette.

During this era, Ike discovered another woman whom he wanted to join The Ikettes. Her name was Ann Thomas, and she was very beautiful. Unfortunately, she couldn't sing a note. Ike came up with the idea of having Ann become the fourth Ikette in the act. Tina met Ann, and agreed that she would be a great visual addition to the stage show. Ann Thomas became known as "the nonsinging Ikette" in the group.

It wasn't long before Ike and Ann Thomas were having sex on a regular basis. On more than one occasion, Tina would walk in on Ike and Ann having sex, and she would calmly leave the room. Tina at this point had no desire to have sex with Ike, and she would rather have him occupied than bothering her.

It also wasn't long before Ann Thomas was pregnant with Ike's baby. This was another occurrence that Tina took in stride. It was like Tina was only biding her time during this era, eager to see where she might find an escape hatch to get free from the nonstop life she found herself trapped in. Ike didn't treat Ann Thomas any differently than he treated Tina, beating her when she displeased him.

The Ike & Tina Turner Revue would have a concert, and Ike would send Tina back to their hotel room. He would then go out and party all night with the band, The Ikettes, or any of the women he had lined up for that night's entertainment. Tina was the star of the show night after night on stage, but she was the only one not having any fun. Ike never allowed her to attend these parties. She would later recall, "The party rooms became party suites. I was jealous and hurt. But I couldn't say anything—no one could say anything to Ike. Because you never knew what he'd do" (4).

When they were back in Los Angeles, another girl named

Ann moved into one of the bedrooms of Ike and Tina's house. Her name was Ann Cain, and Tina was glad to have Ann there to help with the children and to keep Ike out of her hair as much as possible. When Ann started working more closely with Ike on the management of the business, there was a need for another housekeeper. This is when a woman by the name of Rhonda Gramm came into the picture. She too was fascinated with show business, and she and Tina became quite close friends throughout the years.

Instead of Tina getting jealous over Ike bringing all of these women into their house, she seemed relieved to have the attention taken off of her. Ann Cain, however, was extremely jealous of Rhonda Gramm when she came into the Turner operation. Eventually Rhonda Gramm joined the band as the road manager when they went on the road. Since part of Ike's money at gigs was based on how big the crowd was on any given night, someone from Ike's camp had to be at the door to monitor the number of paying patrons. Often, it was Rhonda's job to stand at the door and count people as they entered the club.

One of the many labels that Ike signed with at this point was Loma Records. It was run by a man named Bob Krasnow. A long-time record executive, he eventually became the chairman of Elektra Entertainment. He will never forget the first time he met Tina, at the Turner's Baldwin Hills home in the 1960s. He was expecting a big, glamorous star. Instead, he was shocked to find that when they were off stage, Ike treated her like she was his maid. Recalls Krasnow, "She was in the kitchen with a wet rag, down on her hands and knees wiping the floor, wearing a do-rag on her head" (5).

From the very start, Krasnow could tell that she had all of the raw talent that it took to become a really big star—much bigger than what Ike had turned her into. According to Bob, "She has this sensual persona, but her private mores are so old-fashioned, so traditional. Tina could be your girlfriend, your sister, your best friend—she can fulfill all these emotional niches. Yet when she gets up onstage, she has the power to stimulate you and bring words to life in a way that's uniquely her own" (5).

In December of 1965, The Ike & Tina Turner Revue was one of the guests on a TV special called *The TNT Award Show*. They were seen performing the songs "It's Gonna Work Out Fine" and "One More Time." Also on the show were Joan Baez, Bo Diddley, The Byrds, The Lovin' Spoonful, Petula Clark, Donovan, Ray Charles, and The Ronettes. This was when Tina Turner first came to the attention of producer Phil Spector.

Phil was the producer of all of the hit records by the girl group The Ronettes. He was also romantically involved with The Ronettes' lead singer, Ronnie Bennett. He started out in the music business as a member of the singing group The Teddy Bears. The group had a huge No. 1 hit in 1958 with the song "To Know Him Is to Love Him." After a couple more hit singles as part of The Teddy Bears, Phil decided to become a record producer. From 1961 to 1965, in his own Gold Star Recording Studio, he was responsible for producing hit after hit by The Crystals ("Uptown," "Da Doo Ron Ron"), Darlene Love ("Today I Met the Boy I'm Gonna Marry"), The Righteous Brothers ("You've Lost That Lovin' Feeling," "Unchained Melody"), and The Ronettes ("Be My Baby," "Baby, I Love You"). For years, one of his employees was another would-be producer, Sonny Bono. Sonny had a habit of inviting his girlfriend, Cher, to the studio. Cher made her recording debut as one of the background voices on "Da Doo Ron Ron."

According to Cher, "The first time actually I saw Tina, Sonny, and I were in Sacramento [California]. Ike and Tina were late, and so everyone was waiting for Ike and Tina to come. I was standing there and the whole entourage went by, and it was Ike and then all these guys, and then all these girls who looked like Tina, and then Tina Turner came whizzing by. And I thought, 'This is really Tina Turner, this is so amazing'" (19). Cher and Tina were to become life-long friends.

Phil had developed a way of making a group of singers and musicians sound like an army by layering track on track of sound on top of each other. He called his method of recording "the Wall of Sound." It was expensive to produce, unique, and has since become legendary.

Spector had started out as singer himself, so he appreciated great voices. As soon as he heard Tina Turner singing on *The TNT Award Show*, he was convinced that he had to produce her in the studio.

According to Bob Krasnow, his phone rang one day and, "It was Phil Spector. He said, 'You guys have Ike and Tina?' I said, 'Yeah, we do.' He said, 'Well, uh . . . I want to make a record. With Tina'" (4).

Spector was most insistent that Ike was not to have anything to do with the sessions he wanted to produce. Krasnow played liaison between Spector and Ike Turner. According to the deal that they struck, Phil paid Ike $20,000 for Tina's services. Phil would produce most of the album, but it had to include five songs produced by Ike. Actually, the songs Ike contributed to the album were more "pop" sounding versions of four of Ike & Tina hits as well, plus a new Turner composition. The rerecorded songs included "I Idolize You," "A Fool in Love," "Such a Fool for You" and "It's Gonna Work Out Fine." The new song that Ike wrote was called "Make 'Em Wait." These were excellent treatments of those songs, especially a more rocking version of "Such a Fool for You." Ike's verbal appearance on the album came as part of his familiar spoken vocal on this new version of "I Think It's Gonna Work Out Fine" and background vocals on "Make 'Em Wait."

However, it was the seven new songs that Phil Spector chose

to produce for Tina, which were truly fresh and unique. Tina was thrilled by the compliment of having Spector pursue her services. According to her, "Nobody wanted me to sing in those days. They wanted me to do that screaming and yelling" (5).

Among the songs that Phil recorded with Tina were the power ballads "Every Day I Have to Cry," and "I'll Never Need More Than This." He also chose two R&B classics that he wanted Tina to reinterpret: The Drifters' hit "Save the Last Dance for Me," and Martha Reeves & The Vandellas' "A Love Like Yours." Spector's trademark "Wall of Sound" technique makes these amongst the most excitingly recorded Tina Turner performances of the entire decade of the 1960s.

However, the make-it-or-break-it success of the album was pinned to the one song that was earmarked to be a sure-fire Tina Turner hit single. It was a song called "River Deep-Mountain High." Written by Phil, with Ellie Greenwich and Jeff Barry, it was a strong and gutsy kind of R&B song that would really allow Tina to open up vocally. Reportedly, Phil spent over $22,000 on this track alone. It was to be one of his milestone masterpieces. And in many ways, it was exactly that—a critical hit from the word "go."

Phil Spector personally played "River Deep-Mountain High" for Tina. She reported in the British music publication, *New Musical Express*, "I was knocked out by the Jeff Barry/Ellie Greenwich/[Phil] Spector song the first time I heard it. Phil kinda sang it along with a guitar and I loved it. Then he did the instrumental tracks. Wow! Jack Nitzche's arrangement was really somethin' else!" (20).

Tina was informed that she would be rehearsing the songs that Phil wanted her to record for two weeks, from noon until two every afternoon. One of the details that Tina liked the most was that Ike was not going to be with her. She was "allowed" by Ike to drive herself over to Phil's mansion. For the first time in her singing career, Tina felt like a true professional. This was a project that she completely put her heart into.

Tina was amazed as she arrived at Phil's mansion the first time. She had to be buzzed into the gate to get onto the premises. She eyed the high ceilings and winding staircases. Phil had a mynah bird in the house, and Tina would stop and talk to the bird while she waited for Phil to appear.

While Phil was recording the instrumental and background vocal tracks, Tina made one visit to the studio to see how he worked. She was in awe to find that he had seventy-five musicians and twenty-five singers jammed into the studio just for "River Deep-Mountain High." So much was riding on this one song that Phil reportedly spent hours and hours tinkering with the tracks. According to Bob Krasnow, every important studio session musician in the business was there working on this song, including Glen Campbell, Leon Russell, Sonny Bono, and Hal Blaine.

Cher was later to recall, "I remember when Phillip was playing it, and how excited he was." And Tina remembers, "He was so much behind that project—something he strongly, strongly believed in. I've got to tell you, it was seventy-five backing vocals—it was a choir! The room was full of singers" (19).

After two weeks of rehearsals, the day finally came for Tina to go into Gold Star Studios and record her lead vocal. It was March 7, 1966. When she arrived there at two in the afternoon with Bob Krasnow in tow, it was just Phil and his engineer Larry Levine. Spector had her sing the song over and over and over again. It wasn't long before she worked up a sweat in the sound booth. Finally, drenched in sweat, she removed her shirt and stood there in her bra. They recorded until late at night.

Tony Hall, an English promotional director, was assigned to the task of letting the radio stations in the British Isles know about this dynamic recording. A long-time Tina Turner fan,

Hall recalls, "When we first heard the test pressings, we flipped! This surely was the most exciting record of the year. But how commercial was it? Frankly, I had no idea. I just knew that it would be a crime if all the love put into it by Phil and the Turners were to no avail. The record had to be heard. So far, [in 1966] there was no sign of it in the U.S. Top 100 charts. All the greater challenge to us to get it away in Britain. So I sent out personally handwritten letters to almost every deejay in the country, beseeching them to give the public the chance to make up their own minds" (20).

In America the record failed to find an audience at any radio format. However, in England the record was a roaring success. "The response was really rewarding," explains Tony Hall, "And the reorders started pouring in. It looked like a certainty for Top 20. On the strength of these sales figures, I approached Johnnie Stewart, producer of BBC-TV's high-rating *Top of the Pops* show, to commission his American film unit to video-tape the Turners. Under the guidance of Jim Fitzpatrick in Los Angeles, the Turners were finally tracked down in the middle of a hectic ninety-day tour. The film that resulted was the most exciting of its kind ever seen in Britain. The warmth, pace, and spirit of Tina's vital, visual performance, watched over by Ike and backed by the wild dancing of The Ikettes, was really fantastic. We found it almost impossible to believe that the beautifully Tina was really a happily married mother of four! Up and up rose the record in the charts. Top 20. Top 10. Top 5. Top 3. In America? Nowhere. Frankly, we [in England] were knocked out. As Phil [Spector] himself was quoted as saying, 'We can only assume that England is more appreciative of talent and exciting music than the U.S.'" (20).

Hall was—like the rest of the world—misled about Tina's "happily married" status. If he only knew the reality of what went on behind closed doors in the Turners' private life! Aside from that fact, he certainly knew talent when he saw it.

According to George Harrison, a Beatle who truly knew good music when he heard it, "'River Deep-Mountain High' is a perfect record from start to finish—you couldn't improve on it" (21).

Although it is today regarded as a classic, Tina Turner's recording of "River Deep-Mountain High" at the time was considered to be a "bomb" in America. According to Tina, "It was too black for the pop radio stations and too pop for the black stations." Yet, she had to admit, "It showed people what I had in me" (1).

The song only made it to No. 88 in the United States. Interestingly enough, "River Deep-Mountain High" went to become a huge No. 14 American pop hit in 1970 when it was recorded by The Supremes & The Four Tops. But for Ike & Tina in 1966, it was to become known as the milestone American hit that never was.

Ironically, the song "River Deep-Mountain High" was considered such a non-hit in the United States that the *River Deep-Mountain High* album wasn't even released stateside. Instead, it was only released in Europe at the time. It didn't debut in America until 1969, when it was released by A&M Records and made it to No. 102 on the album chart in *Billboard*.

However, when the single hit No. 3 that summer in the United Kingdom, they were an overnight success. Because of the European success of "River Deep-Mountain High," all of a sudden there was a huge interest in Ike & Tina Turner and their elaborate revue.

Across the Atlantic Ocean, The Rolling Stones were among the biggest fans of the sound of Ike & Tina. The Stones had an upcoming British tour in the fall of 1966, and they thought that The Ike & Tina Turner Revue would be perfect to have on the bill.

On September 23, 1966, "The Rolling Stone's '66" U.K. tour kicked off at Royal Albert Hall in London. Also on the bill that night were The Yardbirds, Long John Baldry, and The Ike & Tina Turner Revue. Tina remembers walking out of her dressing room at Albert Hall, and listening to Jeff Beck, The Yardbirds' guitarist, standing against a wall, playing a masterful guitar solo. Ike too was impressed by the musicianship that he heard on this trip. They toured twelve dates across England with The Rolling Stones, the last one being on October 9, 1966, at the Gaumont Theatre, Southhampton, Hants.

Along the way, Tina Turner met two fans who were destined to become lifelong friends: Mick Jagger and Keith Richards of The Rolling Stones. Throughout the years, they have grown to become two of her best friends and biggest supporters—through thick and thin.

That tour was a lot of fun for Ike and Tina. They had gotten so used to being pigeon-holed into playing the so-called "chitlin circuit" of black American clubs that they had forgotten how great it was to be on large bills at big theaters. According to Tina, "It was fun. It was fantastic. My first experience was when Mick Jagger walked in the dressing room without knocking, and he says, 'I love how you girls dance.' That was the first introduction. I didn't know who he was. And then later, of course, Ike introduced us, and then often he would come into the dressing room, but we were always prepared because we never knew when he was coming in. But that was—that's how Mick is" (16).

Tina recalls the first time she laid eyes on Mick Jagger backstage at one of the shows, "I saw this very white-faced boy in the corner with big lips, and I had never seen a white person with lips that big anyway, so I didn't know who he was or what race he was," she laughs (5).

She was surprised to find that he was among her biggest

Tina Turner is the ultimate "soul survivor." Her initial stardom in the 1960s and 1970s was eclipsed by the ascension to rock & roll superstardom in the 1980s and 1990s.

(Photo: Peter Lindburgh for Virgin Records / MJB Photo Archives)

In the 1960s, Tina and Ike Turner experienced their first wave of success with hits like "A Fool in Love" and "I Think It's Gonna Work out Fine."

(Photo: Harry Goodwin / Star File)

Ike & Tina backstage with Mick Jagger during the 1969 concert tour that exposed the duo to a rock & roll audience and changed the musical focus of their careers.

(Photo: Joe Sia / Star File)

The Ike & Tina Turner Review
in New York City, 1971. With
the famed (and ever-changing)
Ikettes behind her, Tina
commanded the stage
wherever she performed.
(Photo: Dagmar / Star File)

Thanks to hits like
"Nutbush City Limits" and
"Proud Mary," Ike &
Turner reached new heights
in the 1970s. In terms of
sheer energy, no one in the
business could top Tina.
(Photo: Bob Gruen / Star File)

Tina and Ike in 1975, the year of her triumphant role in the rock opera Tommy. *The public had no idea of the torment of her personal life with the physically abusive Ike.*
(Photo: Jill Furmanovsky / Star File)

In 1975, Ann-Margret and Tina were two of the stars of the hit film Tommy. When Tina finally left Ike the following year, Ann-Margret was one of the close friends who helped Tina get back on her feet.
(Photo: Chuck Pulin / Star File)

Ike and Tina in March 1976. Four months later, she fled for her life and never looked back. She had finally reached the end of her rope with Ike's beatings and his drug-induced rages.

(Photo: Bob Gruen / Star File)

Free of Ike, and testing her wings as a solo act, Tina performed at dance clubs like The Saint in New York City in the early 1980s.

(Photos: Charles R. Moniz)

Tina's big breakthrough happened in Manhattan
at a rock & roll club called The Ritz.

(Photos: Charles R. Moniz)

Tina was responsible for raising she and Ike's cumulative family of four boys. The "queen of rock & roll" and her sons in 1982.

(Photo: Bob Gruen / Star File)

fans. "Mick Jagger told me that he was standing in the wings watching the show," says Tina. "He said that basically after that was when he started dancing and moving around. I think he was inspired by the performance because of the energy and the movement the girls and I were putting out. Mick also liked Ike's sound and style because English acts do like blues music" (10).

Tina realized very quickly of Jagger, "he liked black women, liked to play around with them" (5).

Keith Richards has similarly fond memories of first meeting Tina on this tour. "The first time you see Tina is mind-boggling," he claims. "She's so gutsy and dynamic! . . . Tina was great-looking, plus she could move and she had that voice. Usually you can have a voice but you can't move, or you're good-looking but you can't sing. How can anybody have that much? With Tina, there it all is—it's all there" (5).

Richards was surprised to see how exciting Ike & Tina's show was. According to him, it was "kind of like school for us. . . . We were one little blues band. Mick's stage center was a twelve-inch square." Enter Ike and Tina and all of the leggy Ikettes, and there were Richards and Jagger and crew, surrounded by "all these beautiful black chicks in sequins running around backstage, and these fantastic musicians to learn from. We'd do our little bit [on stage], and then we'd watch Ike and Tina and the Ikettes, and we said, 'Wow, this is show business!' They made us realize you got to do more than just stand there and play guitar" (5).

Keith recalls being blown away by the whole "show business" presentation of Ike and Tina's act. It was not only exciting music-wise, but it was also strongly visual and filled with an exciting energy. However, he insists that Tina was the reason that the act was special to begin with. According to Richards, "To me it was all Tina Turner. Ike didn't see it that way. To him he was a Svengali who wrote the songs; he was the producer and Tina was his ticket. He saw himself as Phil Spector, as the driving force behind the star. I saw him as the driving force behind a lot of things. It was the first time I saw a guy pistol-whip another guy in his own band. Ike acted like a goddamned pimp" (5).

Tina remembers how Mick asked her to give them dance lessons backstage, so that they could enliven their act with more energy. "He says, 'I like how you girls dance. How are you doing that stuff?' We would all get up with Mick, and we would do things, and we would laugh, because his rhythm and his hips and how he was doing it was totally off. It wasn't teaching him; it wasn't dance classes. This is what we did backstage—we played around, because onstage he was just doing the tambourine. He wasn't even dancing. This was 1966. Afterwards, Mick came to America doing The Pony. And all of us thought we had done it backstage. Well, I didn't tell people I taught him. I said we would just sit around during intermissions having a good time" (5). Tina showed Jagger how to do The Pony and some other dances, and since that time, she has been accredited as the woman who taught Jagger to dance.

Richards was also impressed by what a warm person Tina always was when he was around her. "Guys would talk about her image sexually, just as a woman," he explains, "But the Tina I knew was different. Tina was somebody to take care of you. Out on the road somebody would always be sick, and she would say, 'Take care of yourself, you have a cold, here's the VapoRub, keep your scarf on, do your coat up.' I saw her like a favorite aunt or a fairy godmother. I always had other visions of Tina—of a mother-earth thing" (5).

This European trip was one of the best and strongest moves that had occurred in their long career. Based on the British success of "River Deep-Mountain High," one of their previously recorded singles on Warner Brothers Records, "Tell Her I'm Not Home," made it to No. 48 on the U.K. Pop chart that year.

While they were in London, Ike & Tina appeared on the British TV show *Ready, Steady, Go!* One of the producers of the show was a woman named Vicki Wickham. Vicki was always a warm and creative woman, and she was very involved in the careers of Dusty Springfield and Patti LaBelle & The Bluebelles (Sarah Dash, Cindy Birdsong, and Nona Hendryx). Tina was always so protected and watched by Ike that she was never allowed to make friends on her own. In London, Ike was kept busy on his own, so Tina became friendly with Vicki and they got to spend some time together. Tina confessed to her how unhappy her life was.

It was Vicki Wickham who took Tina to a fortune teller in London. The woman she took her to was a card reader. In that reading, Tina's eyes were opened to a world that she had only envisioned. The fortune teller claimed that Tina was destined to be among the biggest stars in the galaxy, and that her partner was going to fall away like a dead leaf falling from a tree.

After they were finished with the British concert dates, Ike and Tina flew to Germany and France to make some television appearances and meet the press. Tina's eyes were opened up to the fact that there was a whole world out there beyond the United States. She was especially impressed with France, and she felt very at-home while there.

Based on their new-found European success, in November of 1966, Tina's version of "A Love Like Yours" climbed up the U.K. charts to become a No. 16 hit. According to Tina, "We were breaking the chains that were holding us back from a mass audience" (1).

Tina also claims that this was the period in her life where she realized that she was no longer in love with Ike Turner. Yet, she continued to stay with him. She kept thinking that if they would just have a massive hit record, she would be able to leave him for good. "So for seven years—the first seven years with Ike, I was just realizing what my life was and thinking how bad it was, and I was very loyal to Ike because he had been very good to me in the early days," she explained (12).

Rhonda Graam, who was working as Ike and Tina's road manager, recalls, "She was scared to death of him—everybody around him was, in his own little cult. It was like he had a hold on people" (5).

While Tina and Ike were in Paris, Ike was eager to have some time to himself, so he gave her money to go shopping. Walking through the streets of Paris, Tina began to feel alive again. According to her, shopping became her only escape from what she called "Ike and his awful world" (4).

When the entourage returned to the United States, it was to headline the Galaxy Club in Hollywood on Christmas week 1966. As the year came to an end, the London fortune teller's words continued to ring in Tina's ears—she would become one of the biggest of stars, and her partner would simply fall away. This prophecy was destined to come true. However, it was to take twenty years to blossom into full reality.

7

BOLD SOUL SISTER

From 1967 to 1970 it was the golden age of Ike & Tina Turner. This was the creative height of the band. It was also the era when Tina was at her wildest. While singing on stage she would dance with unbridled abandon—often in unison with the equally leggy Ikettes. Clad in short mini-skirts, she would throw her head back and her long mane of hair would flow behind her like it was caught in a hurricane. The dance steps Tina and The Ikettes did were energetically frenetic and mesmerizing to watch. Behind high-heeled Tina and her back-up girls stood a stoic and stern-looking Ike. He was the guitar-playing leader of the red-hot band he had assembled. He would direct his musicians through their soulful paces while Tina relentlessly commanded the spotlight. To see them perform live was to understand their greatness as a band.

Audiences had no clue about the living hell that Tina's personal life had become. They just knew her as the bold soul sister who seemed to expel an incomparable amount of excitement and heart. She threw herself into her songs and her stage performances. Her hours on stage were the only time that she felt truly alive.

Likewise, no one knew how screwed up some of their business arrangements were. This was largely due to Ike's need to control everything. He was the manager, the dealmaker, the record producer, the bandleader, the booking agent, and—most of all—the decision maker. If anyone stepped out of line, they would be fined, fired, pistol-whipped, or physically beaten. He ruled his world with fear and intimidation. He was insistent that no manager or outside agent was to take a percentage of his money. Ike had been used to doing these things his entire career, and he wasn't about to stop. With proper management, things might have been much better for The Ike & Tina Turner Revue as an act.

In 1967, Ike was again bouncing from record label to record label, accepting quick money for singles' deals or one-shot albums. In this way he made instant cash, but there wasn't a concentrated strategy for career growth. The year before, Kent Records had released an album called *The Soul of Ike & Tina Turner*. It was a compilation of several of the group's singles for Kent. Among them were, "(Am I) A Fool in Love," "Chicken Shack," and a song that Tina must have felt very sincerely— "Hurt Is All You Gave Me."

Their one 1967 album, called *Festival of Live Performances*, was also on Kent Records. It included performances of "A Fool in Love," "He's Mine," "Stop the Wedding," "My Man," and "I Can't Stop Loving You." When their previously released album, *The Ike & Tina Turner Show, Live, Volume 2*, came out in England in February, an eight-day British promotional tour was set up for them.

But when they got back to America, Tina was completely depressed about her life. After "River Deep-Mountain High" came and went, Tina found herself lost at sea, and stuck on a sinking ship with Ike Turner.

She began to think of how to escape. "I had to get out of there because whatever I was doing didn't matter anymore. I had my house, I had my children, I had my own car. I had stuff. I shopped. But I had this horrible relationship I was hiding behind" (5). At one point during this era, she had already tried packing up the four boys and getting on a Tennessee-bound bus. Unfortunately for her, Ike tracked her down and dragged her back into his car.

"I wanted him to find a woman," Tina claims. That way she would be rid of him once and for all. When Tina suddenly announced to him that she wanted their "marriage" to be replaced by a business relationship, Ike did not take the news well. She recalls, "He would really fight harder then, because he thought he was losing control" (5).

Rhonda Gramm explains, "He was afraid she'd leave him. He would keep the fear going. He didn't want her to talk to anyone else—to put thoughts in her mind" (5).

According to Tina, "Sex had become rape as far as I was concerned. I didn't want Ike near me. It was more than not being turned on. It was the fact he was sleeping around. That was not my style" (5).

The sleeping around on the road, or "on the sly," was one thing, but Tina's life with Ike had come to an impasse. She had no life with him, and she had no life apart from him. Furthermore, during this time period Ike began getting involved in drugs. What began with a little marijuana soon progressed to cocaine. It started out slowly at first, but soon his cocaine use made him even more violent and unpredictable.

On one particular afternoon, Ike sent Tina out to the grocery store. She had a feeling that something was up with him.

She decided to hurry, and showed up back at the house earlier than Ike had expected her. There was Ike and "housekeeper" Ann Cain having sex in the middle of the living room. That was when Tina put her foot down. Ike had already gotten non-singing Ikette Ann Thomas pregnant and was paying child support, and now he was screwing Ann Cain in their own house.

Tina told Ike that she didn't want that woman at their house anymore. Not long afterward, she came home to find Ann Cain was there again. Tina was so mad that she ran after Ann with a hammer, determined to hit her over the head with it. Fortunately for Ann, Tina's shoes slipped on the slippery floor, and Ike had to break up the fight.

Tina wasn't the only person who was getting fed up with Ike. At one point, the entire band walked out on him because he was so impossible to get along with. It seemed that Tina was the only one who never deserted him—and if anyone had reason to leave him, it was she.

Since Ike had to hire a whole new band, a new influx of people came into The Ike & Tina Turner Revue. One of the musicians that Ike hired was a baritone sax player by the name of Johnny Williams. Tina liked him the minute she laid eyes on him. Johnny was a well-mannered, light-skinned black man, and he read books, practiced yoga, and was into health food. Whenever Johnny was around Tina, he complimented her on her looks and made her feel good about herself. He was the exact opposite of Ike. She began feeling emotions inside her that had long been dead.

Tina was in love with Johnny, and she began to let Ike know how much she liked the new sax player. At first Ike didn't pay much attention to Tina's flirtation with Johnny, but it soon started to bug him. On one occasion while on tour, Ike was out doing something, so Tina went to Johnny's hotel room and walked right into his arms. She hugged him tightly—just once—and then left as fast as she had walked in. It was the one and only time she ever touched him, and that one thrill had to last her a long time. She knew that nothing could ever come of the flirtation, but the important thing was that it made her feel alive again. It illustrated to her how good life could be without fear—and without Ike.

Johnny was among the topics that came up when Ike and Tina had one of their huge blowout fights one night in 1967. Ike was also pissed that Tina had the nerve to go off and do those recordings with Phil Spector—even though it was Ike who had agreed to that deal. In other words, how dare Tina have a life of her own.

The next day Tina arrived for work severely beaten. Her eye was swollen nearly shut, her lip was cut, and she had obviously been used as Ike's punching bag once again. Johnny took one look at Tina, and tears began to stream out of his eyes. He set his saxophone down and immediately left the stage. Johnny gave notice, announcing that he couldn't work under conditions like these.

The first time that Tina remembers actually seeing Ike snort cocaine was in San Francisco that year. He had a rolled up $100 bill up his nose as he snorted it. According to her, the escalating use of cocaine started making him "evil."

In spite of feeling like her life was falling apart, her live performances continued to astound fans and critics who caught her act. In a 1967 issue of *Rolling Stone*, the magazine's founder, Jann S. Wenner, wrote, "Tina Turner is an incredible chick. . . . She comes in this very short miniskirt, way above her knees, with zillions of silver sequins and sparkers pasted on it. Her dancing is completely unrestrained. She and The Ikettes scream, wail, and Tina is nothing short of amazing" (22).

Recalls Bette Midler, "I saw Tina Turner for the first time at the Fillmore East in the late '60s. She was—and remains—the greatest performer of her time. I've never seen anyone like her before or since, and I'll never forget the excitement of it all. I was in the balcony and I was sure it was going to collapse from the stomping, screaming frenzy of that crowd. My identification was, to say the least, very, very strong. Tina is, to me, utterly unique. She owns it all: great musicality, great intonation, great style, great energy, great moves, and above all, tremendous emotional power, all wrapped up in a fabulous physical package. I owe her a tremendous debt. Thank God she's too much of a lady to collect!" (21).

Critics and fans alike saw her as something special and magical, but to Ike she was nothing more than a meal ticket. In many ways, Tina was no more than a cog in the wheel of the Ike Turner machine. Emotionally, she was no more or less important than the guitar player or the drummer who was in his band. Tina realized that she was being treated as a mere tool in Ike's scheme. "I was the singer," she recalls with resignation (5). She had the one thing Ike would never have—a great singing voice.

In 1968 the group released three different albums on three different labels. Among the three was yet another live performance album release, this time called *Ike & Tina Turner & The Ikettes in Person* on Minit Records. It featured Tina's versions of "Sweet Soul Music," "Son of a Preacher Man," "I Heard It through the Grapevine," and "Respect." An album called *So Fine* was released on Pompeii Records, featuring the dance number "Shake a Tail Feather." And on London Records came a hits retrospective simply called *Ike & Tina Turner.*

In 1968, while all of this was going on, Ike and Tina and the entourage all went back to England for another tour. This tour included both Ann Cain and Ann Thomas—the latter was still an Ikette. It was during this tour that it was discovered that Tina and Ann Thomas were *both* pregnant with Ike's babies. Disgusted with the whole situation, Tina decided that she was through having Ike's children. Ultimately, she went and had an abortion.

While on this European tour, Ike would get adjoining rooms. One was for he and Tina, and the other one was for Ann Thomas. In the middle of the night, he would go into Ann's room, have sex with her, and then come back to bed with Tina to fall asleep.

At one point, they took a trip to Switzerland and rented a sports car. Ike and Tina were riding in the front seat, and Ann was in the back. Some guy in a red Ferrari drove up alongside of them and started flirting with Ann Thomas. When they got to the hotel, the members of their entourage kept teasing Ann about the lover that was chasing her through Switzerland. Ike slowly got madder and madder. Finally, he exploded into one of his irrational rages. He went into Ann's room, dragged her out into the stairwell of the hotel, and beat her up.

Ann Cain was the next one in line for Ike's blows. On a tour of the south of the United States, she picked a fight with him. He came at her with his guitar and broke it over her. When he saw the broken guitar, he began to beat her with his fists for causing his guitar to break. Not long afterwards, Ann Cain reached the conclusion that she'd had enough of Ike Turner, and she quit.

Back home in Los Angeles, Ike had set up a little recording studio in their Olympiad Drive house. It was a demo-recording unit; that way he could do coke and work around the clock in his own home.

The only problem with this new in-house studio setup was that when Ike ran into recording frustrations, he would often take them out on Tina. She recalls, "That was when I was just being led blindly, because I didn't care about anything. I was just getting through this period" (5).

Meanwhile, Tina was becoming a regular visitor to the

emergency room at Daniel Freeman Hospital in Inglewood. One of Ike's favorite things to beat her with was wire coat hangers. He also beat her with telephones, shoes, or whatever happened to be handy whenever he went off on one of his tirades. He would also choke her with his bare hands.

Once, right before a show, he socked her in the face and broke her jaw. When she complained of the pain, he forced her to go on stage and sing anyway. Throughout the set she could taste blood flowing in her mouth. Ike didn't care. She either did what he told her to do, or he simply beat the hell out of her.

On one particular visit to the doctor's office, Tina complained to the physician that she was having trouble sleeping. Could she please have some sleeping pills? Of course he complied. He gave her a prescription for fifty Valiums.

Tina had tried to run away from Ike. That didn't work. She felt trapped in a nightmare that never seemed to come to an end. Perhaps just leaving the world would be the best answer. Thinking that suicide might be her only escape, and equipped with a whole bottle of Valiums, she now had the means to simply and quietly kill herself.

The members of The Ike & Tina Turner Revue were preparing to perform at a new black club in Los Angeles. Tina and the girls were up at the house, trying on the new mini-dresses that they were going to wear that night. Tina went into the bathroom and very quietly took all fifty Valiums.

By the time they arrived at the club, Tina could feel the pills taking effect. She kept thinking that if she could just remain conscious long enough to get onto the stage, Ike would still be paid for the gig. She was in the dressing room with The Ikettes, and she started putting her makeup on. When she went to use her eyebrow pencil, she missed her eyebrow and drew a line all the way up her forehead.

One of The Ikettes took a look at her and knew something

was very *very* wrong. When Ike arrived, Tina was unable to stand up. Instead of terror or sympathy, Ike was simply mad at her for doing anything so stupid, and for having the audacity to ruin his night. They rushed her to the hospital. She arrived unconscious, and the doctors began pumping her stomach.

Later, her doctor told her that Ike was standing over her, screaming, "You want to die? Then die!" (1).

As she began to regain consciousness, Ike shouted at her, "You motherfucker, you tryin' to ruin my life?" (4). To say the least, her nightmare was far from over, and her plan to use death to escape from Ike had been entirely unsuccessful.

Out of the hospital, Tina was not allowed to recuperate. Ike forced her to go back to work immediately. Her stomach was still screwed up from all of the Valium pills she had ingested. She was so sick after performing a show that she would go into the wings and start to cough and vomit. She couldn't even make it back to the dressing room. Ike didn't give her an ounce of sympathy. Instead, he blamed her for screwing up the series of gigs.

According to Tina, this was a major cutoff point in their relationship. She had originally liked him when she first met him. Then, for a while, she loved him. When that subsided, she liked him as a friend again. Finally, she began to hate him and despised being around him.

Meanwhile, they were constantly recording songs. One of the things that one has to admire about Ike is the fact that he managed to record and produce song after song.

Several Ike & Tina albums were released in 1969, all signed to different labels. They included *Cussin', Cryin', and Carryin' On* on Pompeii Records (again featuring "Shake a Tail Feather"), *Get It Together* on Pompeii Records (including "Beauty's Just Skin Deep"), *Get It, Get It* on Cenco Records, and *Her Man, His Woman* for Capitol Records. However, none of them sold well enough to amount to anything. The one album to do well out of this batch was another live performance album for Minit Records called *In Person*. Recorded at the Basin Street West, *In Person* made it to No. 142 in *Billboard* in America.

Yet, the nonstop touring and the pace of their lives continued to be hectic. Among the bookings that they received that year for personal appearances was a performance in Las Vegas. Since Elvis Presley made his big live performing comeback in Vegas, rock & roll and rhythm & blues acts started to carry more weight with the casino crowds. And Ike & Tina were right there.

It was also a year for some musical changes. For the first time since Tina had recorded with Phil Spector, Bob Krasnow came back in their lives. He was now at Blue Thumb Records, and he needed acts to sign to his label. Always one to sign a new recording deal, Ike took Krasnow up on his proposal. With that, Ike signed on for two albums with Blue Thumb.

Bob had an idea he wanted to run by Ike. He felt very strongly that Ike & Tina should record the Otis Redding song "I've Been Loving You Too Long." Ike naturally didn't agree, but eventually Krasnow talked him into it. When the song was released as the duo's next single, it went on to become their biggest chart hit in ages, making it to No. 68 in the United States. The album it came from, *Outta Season*, charted at No. 91 in *Billboard* magazine.

One of the most controversial aspects of the album was the cover concept of the *Outta Season* album. Intended to poke fun at racism, the photo of Tina (on the front) and Ike (on the back) featured them in "white face" makeup, eating big slices of watermelon. Not everyone got the joke it was intended to provoke, but it certainly made some noise on the charts. Original copies of this album are considered true collector's items to-day.

They immediately followed up that album with another disc for Blue Thumb Records, called *The Hunter*. It produced one hit single, a song Ike composed called "Bold Soul Sister," which became a No. 59 hit in America. The album peaked in *Billboard* at No. 176.

The year 1969 was also a very high-profile one for Ike & Tina. On June 20 they were one of the headlining acts at the Newport '69 Festival at San Fernando Valley State College at Devonshire Downs, in Northridge, California. They also joined The Rolling Stones amidst their tour of the United States. The tour opened on November 7 in Denver, Colorado. It also encompassed one of the most controversial Rolling Stones' appearances: the infamous free concert at Altamont Speedway on December 7, 1969, at which four people died—including one by knife wounds. Fortunately, Ike & Tina weren't present for that particular gig. However, they were featured in the film that was made of the Stones during that tour, called *Gimme Shelter*. In the concert film, Tina is seen singing their new hit "I've Been Loving You Too Long."

Tina's friends were horrified when they learned about how Ike would beat her mercilessly. The stories never came from Tina. She was afraid of letting people know about what her life was really like. Bill Wyman of The Rolling Stones recalls, "I heard horrendous stories from The Ikettes about what was going on in the background. It was almost unbelievable, actually. They changed so quickly, The Ikettes, every time you saw them, it was a completely different set, because they just couldn't deal with what was going on, I suppose" (19).

On November 26, 1969, Tina Turner turned thirty. She was starting to come into her own as a person. She was beginning to have an awareness of the world around her for the first time. She was also pushing aside several of the illusions that she had carried around with her about life in general, her life with Ike, and where she was going. She recalls making several new observations during this era.

According to her, "I'd say I was about thirty when a lot of realizations happened. I remember I had always respected airline stewardesses. It was a fantasy, you know—the traveling, the way they dressed in their hats and suits. And on my thirtieth birthday, I remember sitting on a plane. I don't know what happened, but I finally saw that they were really making people comfortable and serving food. I don't mean disrespectfully, but I thought, 'Oh, my God, they're waitresses.' I'd only seen the beauty and the glamour" (7).

During this period of time, all of a sudden Tina also became much more interested in listening to the music that was going on around her. The year 1969 was made famous by Woodstock and several other music festivals. There suddenly seemed to be all kinds of great new music to listen to everywhere, especially in the rock & roll realm. It was the year of The Beatles' *Abbey Road, Hair, Blood, Sweat & Tears, Led Zeppelin II*, and Creedence Clearwater Revival's *Green River*. Whereas, in all of the years before, Tina had just let Ike choose their music and dictate their direction, she began to branch out to discover new material on her own. Ike's musical taste was still—very much—stuck in the 1950s. It was time for Tina Turner to begin to look forward instead of backward. As the 1960s came to an end, so did an old way of thinking for Tina.

One of the songs that she fell in love with was The Beatles' recent single "Come Together." She recalls, "I said to Ike, 'Please, please let me do that song on stage'" (1). He wasn't keen on it in the beginning, but she convinced him to let her start selecting new tunes to interpret on stage and on record.

She was growing tired of always singing rhythm & blues songs about "I lost my man" and "I'm so broke and so blue." She wanted to sing rock & roll. She liked the stance of the songs, and she enjoyed singing them. She especially liked the strong, aggressive kind of music that the male rockers were writing and performing. Among the songs she fell in love with during this era were the Sly & The Family Stone's "I Want Take You Higher," and Creedence Clearwater Revival's "Proud Mary."

It is interesting to note that Ike had the habit of rewriting the same song over and over again. In a whole string of songs he had Tina record, she would publicly call herself a "fool," while the object of her affections was God's gift to women. After "A Fool in Love" came "Poor Fool," "A Fool for a Fool," "A Fool for You," "Poor Little Fool," "Foolish," and "Such a Fool for You." Furthermore, Tina would be required to record these songs over and over again, as Ike jumped from record company advance to record company advance. Well, she was about to get her own songs to sing. At long last, Tina was getting sick of being an unquestioning "fool" for Ike.

8

PROUD MARY

With the two-album obligation to Blue Thumb Records fulfilled, Ike again signed a new recording contract for himself and Tina. This new contract was a more long-term one. It started out with Minit Records—a label they had been on and off of for years. However, only months into the contract the company was absorbed into Liberty Records, which was in turn melded into United Artists Records. This contract would last for the duration of the 1970s.

When the single version of the song that Tina wanted to sing, "Come Together," was released, it peaked at No. 57 on the American singles chart. The album of the same name made it to No. 130 on the LP chart. The *Come Together* album contained Ike & Tina's entry into the rock & roll realm, featuring Tina's searing version of "Honky Tonk Women," as well as a truly rocking interpretation of Sly & The Family Stone's "I Want to Take You Higher." It was the beginning of Tina's career-long habit of taking hot rock songs—from male rockers—and making them all her own. As a single, "I Want to Take You Higher" made it to No. 34 on the Pop chart. The stage was now set for Ike & Tina to score some of the biggest musical successes of their entire career together.

Probably the most revealing Ike Turner composition on the *Come Together* album was an audible train wreck that he wrote called "Contact High." A song about smoking pot, doing coke, and passing out, Tina must surely have cringed at being forced to record such drivel. It also gave the false impression that Tina was a recreational drug user. Nothing could be further from the truth. It was, however, an honest look into Ike's life of false bravado amid a delusional sea of drugs.

Ike & Tina made several notable television appearances during 1970. They were seen on *The Andy Williams Show* and the Sunday night mainstay of American entertainment, *Ed Sullivan*. They were busy and working hard, touring and recording. However, the nonstop grind began to wear on Tina.

At this point, Tina came down with a cold that wouldn't seem to go away. Soon it turned into bronchitis. Her doctor commanded that she get immediate bed rest. Ike would hear nothing of it, and he insisted that she keep on working and quit complaining—and so she did. Soon she had full-blown pneumonia and a fever that she couldn't shake.

Tina tried to tell Ike that she was gravely ill, but he insisted that she just take aspirin. He had several tour dates lined up, and he wanted the money from them. He couldn't be bothered with her complaints. Finally, Tina had to drive herself to the hospital in their limousine. She had never driven such a huge car, but it was the only way she could get there—Ike sure wasn't going to drive her to seek help. The hospital admitted her immediately, and found that she had developed tuberculosis. Her right lung had collapsed, she had a glandular infection, and she was developing lumps in both of her legs because she was so full of toxic infection.

In the hospital one morning, Tina awoke to discover that her room was filled with flower arrangements. Reading the cards, she was delighted and thrilled to see that one of the huge arrangements was from Mick Jagger and The Rolling Stones. She was touched to find that she was genuinely loved and cared about by her friends. Naturally, not a single flower arrived from Ike.

Tina was hospitalized for several weeks. When she was finally released, she went home to a real shocker. Instead of having spent money on flowers to send to Tina, she found that Ike had spent a small fortune on completely redecorating their house—from floor to ceiling—in *Superfly* ghetto whorehouse chic style. Tina was horrified at this sight.

The house was done in wall-to-wall red shag carpeting. There was a blue velvet sofa featuring arms that morphed into octopus tentacles, a waterfall now cascaded down one wall, and there was an enormous coffee table shaped like a guitar. Cabinets that looked like huge snail shells housed a TV set and entertainment equipment, and several bubbling aquariums were homes to tropical fish. The master bedroom now had mirrors on the ceiling, and the kitchen was a bilious shade of green.

When Bob Krasnow came over to the house to see Ike to discuss business, he was equally as shocked by the incomparable tackiness of the new decor. "You mean you can actually spend $70,000 at Woolworth's?!" he exclaimed (1).

Fresh from the hospital, and held together by massive amounts of antibiotics, Tina again hit the road for an endless sea of one-nighters. The only real respite came when they played in Las Vegas. At least there, the Turner clan was put up in grand style. They would play there for long engagements, and there was even enough room in the suite to bring along all four of their cumulative sons.

While they were in Las Vegas during this era, they were invited to appear on an episode of the TV crime series *The Name of the Game*. This particular episode was filmed in Vegas and centered around one of Tina's favorite stars—Sammy Davis Jr. Thanks to Sammy, in the episode Ike and Tina were seen as guest star performers who were featured in a casino segment.

Sammy loved Tina, and when the filming was finished, he wanted to do something nice for her. Perhaps he sensed that Ike *never, ever* did anything nice for her! Davis took Tina's assistant, Rhonda Gramm, aside and told her what he had planned: He wanted to buy Tina a Mercedes Benz as a gift. Rhonda informed him that what Tina would really love was a Jaguar. Sammy loved the idea of surprising her with exactly that.

As planned, Sammy walked her out of the hotel and presented her with the white XJ6 four-door luxury sports car. Tina was knocked out by his kindness. She absolutely loved that car and was deeply touched by Sammy's generosity. Even if Ike placed no value on her, it was bolstering to find that she really did have friends in show business who genuinely did care about her.

One of the most prized liaisons that Tina made in Las Vegas during this time was her friendship with Ann-Margret. A huge movie star in the 1960s, Ann-Margret found a warm reception from casino audiences when she brought her Hollywood glitz to Vegas showrooms.

After the "Ike & Tina" show one night, Tina and Rhonda Gramm went to the Tropicana Hotel to catch the last few minutes of Ann-Margret's show. Afterward, they went backstage to meet her and were delighted to find that Tina was one of Ann-Margret's favorite singers. In fact, she had a stack of Tina's recordings there in her dressing room. It was to be the beginning of a long friendship between Tina and Ann-Margret.

In late 1970, Ike and Tina were in Florida when they booked some studio time and recorded the song "Proud Mary."

A Cajun-flavored rock song by Creedence Clearwater Revival, "Proud Mary" was to get a very unique treatment from Tina, and it would become one of her signature songs.

The whole elongated and ad-libbed rap that Tina has at the beginning of their recording of "Proud Mary" is absolutely priceless. The way she announces that she "never ever" does anything "nice" and "easy," because she does it "nice" and "rough," is a trademark monologue for her. In the song itself, she is able to show for the first time how she can sound melodic when she wants to, but then she shifts gears and demonstrates how she likes to get rough and raucous as well.

Released as a single in the early part of 1971, "Proud Mary" became Ike & Tina's first Top 10 single on the Pop charts. Peaking at No. 4 and becoming their first million-selling single, it finally put them over the top. According to the writer of the song, John Fogerty of Creedence Clearwater Revival, "Tina Turner doing 'Proud Mary' is one of the most electrifying images in rock & roll. Thank you, beautiful Tina, for shooting my song into the stratosphere" (21). It became the second biggest single song of their entire career together.

Ike & Tina's new album, *Workin' Together*, which featured "Proud Mary," likewise became the biggest selling album of their entire career, reaching No. 25 in *Billboard* magazine in the United States. The album also included the amusing Ike composition, "Funkier than a Mosquita's Tweeter," as well as Tina's great interpretations of The Beatles' hits "Get Back" and "Let It Be," and their version of Jessie Hill's "Ooh Poo Pah Doo."

On May 6, 1971, "Proud Mary" was certified by the RIAA (Record Industry Association of America) as their first "Gold" single. The following month, their next single, "Ooh Poo Pah Doo" peaked at No. 60 in the United States.

That same year, The Ike & Tina Turner Revue returned to Europe in hopes of replicating the same recording success they had finally achieved in the United States. The tour was a smash, but somehow the record failed to have the same success in the United Kingdom.

In September, their next album—a live set entitled *Live at Carnegie Hall: What You Hear Is What You Get*—was released by United Artists Records, reached No. 25 in *Billboard*, and was certified Gold for selling 500,000 copies in the United States. The show, which was recorded in New York City's most famous venue, found the duo introduced on stage by famous DJ Frankie Crocker. This particular live album was perfect to demonstrate Tina's new rock & roll vocal stance on songs like "Honky Tonk Women," "A Love Like Yours (Don't Come Knockin' Every Day)," "Proud Mary," "I Want to Take You Higher," and "I've Been Loving You Too Long." Finally they were finished recording live versions of Ike's series of "Fool" songs. To borrow a phrase from The Who, at least now Tina wasn't about to be *fooled* again.

Oddly enough, Liberty Records—a subsidiary of United Artists Records—released still another concert album on Ike & Tina that same year: the single disk *Live in Paris*. Somehow the live releases just kept rolling and rolling.

What Ike Turner was really rolling in at this point was money—and by rights—Tina should have been too. However, he still never actually paid her a cent. He was in charge of all the cash, and she was just expected to accept the few things that he gave her. "Proud Mary," their recording successes, and the money from their concert appearances, had filled Ike's pockets with lots of cold, hard cash.

For a long time, Ike Turner had wanted to be the owner of his own recording studio. That way he could not only save the money that he spent booking studio time, but he could also indulge his every musical whim. With that, he began to make plans for what was to become Bolic Sound Studios. Located at 1310 La Brea Avenue, about five minutes from the Turner house, the one-story building he purchased was totally renovated for his needs. There were two complete sound studios built into the structure. There was a larger studio, which Ike intended to rent out to other recording artists, and a smaller studio, which was for him alone.

Bolic Sound became Ike's own private playground. Now the all-night parties and the cocaine orgies could go on night and day, under the guise of being a business venture.

According to Tina, "When he built it, I thought, 'Wonderful—I'll be rid of him.' But then the phone calls started at three o'clock in the morning. 'Tina, Ike wants you.'" (1). She could be sound asleep in the middle of the night, and Ike would telephone her, demanding that she come to the studio immediately to sing her lead vocal on some opus he had just composed.

In order to protect his domain of drugs, women, and million-dollar sound equipment, Ike had his own arsenal of guns to protect the premises. Furthermore, every square inch of the place was under the surveillance of twenty-four-hour security cameras. The Olympiad house they lived in had a similar system of security devices.

In October 1971, a cover story in *Rolling Stone* magazine blew away any misconception about Ike being just an everyday self-made successful musician. It painted a picture of him as a pistol-packing, drug-crazed lunatic. An "associate" quoted in the story said of Turner, "Ike would storm into the office with a troop of people, six-foot chicks, a bag of cocaine. Really, really crazy. He'd carry around $25,000 in cash in his pocket—with a gun. He'd drive around town, man, sometimes to Watts, sometimes Laurel Canyon, in his new Rolls Royce to pick up coke" (23).

Tina remembers going into the studio for those late-night sessions. There would be an assortment of strange characters draped across furniture, their eyes glazed over and staring into space. There would be Ike in the middle of it, high as a kite on coke, and without the benefit of sleep in days, and would start screaming and yelling at Tina about how she wasn't singing his songs correctly.

At this point, Ann Thomas came back into the scene. Since having Ike's baby, Mia, she drifted back into his life. He put her up in an apartment behind Bolic Sound Studio, so she could be Ike's on-call mistress whenever he needed her attention.

Ann remembers having to hide Ike's walking canes, which he seemed to fancy. Not only did he use them for walking, he used them to beat Ann and the secretaries down at the recording studio. Like Tina, Ann Thomas never quite knew when Ike was going to go off on her physically.

According to Ike and Tina's four children, they, likewise, never knew when their father would suddenly explode into a rage directed toward them. They finally learned to gauge Ike's mood by tracking how many days it had been since he last came back to the house to sleep. If he had only been up one or two days, he could be reasonable. But those times when he had been awake for three or four days, he was a walking time bomb.

In 1972, when it came time to hand out Grammy Awards for the previous year's releases, Ike & Tina Turner's version of "Proud Mary" was one of the nominees that night. Both Ike and Tina were thrilled when it won the trophy as the Best Rhythm & Blues Performance by a Duo or a Group.

The group's next album, 'Nuff Said, on United Artists Records, strayed away from the winning formula of Workin' Together. Instead of giving their fresh interpretations of rock songs, Ike chose to return to his old sound. With that, 'Nuff Said only made it to No. 108 on the charts. The album contained an Ike Turner–produced version of "River Deep-Mountain High." It was a standard version of the song, but it was nowhere near as dynamic as Phil Spector's majestic recording. 'Nuff said indeed!

It was quickly followed up by the album *Feel Good* (United Artists Records/1972). The album featured a dated but fun-sounding dance number, "If You Can Hully Gully (I Can Hully Gully Too)," a rare jazz number for Tina, "Black Coffee," and the Turners' version of The Beatles' "She Came in through the Bathroom Window." The disc made it to No. 160 in *Billboard*. That same year, one single, "Up In Heah," made it up to No. 83 on the Pop singles chart in the United States.

In 1973 came the album *Let Me Touch Your Mind* from United Artists Records. It ended up going nowhere. It featured Tina's version of the songs "Up on the Roof," "Born Free," and Stevie Wonder's "Heaven Help Us All." One of the most interesting cuts is a song called "Annie Had a Baby." When he wrote this song, was Ike thinking of Anna Mae Bullock, Ann Cain, or Ann Thomas? Surely the song applied to all three of them, because they all had given birth to his babies!

That same year also saw two separate "greatest hits" albums—one from United Artists and one from Blue Thumb, and still another live concert album from Ike & Tina Turner, titled *Live in the World of Ike and Tina Turner*. It opens with the "Theme from *Shaft.*" With all of his guns and his cocaine, did Ike Turner suddenly fancy himself an inner city crime fighter? Can you dig it?

However, the real prize was the 1973 album *Nutbush City Limits*, with the incredibly catchy title cut—composed by Tina Turner herself! Finally, she had tested her hand at songwriting. In fact, she wrote five of the ten songs included on this album. She figured that if she and Ike could log enough hit records, she would be able to one day afford to escape from him. Knowing how badly he wanted a hit record, she dug back into her own beginnings, and wrote a song about the place she came from. The song "Nutbush City Limits" made it to No. 22 in the United States, but made it all the way up to No. 4 in the United Kingdom.

Tina wrote another song, which appears on this album with a musical track identical to "Nutbush City Limits." Entitled "Club Manhattan," it tells the story of the place where Tina first met The Kings of Rhythm. She also wrote a song called "Daily Bread," a story-song called "Fancy Annie," and "That's My Purpose." The song that seems the most tailor-made for Tina was one that Ike wrote called "Get It Out of Your Mind." In the context of the song, Tina basically sings "you can have all your women and your drugs, but leave me alone." It doesn't get any more blatant than that. The *Nutbush City Limits* album itself only made it to No. 163 in *Billboard*, but the hit record of the same name gave Tina still another trademark song for her repertoire.

During this period, Tina was slowly gaining back her strength and her determination. She was writing down her thoughts and she was open to new ideas. She had an idea in the back of her mind that she was working up to the day when she would walk out on Ike Turner. Her day of liberation was coming. She knew that she just had to choose her moment, and she was going to be free.

9

I'VE BEEN LOVING YOU TOO LONG

Tina recalled a conversation that she had with Ike during this era, where he got exasperated with her for something. While arguing with her, he asked her what she ever did for him? She looked at him blankly and told him that he must be blind. She gave him manicures and pedicures; she dyed his hair when it started to go gray; she raised their kids; she looked the other way while he had sex with every available woman who crossed his path; and she was the star of his entire entertainment enterprise! Furthermore, she took his abuses, both physical and mental. But Ike didn't see it that way. She started talking back to him, but he was so used to ignoring her that he barely heard what she was saying.

"I kept saying things, but he didn't listen," she remembers. "Then he listened and he didn't like what he heard, and he tried to stop me saying it" (1).

Whatever home life Tina and her four sons had was torturous at best. The boys would scatter as soon as they saw Ike coming back to the house. They didn't want to be anywhere near him. When Christmas time rolled around, Ike forbade Tina from buying any "motherfuckin' presents" (4).

At the time, Ike had a new circle of people hanging around him. The drugs and money drew a certain element of odd characters to Ike. He was hanging out with a lot of hippies, and he was interested in the occult and voodoo. Tina was leery about even going down to the studio because the atmosphere was so drug-laced and uncomfortable to be around.

Through this part of the middle 1970s, Tina claims that the only thing that got her through all of Ike's abuses and nonsense were the fortune tellers she was seeing. Ike would come home and pass out, and he had so much cash in his pants pockets that he wouldn't miss a couple of dollars she carefully removed.

Because Ike was capable of watching her every move in the house through the monitor cameras he had at the house, Tina had to sneak out to see her "readers." She would tell Ike that she was going out shopping, and she would make a beeline for another of her soothsayers. Some of them would read tea leaves. Some would read tarot cards. But the messages all seemed to be the same. They all agreed that a bigger, more fulfilling life was awaiting her in the future.

One of the readers told her that "one day you will be among the biggest of stars and you will live across the water" (5). According to her, listening to the fortune tellers was "the beginning of my escape from Ike Turner. . . . It's possible to push a person too far, and I was pushed beyond the limit" (1).

In a 1993 magazine article, Tina outlined the physical abuse she had to endure as a day-to-day way of life with Ike. "This was always bruised," Tina said as she pointed to her jawbone. Motioning to her inner lower lip, she explained, "This was always just torn apart, because it hits the teeth. So the mouth was always distorted, and the eyes were always black. If you look at some of the earlier pictures, my eyes were always dark. I couldn't get them clear. I thought it was smoke or whatever. But Ike always banged me against the head" (5).

It was a miracle that Tina wasn't left with permanent damage from the beatings she received at the hands of cocaine-crazed Ike. "How could I have survived? Only once I got knocked out. Only once. And that was when I got this," she explained, motioning to a scar outlining the outer part of her right eye. "Black eyes, busted lips—somehow I just ignored it, but people knew. I thought that they thought it was a car accident. I made something up in my head in terms of the public" (5).

Her visits to doctors only yielded temporary relief. "In those days, believe me, a doctor asked you what happened and you say, 'I had a fight with my husband,' that was it. Black people fight. They [medical doctors] didn't care about black people," she said with resignation (5).

The people around her were helplessly stunned by what they witnessed in the presence of Ike and Tina. Recalls Bob Krasnow, "I felt great responsibility for Tina, and I'd be there while it was going on. I was young, and I hero-worshipped Ike in a perverted way. Had I been more liberated or more experienced, I would have spoken up. I didn't" (5).

The cocaine only made Ike's outrages become more dramatic and more violent. "The whole thing took this huge turn for ugliness," says Krasnow. "Tina was the focus of a lot of this horror, but the whole world suffered. In those days there was no Oprah Winfrey, no publicity dealing with abuse, no abuse [telephone] hot lines. She was out there by herself in a man's world—she was on the road with B. B. King and Chubby Checker. She was the only woman in this world . . . a demeaning man's world" (5).

Still, Tina found her own inner strength during this time. "I started coming into my own those last years with Ike, because I was in charge of the girls [The Ikettes] and the basic performance. I had also gotten involved with arrangements. I don't play, but I was able to communicate verbally with the musicians—Ike's musicians. So by the time I got my [own post-Ike] band, I was equipped," she explains (7).

The worst on-stage degradation that Tina had to endure was having to mimic performing fellatio to her microphone during the song "I've Been Loving You Too Long." This was Ike's idea. It got to the point where Ike would moan and groan into his microphone like he was having an orgasm, just to make the song all the more erotic. Tina now hates that song and refuses to ever sing it again. It still conjures up memories of her life being a living hell with Ike during these last stages of their marriage.

Yet, through it all, she had her own sense of dignity, and she knew that she was mounting the courage to leave Ike Turner once and for all. "O.K., so if I was a victim—fine," she concedes. "Maybe I was a victim for a short while. But give me credit for *thinking* the whole time I was there. See, I do have pride. I've got to get somebody else to say, 'Yes, Tina, I do understand, and there are no 'buts'" (5).

Ike had the habit of showing up at the house with some pretty girl in tow whom he wanted to impress. He would drag them up to meet "Tina Turner." There Tina would stand, being gracious to these women, so that Ike could dazzle them into having sex with him.

Tina recalls, "There was all kinds of sex going on at the house, and I had caught him on the sofas, and women on their knees. I said to him, 'You can't do this in this house.' I really felt this house was mine. Ike was at a stage of showing off. He built a recording studio not far from the house. He wanted to let people know he had an apartment in the back of the recording studio, that he had recording-studio living quarters and the building next door as an agency, and wanted to come up and show off the house, which was decorated like a bordello" (5).

According to Tina, one afternoon Ike showed up at the house with a pretty woman in tow. Tina figured that it was just another of the girls whom Ike wanted to impress and then have sex with. The woman's name was Valerie. She was white and Jewish, and she was married to a black jazz musician.

Tina met several white women in mixed marriages at the time. Herbie Hancock was married to a woman named Gigi, who was German. Wayne Shorter had wed a Portuguese woman by the name of Anna. Her friend Maria Booker was also married to a black musician.

She realized that Valerie was part of this same circle. Comparing Valerie to the type of women Ike usually showed up at the house with, Tina says, "All of them weren't bitches or sluts" (5).

Ike had hired Valerie to be one of the secretaries down at the studio. When she told him that she was a "chanter," he assumed that it was some sort of fascinating branch of occult or witchcraft. When she explained to Ike and Tina that chanting was part of the Buddhist religion, Ike was instantly disinterested. However, Tina was just as quickly interested.

Valerie explained to Tina how chanting was part of Nichiren Shoshu Buddhism. Tina was fascinated. Valerie told her about *shakubuku*, which is the initial phase of Buddhist teaching. During that first meeting, she presented Tina with a book and prayer beads. She also taught her the chant "*nam-myoho-renge-kyo.*" Tina wrote it down on the spot. According to Tina, something inside her just lit up at hearing Valerie's explanation of Buddhism.

While Ike was down at the studio for long stretches, and Tina was all alone in the house, she started trying out this idea of chanting. Just to underscore her Baptist upbringing, she would recite "The Lord's Prayer," and afterwards she would recite the Buddhist chant five times. She explains, "I never let go of the Lord's Prayer until I was sure of those words" (5).

It didn't take long before positive things started happening for her. In the beginning, there were small signs that her life was changing for the better. She had been having a problem with face makeup, having developed an allergic reaction to what she had been using. She had been looking for a certain brand that her skin would be tolerant of, but had been unable to locate it.

She started chanting for the first time, and moments later the phone rang. It was a girl from Bloomingdales department store—the makeup Tina had been looking for was suddenly in stock. Was it the chanting? Or was it just coincidence? Tina was intrigued, so she continued chanting.

The next step entailed buying a personal Buddhist altar or *butsudan*. It is essentially a little cabinet that holds incense for the sense of smell, a candle for light, a sacred scroll, and other objects. These are not objects to be worshiped, but they are objects that allow one to focus.

What was it that Tina was seeking? "Change," she explains. "The practice—in the early stages of it—when it was introduced to me, was that it could change your life if that's what you were looking for. And at that time, that's definitely what I wanted" (16).

It opened up her eyes to a whole new world of possibility. "What's reality sometimes is not exactly real," says Tina. "Because you keep saying, 'What did I do?' You get on your knees every night and you say 'The Lord's Prayer,' and you say, 'Somebody must send some help to me, because I've never done a thing in my life to deserve this.' And that's when I started to chant" (5).

Other than Valerie's introduction to Buddhism, Tina was on her own to explore this new spiritual side of herself. "I had to teach myself, because I didn't have the freedom to actually go to meetings, or for people to come to me. So I remember working really hard. And I am happy that I did it that way, because it was on my own that I really struggled for it, and it changed my life. . . . How I view it is that it is something that one depends on like—think, like I need my refrigerator, I need the clothing on my back, I need shelter. And chanting takes care of that spiritual side, that subconscious mind that I tap into. My reality is God has given us the faith, but we have to find it. We have to work on it, to find the God within us, that—say that 'core.' And when you chant, when you get into the rhythm, the sound," she explains (16).

According to Tina, chanting channels her into "the mystical law of the universe. I'm saying a word, but it sounds like '*hmm-mmmm.*' Is there anything that is without that? There's a hum in the motor of a car, in the windshield wipers, in your refrigerator. An airplane goes *rowwmmmmnnn.* Sometimes I just sit and listen to the sounds of the universe and to that hum that is just there" (6).

There was an empty room in the house, and Tina stashed her *butsudan* there. Whenever Ike was away she would chant and read her book. She felt herself getting stronger and stronger each time she did it. Ike discovered the *butsudan* one day and totally freaked out. According to Tina, he couldn't understand it at all, and it frightened him. He yelled, "Get that motherfucker out of this house!" (4).

Looking back on this era of self-discovery, she says, "I was introduced to Buddhism and started to really care about what that was about, and I had no idea what the subconscious mind could actually do, and I realized that" (12).

There were all sorts of signs that things were going to improve for Tina. One of the positive things that happened to her was that she personally met the woman who for years had been her heroine. "My one idol was Mrs. Jacqueline Kennedy Onassis," claims Tina. "Her grace, her style, her intellect was how I modeled myself in terms of how I wanted to present myself off stage, so to speak. For my work, of course, the guys—The Stones, Rod Stewart. The rock & roll guys. That was what I wanted and that's what I did. And that's how it is" (16).

After years of meeting all sorts of celebrities, Tina was rarely in awe of anyone. But Jackie Kennedy Onassis was different. She was strong and classy, and she had risen above tragedy. Tina wanted to be just like her. "The first time I met her, I was nearly in tears. In those days I wasn't thinking about anybody in my circle or the clubs where I was. I was thinking that nobody was at the level of what I wanted in my life" (5).

Regarding her encounter with Jackie, Tina explains, "We were checking into a hotel, and for some reason she was there, and at the time she was with Mr. Onassis. I was standing at the reception, and I looked down, and I wasn't sure that it was her. But then she made a gesture of how she usually carried her person, and before I knew it I was running towards her. I was totally out of control. And by the time I got to the swinging doors, I said, 'Oh, Mrs. Kennedy, oh, I mean Mrs. Onassis.' And she turned very gracefully, and I said, 'I'm Tina Turner. I just wanted to say hello.' And she extended her hand and had this big smile on her face, and I thought, 'I'm saved.' She could have been rude. Actually, she could have been, but wasn't. She was very kind. And who was rude was the lady standing with her; she was looking down her nose at me like I was some disease. She [Jackie] says, 'Oh, hello. My children would be pleased.'

And we had just played Hyannisport, and I had been with Robert Kennedy's family and we had been boating and dancing with them, and so they had told Caroline and John John, and therefore, she knew who I was. And I was very excited and she shook my hand and left, and as I turned there's Mr. Onassis, and I said, 'Hi.' I had to control myself. And I went to my room, and the sofa was just going," she says, mimicking nervous shaking. "I can understand now sometimes when some of the fans come. I try to be as compassionate as I can, because I can relate" (16).

At this point in time, the lives of Ike and Tina Turner couldn't be any more different. He was busy spending time at Bolic Sound, snorting cocaine, and recording track after track of music, often overworking songs to the point where they had no point. He had also become an out-of-control coke addict. In fact, by this time, he had snorted so much cocaine that he now had a hole in the cartilage that was in between his nostrils. To numb the pain, he simply did more coke. Ike was in the middle of his most self-destructive phase.

Tina, on the other hand, was on the road to self-discovery and empowerment. For years she had unleashed an incredible amount of power and energy on stage as the invincible "Tina Turner," and then went into a shell when she was off-stage. That was all changing as she began tapping into the incredible strength within her via Buddhism. She continued chanting, and good things just kept happening. The next sign that change was underfoot came in 1974 when she received word that the producers of the forthcoming movie *Tommy* wanted her to be one its stars. This was to be another very important step on the path to her escape.

10

THE ACID QUEEN

While Tina was finding herself by chanting, Ike was losing himself in a sea of drugs. Bolic Sound Studios was supposed to be a huge "cash cow" for him, since the large studio could be rented out to pay all the bills. Unfortunately, all of the late-night parties did little to help the studio. Several of the soundboards were ruined by having cocaine and coffee dumped down into their inner workings. Good musicians wanted nothing to do with booking recording time there. And the things that Ike was producing, no one was buying.

The one R&B album that the duo released in 1974 was called *Sweet Rhode Island Red*. It contained versions of two recent Stevie Wonder songs: "Living for the City" and "Higher Ground." It completely failed to make the charts.

Disenchanted with the way that the duo's rhythm & blues records were selling, Ike decided to branch out stylistically. Along these lines came two completely different concept albums, one of them gospel, and one of them country. The album entitled *The Gospel According to Ike & Tina Turner* was an interesting curiosity. Aretha Franklin had just scored a huge hit with her own gospel album, *Amazing Grace*, so Ike must have figured that this would be a good avenue to travel down. The resulting album included such gospel standards as "A Closer Walk with Thee," "What a Friend We Have in Jesus," and "When the Saints Go Marching In." It was an odd choice for the duo—Ike was a drug addict who never went to church, and unbeknownst to him, Tina had become a Buddhist. Reflecting this dichotomy, the gospel album completely failed to find an audience.

In another bizarre move, Ike decided that Tina should do a solo album of all country & western songs. It was recorded at Bolic Sound, and it employed country music's Tom Thacker as the producer. The resulting 1974 album was entitled *Tina Turns the Country On!* It included Tina's version of several recent country songs such as "Help Me Make It through the Night," "Long Long Time," and "I'm Moving On." The Pointer Sisters had just won a Grammy Award for their first country song, "Fairytale." This was possibly the motivation for Ike to steer Tina in this direction. It does have the distinction of being the first official Tina Turner solo album. Several songs were recorded for this album, including another ten cuts that remained unreleased for years. They are now available in several CD compilations including one called *Soul Deep*, and another called *Simply Tina*. The other country songs included Tina's version of Tammy Wynette's "Stand by Your Man" and Loretta Lynn's "You Ain't Woman Enough to Take My Man." The song she should have sung would be one called "If You Are Woman Enough—PLEASE Take My Man!"

The one Ike & Tina single to make the charts in 1974 was called "Sexy Ida, Pt. 1." It made it to No. 65 on the American Pop charts. Recording-wise it was something of a "bust" for the duo. In addition, Ike had started recording and releasing his own solo albums, none of which ever sold any significant amount of copies. Ike was completely losing his grip on what was viable in the marketplace.

He was also making some bad investments with his money. His once-profitable enterprise was starting to lose money right and left. It seemed that their live appearances in Europe were the only things producing money. The American audience is very fickle. Without the benefit of any new hit records, the number of dates they could play in the states was dwindling.

According to Tina, "There were a lot of ups and downs, but Ike kept our act going because he had a dream to have a certain amount of songs in the Top 10. He wanted to be successful with charted music and be known for that and to receive that type of recognition from the industry. As a producer/musician, I think that's what most people strive for. He worked for that" (10).

Ike decided to upgrade Bolic Sound from a twenty-four-track studio to a thirty-six-track studio. This only gave him more room to tinker with his songs, to the point where he would layer so many sounds onto the tracks that they seemed to make less and less sense. He would start out with good song ideas, but by the time he was done tinkering with them, he would ruin them. "The more tracks they gave him in the recording studio, the more tracks he used," explains Tina. "So he overwrote a lot of music. Things sort of got lost due to the mixture of drugs and mechanics" (10).

Furthermore, the couple's four sons were getting involved in drugs as well. With the example that Ike was setting, and the fact that there was always a ton of cocaine to be had at Bolic Studio, it was easy to see how the boys could fall into that trap as well.

Ike's own drug use, his physical violence, and his erratic behavior all escalated even further during this period. Tina never knew when she was going to get hit, for what reason, or with what object. He would suddenly lock the door of whatever room they were in, and Tina would know it was coming.

Ike's incredible rage and physical abuse wasn't reserved for Tina alone. He also beat up Ann Thomas. He would beat Rhonda Gramm while she was driving the car he was riding in. He would grab her hair and pull handfuls of it out.

Tina proclaims, "He was an evil and possessed person" (4). At night in bed, Ike would insist on sleeping on the crook of Tina's arm. If she moved, he would punch her in his sleep. She was his prisoner, and she was resigned to being routinely maimed and beaten by him.

On plane rides, Ike would insist on booking three coach seats in a row. Tina would have one end seat, Ann Thomas would have the other end seat, and Ike would sit in the middle. During the flight he would take off his shoes, and stretch out across the three seats—his head in Ann's lap and his feet in Tina's lap. He did everything he could to degrade Tina.

Fortunately for Tina, in 1974 she got a nice long vacation from Ike. That was when the film version of *Tommy* was being shot in London. The producers were very interested in Tina, but they had no interest in putting Ike in the film.

Producer Robert Stigwood was bringing The Who's classic concept album to life, and he was planning to mix the cast of movie stars with several rock stars. The familiar screen actors included Tina's friend Ann-Margret as Tommy's mother, Oliver Reed as her second husband, and Jack Nicholson as the doctor. In the rock star department came Roger Daltry as adult Tommy, Elton John as the Pinball Wizard, Eric Clapton as the Preacher, Arthur Brown as the Priest, and Keith Moon playing perverted Uncle Ernie. Casting for the role of the Acid Queen was still up in the air. Reportedly, the film's director, Ken Russell, had also been considering David Bowie as the Acid Queen. During this era, Bowie was amidst his makeup-wearing, gender-bending, unisexual phase, so it could have worked in that context.

However, Tina's name kept coming up. A script was sent to her, and when she read it, she was convinced that the role was perfect for her. Like most of the rock star appearances in the film, the Acid Queen only appeared in one sequence. Just as Ike had done with Tina when he cut the deal with Phil Spector for her to record "River Deep-Mountain High," he likewise agreed to this deal. When the contracts where signed, Tina flew over to London to join the production. Tina has always wanted to act, so this seemed like the perfect opportunity for her.

The funny thing is that Tina had never even heard the original *Tommy* album by The Who, so she really had no idea about the whole storyline or some of the drug connotations in the story when she took the role.

When she initially met Ken Russell, he was shocked to find that she wasn't six-feet tall like her on-stage persona might suggest. To give her height in the film, the wardrobe department made sure they outfitted her with a pair of outlandishly high platform shoes. She thought the shoes were "awful," and she found the tacky short skirt that she was to wear "horrible." But she decided to take the look even further, and added some additional touches all her own: fishnet stockings, bright red lipstick, and fingernail polish. When she put it all together, Russell still wasn't convinced he had made the right casting decision. But Tina knew how to turn on the wattage when the cameras started rolling. According to her, she did her best Vincent Price–like evil genius imitation, complete with big bulging eyes and a head that quivered with madness. Russell instantly loved it and delightfully shouted for "more!"

When it came time for the Acid Queen's big scene, Tina was shocked to find that her beautiful female twin "assistants" entered the scene bearing a dramatically large hypodermic syringe. "My God, is this movie promoting drugs?" she asked out loud in shock. She had no idea that the "acid" in her character's name referred to LSD! Nonetheless, she had a great time bringing the Acid Queen to life in front of the cameras.

Tina's experience of filming her role in *Tommy* went pretty much without a hitch. According to her, "My part was small, but it was my part. It gave me strength. I could feel myself growing" (1).

Her friend Ann-Margret, on the other hand, had a very well-publicized accident on the set of *Tommy*. There was one scene in the movie called "Champagne." Pete Townsend of The Who wrote the song especially for the movie. During the scene, Ann-Margret's character of Nora throws a champagne bottle through a television screen, and a sea of baked beans (yes baked beans!) starts flowing out. Ann-Margret, or "Nora," was to gleefully play in the resulting baked bean mess. Unfortunately, she got too close to the broken glass of the TV screen, cut her arm, and required twenty-seven stitches to piece her back together.

When Tina was done filming her part in *Tommy*, she got an offer to return to London—again without Ike. According to Ann-Margret, "I've always admired the talent of Tina Turner, an immensely gifted, intelligent, and proud woman. I'd seen her in clubs several times, but during *Tommy* we got to know each other well. After the film ended, Roger arranged for us to stay in London and shoot my next TV special there. Tina flew back home to California. A few days later, we called and asked her to come back and guest on the show. She returned immediately, with only the clothes on her back. Then's when I learned how little money she had, and the extent of the tough time she had gone through before leaving Ike Turner" (24).

On the special, entitled *Ann-Margret Olson,* which aired in 1975, the two women had a great time singing and dancing together. Tina was able to confide in Ann-Margret and tell her about the hell she had been living through the past fifteen years with Ike. Ann-Margret let Tina know that she would be there for her if she ever left Ike.

Regarding the special, Ann-Margret fondly recalled, "I performed a medley—'Nutbush City Limits,' 'Proud Mary' and 'Honky Tonk Women'—with my friend, the *dynamic* Tina Turner" (24).

After returning to Los Angeles, the Ike Turner nightmare continued for Tina. One night in the studio with him, he claimed she wasn't singing the song the way he wanted to hear it—so he threw an entire pot of boiling hot coffee in her face. The majority of it hit her in the neck. The first second that the scalding liquid hit her, it felt like the sensation of cold. Then, seconds later, Tina was aware that she had been severely burned. It was so hot that a layer of skin peeled off of her. She started screaming with pain. To make her stop screaming, Ike began beating her. It turned out that she had third degree-burns.

According to Tina, he would beat her up, then force her to have sex with him, and then he would go back to playing his music—like nothing had happened. Says Tina of Ike's frame of mind during these outrages, "It was like, 'Goddamn it, *SHE* made me do this!'" (4).

Meanwhile, the film *Tommy* was being edited for its gala release. The plot of the film—like the rock opera it came from—is the story of a little boy who witnesses the murder of his military pilot father at the hands of the his mother's lover (Oliver Reed). His mother, Nora (Ann-Margret), drums into Tommy's head that he never saw anything, never heard anything, and wasn't to speak of anything, Traumatized by the event, he becomes blind, deaf, and dumb. After a series of bizarre experiences at the hands of his perverse relatives, Tommy grows up to become a young adult (Roger Daltry). Trying to shock the sensations of sight and sound back into Tommy's life, his stepfather takes him to see the exotic and erotic Acid Queen. That's where Tina makes her entrance, in a scene-stealing sequence where she attempts to make Tommy respond to her hypnotic drug therapy. As the story progresses, Tommy develops an incredible ability to play pinball like a wizard. After Tommy becomes an idol of the young, he regains his sight and hearing, and is elevated to prophet status. The film has not one word of dialogue, as all of the characters sing their musical soliloquies. The result is one of the most colorful and over-the-top rock movie musicals ever made.

To be part of the gala opening of the film when it was released in 1975, Tina was in New York City, along with Elton John, Ann-Margret, and several of the other stars. This was a very empowering experience, to be held in such high regard and to receive a tidal wave of credit and praise—apart from Ike.

Time magazine raved, "There has never been a movie musical quite like *Tommy*. A weird, crazy, wonderfully excessive version of The Who's rock opera!" (25) Claimed movie critic Leonard Maltin, "Energetic rendering of The Who's best-selling rock opera with standout musical performances by Clapton, John (singing "Pinball Wizard"), and Turner!" (26).

The all-star original soundtrack album of *Tommy*—complete with Tina's searing "Acid Queen" number—scaled the American charts to land at No. 2. It was the highest charting album that Tina had appeared on—to date. It was certified "Gold" for over a half million copies sold in the United States alone.

In order to fully capitalize on the public's increased interest in Tina—without Ike—Liberty/United Artists Records wanted a rock & roll album by Tina alone—entitled *Acid Queen*. Since Ike negotiated the deal, he allowed outside producers Denny Diante and Spencer Proffer to produce half the album alone with Tina, but they had to co-produce the other half of the album with him involved, and with Ike writing the songs. The most fun Ike-written cut is an ode to the musician who used to play his music at the Nutbush picnics, "Mr. Bootsey Whitelaw." The song is a musical warning about avoiding Bootsey's sexual advances. But it was the first five Ike-less rock & roll cuts that really made this album special. On it Tina cut The Rolling Stones' "Let's Spend the Night Together" and "Under My Thumb," The Who's "I Can See for Miles" and "Acid Queen," and Led Zeppelin's "Whole Lotta Love."

A great album, *Acid Queen* only made it to No. 155 in *Billboard* in America. Only one single was released from it, "Baby Get It On," which Ike wrote. The song peaked at No. 88, and was accredited as being an Ike & Tina Turner cut. What was truly important about this album was that it was her first rock & roll solo album, and it set the stage for greater success to come.

Tina kept chanting more and more frequently during this period. Ike's violent behavior gave her good reason to do that. Since the whole *Tommy* project was a huge success for her, the press was constantly interested in her—her alone—and not Ike. He would go into rages over this. And, while he was arguing about that, he would bring up "River Deep-Mountain High"—another deal he made without consulting Tina.

In the past, whenever she started thinking about leaving Ike, she was conflicted. According to her, "There were tons of things involved. Where was I going to go? Was I going to leave my children in that mess?" (8). She couldn't go back to her mother's house because Zelma was living in Ike's house in East St. Louis. Tina would never be safe there. Her sister, Alline, lived in the Baldwin Hills area of Los Angeles and was just terrified of Ike Turner and his temper. Tina wouldn't be safe there.

But, finally, she had reached the end of her tether. The first time she ran away, she went to her cousin's house. It only took Ike three days to locate her there. He forced her to go back home with him, and then proceeded to beat her up again.

Then, just to demonstrate his anger toward her, Ike picked up a fireplace iron. Tina figured he was going to beat her with it, but she unflinchingly stared him in the eye. In the past he had broken her jaw and her ribs. What more could he do to hurt her? She was through being afraid of him. He ended up not hitting her with the iron poker after all. Instead, he bent it with his bare hands just to make his point.

Tina ran away again, this time taking the children. She went to the house of a friend—Maria Booker. Ike never thought of looking for her at Maria's house in Malibu. She stayed away for two weeks. She came back and told Ike that she was through playing this game and that she was leaving him. He didn't beat her immediately. But the beatings did continue.

When the Ike & Tina Turner hit recordings dried up during this era, so did the American tour dates. Ike kept recording an endless sea of material, but none of it would ever yield another hit. There were, however, tour dates to do in France, Germany, England, Australia, and the Far East. Little did Ike know that this was to be the final global Ike & Tina tour—ever.

Since Ike insisted on being paid for their live performances in hard U.S. currency, on these foreign tours he would have quite a bit of money with him. He had taken to carrying it around in a briefcase because he trusted no one. When the tour got to Paris in December of 1975, the briefcase was somehow lost with over $86,000 in cash in it. Ike insisted that the entire entourage submit to lie detector tests to locate the culprit. However, Ike was left with no one else but himself to blame. It was surmised that Ike was so stoned he had simply set it down somewhere and walked away.

In January 1976, The Ike & Tina Turner Revue rolled into Indonesia. At a club in Jakarta, Ike got into a fight over a below-standard sound system. It ended up in a battle with the local police, and the band had to flee—abandoning $22,000 worth of their own equipment.

Back in Los Angeles in March 1976, Rhonda Gramm had finally had enough of Ike, so she quit. Ike promptly had her house repossessed, as he was the deed-owner. Barely registering the changes that were going on around him, Ike Turner returned to Bolic Sound Studios and his habitual intake of cocaine. His physical fights with Tina continued into 1976. He was, however, oblivious to the fact that the party was about to come to a crashing end for him.

Tina's superstar friend Cher recalls, "I was doing the *Cher* show, and Ike & Tina came on, and Tina and I got along really, really well. I remember she came backstage and she was alone. And, I remember she was asking me how difficult it was for me to leave Sonny." According to Tina, "[Cher] said that Sonny didn't hurt her in the sense of violence, but other than that, we just sort of came right along the same kind of way" (19). Tina took note of how smoothly Cher had been able to leave Sonny Bono and have her career continue to flourish and grow without him. Like the old Sam Cooke song, "Change Is Gonna Come," Tina was beginning to see a new era about to start for her.

She was getting stronger by the day. She had come to the conclusion that she was even willing to walk away from show business if it meant getting Ike Turner out of her life for good. "Music life was not attractive. It was dirty. It was a chitlin' circuit—eating on your lap. And that's why I say, 'I was always above it.' Why, I don't know, but I knew I didn't want it. I'd rather go and clean a white person's house, where it was nice, than sing in dirty old places and deal with Ike and his low life," she claimed (5). Liberation day for Tina Turner was right around the corner.

11

THE LAST STRAW

It was July 4, 1976, and it seemed like any other combative day in the life of Ike & Tina Turner. They were flying to Dallas to begin a regional concert tour. The first date on the tour was set for that night at the Hilton Hotel in downtown Dallas. On the flight from Los Angeles to Dallas, things very quickly got off on the wrong foot.

Tina and Ike arrived at the airport with Ann Thomas, their current bandleader, Claude Williams, and a new white girl from Canada whom Ike was sleeping with. That day, Tina was wearing a white Yves Saint Laurent suit. At the airport, when Ike tried to give her some of the gooey, melting chocolate candy he was eating, she made a negative reply. With that he hit her.

When they boarded the plane, it was the usual seating arrangement, with Ike in the middle seat, Tina on one side and Ann Thomas on the other side. He intended to lay across them on the flight in his usual grand style. Tina wasn't in the mood for this demeaning arrangement today. With that he kicked her and gave her a dirty look.

They arrived at the Dallas airport and got off of the plane. As they walked to their waiting limousine, Ike was giving Tina evil looks. She knew a fight was brewing, and today was the day she was prepared to fight back. According to her, "When someone is really trying to kill you, it hurts. But this time it didn't hurt. I was angry too" (5).

Recalls Ike, "Whatever she said to me, man, I was really out there. I slapped the shit out of her. She did it again. Bam. I slapped her again. And when I slapped her that time, she jumped up in the limo and put her knee in my chest. I said, 'You motherfucker.' I grabbed her by the windpipe to pull her off of me. And I punched her and punched her. When I hit her, there was blood coming from my eye or something" (17).

This time Tina was through taking his abuses. In the back of the limo she remembers going at Ike for the first time in her life "Digging, or just hitting or kicking." He just kept on beating her, and she kept on fighting back. "By the time we got to the hotel, I had a big swollen eye. My mouth was bleeding" (5).

Ike Turner had hit her for the last time; she had made up her mind. "I knew I was gone," she claims. "I was flying. I knew that that was it. By the time we got to the hotel, I'm not lying, my face was swollen out past my ear. Blood was every place" (6).

The people who were at the front desk of the Hilton were stunned at the sight of a bleeding Ike and Tina. They looked like they had just walked away from the wreckage of a head-on car crash.

"We walked upstairs," says Tina, "and Ike knew. So he went and laid across the bed. And I was still saying, 'Can I get you something?' And I started massaging him, as usual, massaging his head. And he started snoring. And I leaned over and I said . . . 'goodbye'" (6).

She didn't waste any time getting the blood off of herself or changing her clothes. The time for the great escape had come, and this was it. Her head was so swollen she couldn't even put on her wig, so she just left it there. She put a hair wrap on her head. She threw on a cape, grabbed a small piece of hand luggage with some makeup and toiletries in it. With that, Tina headed for the door. "I knew I would never be given my freedom. I would have to take it," she says with defiance (5).

"I ran down the hall, and I was afraid I was going to run into his people—his band and his bodyguards. So I went through an exit and down the steps. I was so afraid . . . because everybody was aware that Ike and Tina were supposed to be on in half an hour. Then I turned and went through a kitchen, just running. I just dashed through and went through the back door, and I remember throwing myself up onto trash cans just to rest, just to feel I had gotten away. Then I composed myself and thought, 'Now what?' I started to run fast, just run" (5).

The alleyway ran right into the freeway. Across the busy freeway was another hotel, the Ramada Inn. Tina hoped this would be her haven of refuge. She arrived at the front desk bleeding, swollen, and desperate. She asked to see the manager.

If she had decided in advance that she was leaving Ike this very day, she might have prepared herself better. But she knew it was time to finally make her break for freedom. When she looked in her pockets, she discovered she had left Ike with next to nothing on her—only thirty-six cents and a Mobile gasoline credit card.

She told the manager of the Ramada Inn who she was, and informed him that her husband had beaten her up and that she didn't have any more than a quarter, a dime, and a penny on her. She asked him if he could give her a room to stay in, and she swore that she would pay him back. Seeing the seriousness of the matter and recognizing who she was, he gave her his best suite. He also put security guards on the door and offered to get her any food she wanted. Her face was so swollen and bruised that all she could eat was some soup and crackers.

After the hotel manager left, she washed the blood off of her white pants suit and draped it over the room's heater so it would dry. Still aching from the fight she had just had, she tried to figure out what to do. According to her, "I needed to call somebody with money. My family didn't have the money for a ticket. That's the whole thing always. I didn't know anybody with money. They were all Ike's people" (5).

She called a man named Mel Johnson, who was a friend of Ike's from St. Louis. Currently, Mel was a Cadillac dealer in Los Angeles. However, she sensed that calling Mel was a mistake. After she hung up the phone, she called Ike's manager, Nat Tabor. He knew the situation between she and Ike, and he offered to help her. He had friends in that part of Texas, and he sent these people—an older white couple—to pick her up, take her to the airport, and give her some cash.

The next day, everything went as planned, and as the plane was preparing to land in Los Angeles, Tina had a sudden sense of fear that Ike could have flown there ahead of her and would be waiting at the gate when she got off the flight. She made up her mind that she would simply start screaming her head off until the police came. There was no way she was ever going back to him again.

She had done her best to disguise herself so that no one would recognize her. With her own hair still wrapped on her head, and huge dark glasses on, she hailed a cab. The first thing the cab driver said to her as he turned around to inquire where she was going, was to ask her if she was Tina Turner. So much for her disguise.

She spent the Fourth of July weekend at Nat Tabor's house. She ended up spending a week there and finally realized that she would have to face her problems. There was absolutely no hope for a reconciliation with Ike. According to her, "What made me leave was the beating. I thought, 'I'm not going to be dragged down in the dirt one more time" (2).

Nat phoned Ike to see if he could amicably pave the way for the formal separation. Ike went into a tirade on the phone, threatening the lives of Nat and his family. Tina told Nat that she was going to leave, as she did not want to endanger him or his family any further. She decided to go back to Maria Booker's in Malibu again. While she stayed there, she and Maria chanted together. However, they both realized that Tina couldn't stay there for long because Ike would eventually come looking for her there.

Maria made arrangements for Tina to move in with her sister, Anna Maria Shorter, who lived on Lookout Mountain. She was married to Wayne Shorter, a jazz musician with the group Weather Report. Anna Maria was a Buddhist chanter as well, and she and Tina chanted to strengthen Tina. Next, she moved in with a girl who was a college student, who chanted and worked as a masseuse. From there Tina moved back in with Anna Maria.

Without a cent of her own, Tina paid her way at her friends' houses by cooking and cleaning, and felt blessed to do so. However, she did much more than just clean. She would tackle tasks that no one likes to do for themselves, such as organizing closets and straightening up things for them. It was not just work; it was a way of working through her own frustrations.

"I want to tell you something," says Tina. "I enjoyed it. Because I was paving my way. What was I supposed to do, sit there and be a star? There were two things I could do. And I couldn't sing there. But I learned to clean from the white woman in Tennessee. It was physical. I'd just see the closet transformed and it was wonderful. It was what I do in my own house. Except the house was missing" (8).

A couple of months went by. Tina was able to get in contact with her son Craig, and she had his girlfriend sneak into the Turner house and take some of Tina's clothes out of the closet. Finally, she was able to have some of her own things to wear. Tina also had her bring her .38 pistol, just in case she had to defend herself against "pistol-whipping Ike Turner"—as he had been known in East St. Louis.

Meanwhile, Ike secluded himself at Bolic Sound. According to his son, Ike Turner Jr., Ike did so much cocaine that he stayed up for fourteen consecutive days. Ike Jr. tried to be loyal to his father. That is until one night when Ike bashed his son over the head with a loaded .45 pistol. As Ike Jr. was being stitched up at the hospital, he knew that he too would have to escape.

After Tina left Ike, all of the scheduled tour dates had to be canceled. No one was going to buy concert tickets to see Ike without Tina. Pretty soon, the concert promoters started filing lawsuits. Furthermore, the recording contract with Liberty/ United Artists Records was due to lapse. While he was alone in the studio, Ike kept writing and recording songs of hurt and revenge. They were songs that no one was even remotely interested in hearing.

One day Anna Maria and Tina decided to go out to the store. Tina wore her head wrap and dark glasses. However, when a car pulled up beside them and gave them a good hard look, they knew that they were being followed. That night, while chanting, suddenly Anna Maria announced that she was going to turn the lawn sprinklers on—full blast. In case anyone wanted to come up to the house, they were going to get soaking wet.

Sure enough, a knocking came at the door. It was Robbie Montgomery, one of the former Ikettes. Anna Maria did her best impersonation of a Portuguese maid, and told Robbie that no one was at home but her. As Tina looked out the window, she could see Ike, his Rolls Royce, and five or six cars full of people, all dressed like extras for a *Shaft* or *Superfly* film. There was Ike in his boots and a jumpsuit—hoping to drag Tina back by force.

Tina and Anna Maria called the police. When the police arrived, Tina announced to them who she was and informed them that the man in the jumpsuit was Ike Turner and that she had no intention of going back to him. The police made him leave the premises upon the insistence of the property's owner.

Although they all left that night, now Ike knew where Tina was. Ike phoned Maria Booker and asked her to line up a meeting between he and Tina. Tina was feeling very strong and self-confident at this point, so she agreed. She was tired of living this fugitive lifestyle.

Ike arrived at Anna Maria's in a car with a driver. She got in the car with him for their talk. According to Tina, Ike nervously fumbled with his hat while he spoke to her. She knew that he didn't dare lay a hand on her this time. In that meeting, she let him know that she was never going to go back to him— end of topic. He drove her back to Anna Maria's.

Two days after their meeting, Ike sent all four of their sons to go live with Tina. They arrived with their clothes and pets. Then he sent over $1,000—enough money to rent a house—and pay for one month's rent. Tina knew that he was just setting her up. There was an added complication in Tina's life too. Since it was she who legally had walked away from the tour dates, the lawsuits now were arriving in her mail. It was she who was legally liable for the missing dates she had failed to fulfill.

She got in touch with Rhonda Gramm and asked if she would help her piece things back together. With Rhonda now playing booking agent, she began to book television appearances for Tina, shows that she could appear on without requiring a band or an act. She supported herself by appearing on TV game shows like *Hollywood Squares* and a series of variety programs—including the *Cher* show. Since Cher had left Sonny, she felt a special kinship with Tina. She was also seen on the *Donnie and Marie Osmond* show, *The Brady Bunch Variety Show*, and even a *Laugh-In* revival. Tina Turner was starting her career all over again, this time as a solo star.

After years of feeling trapped and isolated, Tina began to realize that she had several friends who were very supportive of her. One of her closest allies turned out to be Ann-Margret.

Recalls Ann-Margret of this era, "We spent more time together. She and her assistant Rhonda came to our house many times for dinner. Roger and I went to hers. She once admired a dress Bob Mackie had made for one of my specials, and I gave it to her. Roger and I truly believed in Tina as a person and a performer, and we wanted to do anything to help restore her self-confidence and self-esteem. We've remained friends ever since" (24).

Initially, Tina filed for divorce from Ike only weeks after the Dallas fight. Nat Tabor had filed the initial divorce petition on July 27, citing "irreconcilable differences." Once Ike had threatened Tabor's life, he was off the case. It was Ann-Margret's husband, Roger Smith, who put her in touch with Arthur Leeds of the law firm of Gottlieb, Locke and Leeds.

The papers that they filed startled everyone. Although she was entitled by California law to "community property" which had been acquired during her marriage, she did not seek or want 50 percent of everything that Ike owned—like she could have legally taken it from him. She only wanted two things— her freedom and her stage name of "Tina Turner." Leeds did petition for $4,000 a month in alimony and an additional $1,000 a month in child support. Although, Tina never expected Ike to agree to that, at this point she didn't really care about the money at all.

Then Tina got a phone call from Mike Stewart at United Artists Records. He wanted to set up a meeting between himself, Tina, and Ike. She agreed. In the context of that meeting, she informed them both that she had no intention of ever singing with Ike again, in a recording studio or on a stage—ever. Ike's plan to lure her back to him with record company money had backfired, and now he was really pissed off.

Furthermore, Ike had it in for anyone who helped or sheltered Tina. The first one to receive damages at the hand of Ike was Rhonda Gramm. It seemed that twice her house in Reseda was set on fire. Rhonda came to live with Tina for a few days, then she went back home. When her windows were blown out by gunfire, she moved back with Tina again.

Tina very quickly learned how to become resourceful once she had her own place. The first house that she lived in she had furnished using grocery store trading stamps.

She had no income of her own. In fact, at one point she had to rely on government food stamps to keep food on the table. "I'm not ashamed of it," says proud Tina. "It was like playing house" (2).

The hill in back of the house that Tina was renting on Sunset Crest Drive was covered with vines, which made it easy to scale up. So, Tina's son Craig rigged Coke bottles together with strings to form an alarm against anyone who tried to sneak up.

One night they were in the house when the sound of gunfire in the front yard startled them. Someone had blown the windows out of Rhonda's car. Another night, a police officer came to the door to warn Tina that Ike had hired someone to kill her, and that she should be aware of the threat. Arthur Leeds also received threats on his life during this period of time.

Tina took to having her pistol with her at all times for protection. Driving in West Hollywood one day, she ran a red light. While the police officer was writing up the ticket they spotted the gun in her purse. She was taken in to the police station to be booked. However, when she got there and they found out who she was, they simply confiscated the gun and let her go free. They too knew all about Ike Turner, and they knew all of the illegal things in which he was involved. One of the ideas that came out of her meeting with Mike Stewart was Ike's suggestion that Stewart could start managing her career for her. Although Tina knew that Mike was still too close to the Ike camp, she didn't have any other offers.

She got ahold of Mike and started working with him. Stewart lent money to Tina while she mounted a stage act and reinvented her singing career as a soloist. Mike recalls that Tina never complained about this new position in which she now found herself. One night, Stewart took Tina to a movie premiere, and according to him, "You would have thought I was with Madonna today. The paparazzi swarmed. She was a celebrity" (5). The public still revered Tina as a big star apart from Ike.

With assistance, money, and help from Mike Stewart, Tina mounted a stage act of her own. She was all finished singing Ike Turner songs like "A Fool in Love" and "I Idolize You." Another song she would never, ever sing again was "I've Been Loving You Too Long," which brought back awful memories of that demeaning microphone fellatio routine.

She wanted to have a completely new act and a fresh, contemporary look. According to her, "I had been tired of this singing and this whole image of how I looked. I hated how I looked. . . . The hair and the makeup and all the sweat—I hated all of it" (5).

It was now 1977, the year when disco was sweeping the country. Several of the '60s acts, like Aretha Franklin and Dionne Warwick, were having trouble keeping up with the new wave of disco divas like Gloria Gaynor, Donna Summer, and Sister Sledge. So Tina reinvented herself.

Thanks to Ann-Margret, Tina started working with designer Bob Mackie, who also worked a lot with Cher. Wearing tuxedos on stage and glittering gowns from Bob Mackie, Tina fashioned a whole new image for herself that had absolutely nothing to do with Ike. She added songs to her act like The Trammps' "Disco Inferno." Naturally, she had to retain some of her signature hits like "River Deep-Mountain High," "Proud Mary," and "Honky Tonk Women."

Since she was starting over again, cabarets and casino lounges were the only venues that she was able to perform in for awhile. She was just happy to be working. She hired dancers, and she sang ballads for the first time in her career. She had been so used to screaming her lyrics—as per Ike's insistence—that it was refreshing to sing whatever songs she wanted to sing.

The act debuted at a small club in Vancouver, British Columbia. It was far enough away from the Los Angeles and New York City critics to test the waters of her new act and her new persona. The act was not without its glitches. At one point in the show, Tina was to make her entrance in a man's suit, in a sort of "Big Spender" production number. Velcro held the black suit, shirt, and hot pink necktie together at the seams. At one point during the number, the dancers were to breakaway the suit to reveal Tina in a form-fitting short shirt and nylons. On opening night the Velcro didn't release, the stockings were falling down, and it was a potential mess. Undaunted, Tina kept on singing and nudged one of the dancers to fix the situation, making it look like it was just part of the act.

Onstage mishaps aside, she finally had her own band and her own dancers, and she was feeling like a million bucks. To top it off, when she came to her grand finale number, the crowd stood up and gave her a standing ovation. Miraculously, it was the first one she had ever had in her career. It felt wonderful.

One of Tina's most famous Bob Mackie outfits from this era was a gold one that had wings attached to it. After years with Ike, it felt wonderful to have some fun with the glamour and glitz of it. "The wings and Las Vegas style. I mean, you look for glitter," she recalls. "It was the first time I had a chance to dress in such costumes. I enjoyed it" (16).

Booked on the nightclub cabaret circuit—in places like Reno and Lake Tahoe—Tina was putting herself and her career back together. She took an advance on song royalties she had written (like "Nutbush City Limits"), and moved herself into a new home in Sherman Oaks. She kept it a secret from Ike, but it wasn't long before he found out her whereabouts.

She was inside her house late one night, with her son Craig and his girlfriend, Bernadette, when they heard gunfire. When they looked outside, they found that someone had encircled Bernadette's car with gasoline and set it aflame. Ike was obviously up to his old tricks. Since his own career was in the dumpster, he had nothing better to do than to devise these threatening pranks.

To have some sort of income, and to fuel his hope that one day Tina would come back to him, Ike started salvaging some of the tracks he had in his studio with Tina's lead vocal on them. In 1977, United Artists Records released an Ike & Tina album called *Delilah's Power*. It included several cover tunes like Three Dog Night's "Never Been to Spain," Lena Horne's "Stormy Weather (Keeps Rainin' All the Time)," and The Archies' "Sugar, Sugar." Neither the album nor the single "Delilah's Power" made it onto the charts.

Tina's interest in visiting psychics continued in this era. In 1977 she went to see a woman named Carol Dryer. It was Carol who read Tina's soul aura and announced to her that she had once lived in ancient Egypt. This further underscored her interest in reincarnation, Egypt, and the mystical powers of the universe. Dryer claimed that Tina was now working out, in this lifetime, some of the mishaps that had occurred in her former life in the land of the Pharaohs. Tina was fascinated by these theories and continued to delve into reincarnation and Buddhism.

She was beginning to have problems with the four boys as well. She was doing the best she could to raise them. She would not let them speak improper English or speak in slang words or phrases. But now that she was the breadwinner in the family, she had much too much to concentrate on without having to watch out for them and keep them out of trouble. She hired the woman who was once her nemesis—Ann Cain—to move into her house and take care of the boys for her.

Finally, the arrangements for Ike and Tina's divorce were approaching. It seemed that Ike had his hands on all sorts of holdings, from jewelry and real estate to a lot of money in songwriting royalties. Tired of fighting with Ike Turner's camp, Tina instructed Arthur Leeds to forfeit all of the money, walk away from the assets, and just end the whole mess. She was to receive her two Jaguar automobiles and all of the songwriting royalties from the songs she had composed. As far as she was concerned, Ike could keep everything else.

When she decided to take not a cent from Ike, the judge asked her, "Young lady, are you sure?" (8). She was dead sure. She didn't want to be obligated to him in any way, shape, or form. She had her own life and her own future to concentrate on now.

As she explains, "It's not about leaving with money. You leave with knowledge. Inner strength. All the discipline I have to have now came from being with that man. . . . I knew what I was doing, and I knew why, and I got out. You don't step out and do what I did with my life if you don't have some control there" (8).

The terms of the divorce were finally ironed out in November 1977, and the final decree was to be issued on March 29, 1978. Finally, she was legally free from Ike Turner. That was not to say that he still didn't reappear from time to time to harass her, but no longer did he have a legal hold on or claim to any of the matters in her life.

According to her, "My success and triumph was in leaving Ike" (11). Her day of independence had finally come. It had been a sixteen-year nightmare roller-coaster ride, but now Tina was finally free from Ike Turner.

12

TINA REBORN / PUTTIN'
ON THE RITZ

Experiencing her newfound freedom, Tina was on the path of redefining her career as a solo artist. For the first time in her life she was getting to truly make her own decisions. And, she was no longer living in the fear that she had existed with during her sixteen years with Ike.

"Once the divorce came—I had cut my hair," she recalls. "I had gone shopping, even though I had no money. I got through it, though, but it was really fun. It was a freedom that—unless you've ever been in some form of bondage that you—it's very hard to explain it. To have the freedom to get in your car and just ride, sometimes, because I'd never had that chance or that opportunity. I met new people, new friends. I moved from that side of California to an opposite side and I met friends, and . . . I learned how to drink a bit of champagne and wine. I learned some things. I learned about another life, and I liked it, you know?" (12).

Part of her new life included selecting the material for her albums on her own. She was truly trying out her wings, and it felt great. In 1978 Liberty/United Artists released her third solo album, entitled *Rough*. It was a mixture of contemporary rock songs and cover versions of recent hits from other artists. Three of the most notable cuts include her interpretation of Bob Seger's "Fire Down Below," Dan Hill's "Sometimes When We Touch," and her first recorded version of Elton John's "The Bitch Is Back." Still trying her hands at country, she also recorded Willie Nelson's "Funny How Time Slips Away." There was one single released from it, titled "Root Toot Undisputable Rock & Roller." The album was produced by Bob Monaco.

Also in 1978 came Tina's next appearance in a major film. She was seen in the highly publicized rock & roll motion picture *Sgt. Pepper's Lonely Hearts Club Band*. Producer Robert Stigwood had been so successful at bringing The Who's *Tommy* to the big screen that he was anxious to repeat the formula with another big rock star feature fashioned after a famous album. So, he optioned The Beatles' 1967 masterpiece album *Sgt. Pepper's Lonely Hearts Club Band*, and set about turning it into a huge spectacle, starring The Bee Gees and Peter Frampton as the four members of the band.

Since several of the songs contained on it suggested characters, like "Being for the Benefit of Mr. Kite," "Lovely Rita," and "Lucy in the Sky with Diamonds," different actors could play each of them. One of the most famous aspects of the album was the original cover, on which The Beatles were depicted standing in marching band outfits, surrounded by cardboard cutouts and photos of famous people on bleachers behind them. To replicate the album cover concept, during the last minutes of the film, The Bee Gees and Peter Frampton were likewise surrounded by a team of famous faces on bleachers behind them. The notable stars included one of the oddest lists of movie stars, rock stars, and Broadway stars billed as "Our Guest at Heartland." Tina Turner was very prominently displayed in the front row, singing the song "Sgt. Pepper's Lonely Hearts Club Band" while standing next to Chita Rivera and Carol Channing. Tina was wearing one of her scant Bob Mackie outfits. Also on the bleachers were Minnie Ripperton, Dr. John, Connie Stevens, Bonnie Raitt, Sarah Dash, Nona Hendryx, Frankie Valli, Anita Pointer, Helen Reddy, and dozens of other rock and pop stars. Unfortunately, when the film was released, it was a huge bomb at the box office. However, it reinforced the fact that Tina Turner was still a huge star in Hollywood circles.

The following year came her fourth solo album, *Love Explosion*, her next excursion into defining her own solo sound. She did a fun version of The O'Jay's "Backstabbers" and she made her first forays into disco music with songs "Love Explosion" and "Music Keeps Me Dancin'" She even performed a ballad made famous by Barbra Streisand "Just a Little Lovin' (Early in the Morning)." The album was produced by Alec R. Constandinos.

Neither of her first two post-Ike solo albums sold a significant amount of copies. Tina was happy just the same. She had a career, and if she survived with what she currently had, she considered herself blessed. "Once you've experienced a type of bondage and then gotten free, you really learn what being free is all about, and it's about just being comfortable and free. So I didn't put any value on not having an immediate hit record or not being in the limelight. I was fine where I was. I watched myself to see what I could do with people. It was a studying time after I left Ike" (10).

While Tina was releasing solo albums, Ike was busy releasing more Ike & Tina Turner albums. In 1979 United Artists brought out a greatest hits compilation called *Soul Sellers*. In 1980, Ike sold more tracks from in the vaults to Fantasy Records, yielding an album called *The Edge*. It included cover versions of Shirley & Company's "Shame Shame Shame," Bill Withers' "Lean on Me," Elton John's "Philadelphia Freedom," and Alice Cooper's "Only Women Bleed"

Ike had no idea how good he had it with Tina until she was gone. He walked around grumbling about how he made her a star. In reality, she made him a star. Sure, he was the business-man who gave her the breaks, but he would never have achieved the greatness he did without her.

Furthermore, his resources were now dwindling, and the demand for audiences to see Ike *without* Tina was pretty nonex-istent. Once the cash ran out, the party that didn't look like it was *ever* going to end suddenly came to an end. Observed Ike, "Before Tina and I broke up, I had twenty-five people around me every day, telling me they loved me. 'Oh Ike, I love you, I love you, I love you.' All that bullshit. To them bastards it ain't nothing but a word, man. They don't mean shit. Then I found myself alone for the first time in, what, thirty years? None of the 'I love you' assholes were there then. None of them. When they thought I had no money, they was all gone" (17).

While Ike was falling apart, Tina was getting herself in tip-top physical shape. To clear up many of her health problems, she sought the advice of a homeopathic doctor. According to her, "Af-ter my second visit to the hospital, my eyes became clear. The whites of my eyes were never clear. They were always just not white. And I started to feel healthy. I had a glow, a light about me. I started to get energy, to feel strong, to enjoy my work more" (5).

In 1979, Tina Turner taped a TV special called *Olivia New-ton-John's Hollywood Nights*. On the show, Olivia invited several female rock and pop stars to be her guests for a big all-girls pro-duction number. Olivia asked Toni Tennille, Karen Carpenter, and Tina Turner. Other guests on the show included Olivia's *Xanadu* film co-star, Gene Kelly, as well as Andy Gibb and Elton John. It aired on April 14, 1980, on ABC-TV.

It seems like an odd TV project to change Tina Turner's career, but that was the outcome of this one. Rava Daly, who was one of Tina's dancers in her cabaret act, kept suggesting to Tina that she should get in touch with Olivia's boyfriend at that time, personal manager Lee Kramer. Daly knew that Kramer was on a quest for new management clients. After Tina appeared on Olivia's show, she felt confident enough to make the phone call.

She came in for a meeting with Kramer at his office, and she brought Rhonda Gramm along with her. Kramer introduced her to a business associate of his, Roger Davies. Tina liked both of them, especially Davies. She was very frank in outlining the fact that she was in debt and was looking to turn her career around. At the time she owed Mike Stewart $200,000, she owed the IRS $100,000 in back taxes, plus penalties of another $100,000. She truly needed some career advice. Most of her debts to the promoters of the aborted 1976 Ike & Tina tour had been repaid at this point.

Tina played Roger some songs that she had recently recorded. She wanted his opinion on the material. Roger was not very impressed by what he heard, and he told her that he didn't think these songs were what radio was interested in at the moment. Instead of being incensed by his comments, she was impressed with the fact that he wasn't some "yes" man. Tina liked the way he communicated his thoughts. He was direct but tactful.

Kramer was enthusiastic about signing Tina as a client, but Roger wasn't convinced yet. He wanted to see what she could do on stage first. Tina was about to start a two-week engagement at the Fairmont Hotel in San Francisco, and she suggested that they come up and see her there. Lee Kramer and Roger Davies finally made it up to San Francisco on the last night of her engagement.

Davies especially loved what he saw that night. Although the Fairmont Hotel was a pretty staid and stiff setting to see an act like Tina's, he was knocked out by the energy she expelled on stage. He was so impressed that they stayed for the next show as well. They were thrilled to find that she was even better during the second show. They decided to sign her immediately.

Roger and Tina both agreed that she should aim for more of a rock & roll type of show. However, he was to find that directing her out of the cabaret circuit was not as easy as they anticipated. Davies decided to study her act some more and see what needed changing first. For the time being, she played a lot of dates in Canada, unable to get the kind of bookings they wanted for her in the United States. Recalls Davies, "There was a terrible stigma attached to her because she walked out on the tour and because everybody still thought she was with Ike" (2). Roger didn't want too many drastic changes in her act . . . only change the band, fire the dancers, find new material to sing, and ditch the clothes.

Tina was willing to take his advice. According to her, "I kinda sensed that I would eventually be successful and decided not to give up until it happened" (11).

In late 1979, an interesting proposal for Tina's services came to Kramer and Davies' office. It was an offer to tour and perform for five weeks in South Africa. It would make her $150,000. However, Davies was unable to go with her, as he was accompanying Olivia Newton-John to London for the British debut of the film *Xanadu*.

If Tina accepted the African tour, she would be accompanied by a young management trainee, Chip Lightman. She had no idea who he was, but the money was too enticing. She also took along her son Ronnie, who was presently playing the bass in her band. The tour included dates in Johannesburg, Durban, and Capetown. Although this was a controversial period in South Africa because of segregation, Tina noted that the audiences seemed mainly racially mixed.

She returned to the United States, then she and the entourage left on their next tour in Australia and Southeast Asia. This time around, Roger was with her. After a show in Manila, he told her that she had to fire everyone immediately. She needed to be more rock & roll, and the Bob Mackie costumes had to go. She also let Rhonda Gramm go. Ms. Turner recalls, "Roger had me get rid of everybody" (2).

In 1980, Tina debuted her new band at the Fairmont Hotel in San Francisco. From there she headed to Europe: Poland, Czechoslovakia, and three sold-out nights at the Hammersmith Odeon in London. Then it was off to the Middle East: Bahrain, Abu Dhabi, Dubai. She recalls, "We more or less survived off of Poland, Hungary, Yugoslavia, even Teheran—places like that" (2). She had gigs all over the world, but the bookings she was offered in the United States were not the types that either she or Roger wanted. The problem was how to reintroduce her to American audiences.

Then a possible management problem arose. Olivia Newton-John had severed her relationship with Lee Kramer, and she wanted Roger Davies to quit Kramer's management firm and take her on as a client. He agreed. Now Tina had to make a decision—remain with Kramer, or stick with Davies. She chose Davies. Now Roger Davies had two entirely dissimilar clients: Olivia Newton-John *and* Tina Turner.

In this era, the American music scene was in an odd space. Disco devoured the whole music business from 1977 to 1979. Then, suddenly, in 1980 and 1981 New Wave rock was the rage, and everyone from Carly Simon to Linda Ronstadt was going punk. Then the bottom dropped out of that, and the music business went into a huge sales slump. Everyone seemed to be looking for the next big thing. The big thing that was right around the corner was MTV, which was in the planning stages at this point.

Tina still wasn't in the right position to get the kind of record deal that she needed. She cut several demos, including The Rolling Stones' "Out of Time," Murray Head's "Say It Ain't So," and a song by Australian group The Sherbs called "Crazy in the Night." However, none of these songs seemed to spell "hit."

In Greenwich Village, New York City, a man named Jerry Brandt owned a rock club on East 11th Street called The Ritz. Located between Third and Fourth Avenues, the club had originally been a dance hall that had been long abandoned. It had a large, flat dance floor and a big stage where the dance bands would perform. With nice high ceilings, the upstairs had a wrap-around balcony wide enough for tables and chairs on it. In its new incarnation as a rock club, it worked perfectly. It was a hip and happening place during this era, featuring established acts, along with many new wave and punk acts.

After months and months of playing places like Yugoslavia and Abu Dhabi, Roger Davies felt that Tina was ready for the big time, and being seen in New York City was crucial. The Ritz seemed like the perfect venue to showcase her return to the mainstream. After all, ten years had passed since Tina had last played Manhattan.

Davies phoned Brandt, and the club owner loved the idea of having Tina Turner perform at The Ritz in the summer of 1981. Roger announced up front that he didn't care if they paid anything for this gig—the important thing was for Tina to be seen by the right people.

Enthusiastic, Brandt took out full-page ads in *The Village Voice*, and there was a buzz all over town that Tina Turner was back. Invitations also went out to several celebrities and press members. A varied list of stars showed up for this first Ritz engagement, including Mick Jagger, Andy Warhol, Diana Ross, Mary Tyler Moore, and Robert DeNiro. Tina felt like she was holding court. She ended up playing three nights of packed houses, and she got great reviews. Tina was back and The Ritz had her!

This first Ritz engagement was such a smash that Brandt booked Tina for a return run at the club in October of 1981. That second visit to The Ritz proved equally successful. Among the stars who came that time included Rod Stewart—who brought along record producer Richard Perry.

Rod was very excited to see Tina back in full form, looking and sounding great. It just so happened that Stewart was going to be the musical guest on the TV show *Saturday Night Live* that very Saturday night. He invited Tina to be his special guest on the show, turning his hit "Hot Legs" into a duet. She jumped at the opportunity. It turned into a high-profile return to network television for her.

One of the songs that Tina was performing in her act at the time was her torchy rock version of The Beatles' hit "Help!" When she got back to Los Angeles, she went into a recording studio with Richard Perry and made her first attempts at turning it into a hot hit record. But somehow, that particular track wasn't coming out as excitingly as she was doing it on stage, so it was scrapped.

In the fall of 1981, The Rolling Stones were on tour, and Roger Davies and Tina went to see the group perform at the L.A. Forum. When they got backstage to visit the boys after the show, Keith Richards asked Turner why she wasn't on tour with them. She simply told them that they had never asked her. Well that was quickly remedied. The Rolling Stones were booked for three dates in November at Brendan Byrne Arena in New Jersey, just across the Hudson River from New York City. They asked her to open for them for the engagement. She instantly accepted. Furthermore, Mick Jagger invited Tina to duet with the band during the concert on the song "Honky Tonk Woman."

That night in New Jersey Tina hit the stage in a sexy pair of black leather pants and leopard print boots. She recalls that playing on the same stage as The Stones proved to be a huge bonding experience between her and the hot new touring band she was now working with. For all of them, this was truly the big time!

Not to be outdone by The Stones, Rod Stewart again came to Tina's aid, this time with an invitation of his own. On December 18, 1981, he was performing at The Great Western Forum in Inglewood, California, in a concert set to be broadcast via satellite around the world. He invited Tina Turner and Kim Carnes to be his guest stars on the telecast that night on the song "Stay with Me." When the concert was released as an album the following year as *Rod Stewart Absolutely Live*, the Stewart, Carnes, and Turner trio version of "Stay with Me" is the grand finale on the disk.

Playing in front of a stadium audience with The Stones and Rod Stewart really opened her eyes up to a whole new realm of concert possibilities. She could feel her dreams expanding and focusing. Tina claimed, "I wanted to be like The Rolling Stones and all the guys out there that were packing the stadiums" (12).

Her road back to mainstream recording happened one piece at a time. She had offers to do one or two cuts on a couple of albums featuring varied artists and a couple of one-shot singles. The first one came in 1982 when she ended up with two tracks on the Warner Brothers soundtrack album for a Daryl Hannah and Peter Gallagher film called *Summer Lovers*. One of the songs was her freshly recorded "Crazy in the Night" and the other one was called "Johnny and Mary," which Richard Perry produced for her. On that soundtrack album she was in very good company, as it also included new music by Elton John, Nona Hendryx, Heaven 17, Chicago, and Depeche Mode.

Recalling his frustration over trying to find Tina a label contract, Davies says, "It wasn't easy to get a record deal. A lot of people still thought she was with Ike" (11).

In 1982 Tina received another offer to record. There was a production team in England who called themselves B.E.F. (British Electric Foundation). The team was actually just a duo of producers—Martyn Ware and Ian Craig Marsh—both members of the group Heaven 17, who had also had a cut on the *Summer Lovers* album. There were no "musicians" per se in this "group," it was just the two men and their synthesizers. They wanted to record an album comprised of their own tributes to some of their favorite rock stars and wanted to use singers who weren't heard from much anymore. Among the British singers they had lined up for their album were Sandie Shaw and Gary Glitter. They wanted to record a version of The Temptations' hit from 1970, "Ball of Confusion (That's What the World Is Today)," and Sam Cooke's "Change Is Gonna Come" with Tina as the singer. Why not? And so, Roger and Tina flew to London.

Martyn Ware recalls, "The first time Tina and I met in the studio, her first words were 'Where's the band?' I was surrounded by what was the latest recording equipment and synthesizers, engrossed in creation of the whole rhythm section without the aid of any musicians—which at that time was a very revolutionary technique. I believe that Tina's openness to ideas is what has enabled her to become popular with a new audience. Tina was charm and professionalism personified, as she has been in all of our following recordings together" (21).

When the B.E.F. album *Music of Quality & Distinction, Volume 1* was released in April 1982, "Ball of Confusion" made the album, but "Change Is Gonna Come" did not. It went on to became a big hit in England—which was the only country in which it was marketed. ("Change Is Gonna Come" can be found on the 1994 Tina boxed compilation, *The Collected Recordings, Sixties to Nineties.*)

To coincide with the B.E.F. album release, Roger booked Tina at the Hammersmith Odeon theater again in London to mark her comeback in progress. At the time, he was actively seeking a solo recording contract for her.

When United Artists and Liberty Records were rolled into Capitol/EMI Records in America, Tina Turner had been one of the acts that was dropped from the label. When Roger approached the executives at Capitol, they were unenthused about signing her again for the American market. However, intrigued by the noise that the *Music of Quality & Distinction, Volume 1* was making in the United Kingdom, their international division was interested in her for the British market. What started brewing was a possible deal for the international audience. With that, Tina went into the studio with one of Capitol's house producers, John Carter, to record a couple of songs to test the waters within the company. The songs that Tina cut during those sessions included The Animals' "When I Was Young" and The Motels' "Total Control." Still, the actual deal remained unsigned—because she hadn't had a major hit since "Proud Mary" in the early 1970s, Capitol wasn't sure if they wanted her or not.

Meanwhile, in December 1982, Tina was booked for another return to The Ritz in New York City. Roger Davies was startled when he received a phone call from the Capitol/EMI Records office in New York, wanting to add sixty-three people's names to the guest list for the show that very night. What had happened was that EMI was getting ready to release a big David Bowie album, *Let's Dance*, and there was a huge listening party for it. When David announced to all of the Capitol/EMI executives he was with that he was going to see his all-time favorite female singer that very night, the company heads asked who that was. Replied Bowie, "Tina Turner."

With that, everyone at the company meeting wanted to come along too. In addition, Bowie wanted to bring along several of his friends, including his co-star from the film *The Hunger*, Susan Sarandon, as well as Keith Richards and Ron Wood from The Rolling Stones, and tennis star John McEnroe.

Tina had no idea that all of this was going on. However, when she hit the stage at The Ritz that night, there seemed to be some sort of a buzz in the crowd. She figured that there must have been some movie star in the audience. Little did she know that half of the staff of Capitol Records was there, along with Bowie and company.

The show was incredible that night, and she was surprised and delighted to have her buddies Bowie, Richards, and Wood there at the Ritz. They invited her back to an after-concert party at Keith's apartment in the Plaza Hotel. They ended up drinking champagne and singing songs all night long. Tina and Roger didn't leave Keith's until 8:30 the next morning.

Well, that night at The Ritz really turned the heads of the executives at Capitol Records. After seeing her in action, they agreed to sign Tina in America also—since she was now signed to a singles deal with EMI Records for England only. When the British executives heard the two songs that she had recorded with John Carter at the helm, they were deemed "too American" sounding to have a big impact on the international market. Capitol wasn't impressed with them either, and declined releasing them. Roger was insistent that he and Tina go back to England to record.

Davies arranged for Tina to return to the studio with the B.E.F. guys to produce her first British single that was part of her new deal. Ware and Marsh were thrilled by the idea of working with Tina again. Since the record company was not going to pay to get them to Europe, Roger lined up a concert over there to finance the recording of the song. The only concert he could put together was in Stockholm, Sweden. The engagement called for Tina to sing with a twenty-one-piece orchestra. She had never performed with a full orchestra, why not? Tina was such a hit in Stockholm that she made the front page of the newspaper there the morning after the show.

Roger and Tina arrived in England, only to find—to their horror—that Ware and Marsh had been so busy with their group, Heaven 17, that they hadn't custom written a new song for the session as planned. Here Davies had booked famed Abbey Road studios for the recording, it was the night before the session, and they didn't have a single song!

There was an emergency meeting in Roger's hotel room at Grosvenor House, where Ware and Marsh brought over a stack of their favorite singles that they thought Tina might do a good job of covering. When she saw that they had brought with them only rhythm & blues songs to suggest for her, she asked them if they were into any rock & roll. She explained that she had no interest in R&B, since that was part of her life in the old Ike & Tina days. While brainstorming, Tina, Roger, Martyn, and Ian all agreed that they were into Bowie, so off Roger went to purchase every David Bowie cassette he could find. When he returned, the one song that they seemed to agree upon was "1984." They liked the idea of that one, as well as one of the R&B songs they had played earlier in the evening—Al Green's "Let's Stay Together." Okay, now they had two songs to work on the next day in the studio.

Everyone involved in the session that day was thrilled with the results. She sang "Let's Stay Together" only once, and Roger and the producing duo all claimed that was *it*—a perfect performance. With that finished, they went on to "1984." According to Martyn Ware, "The highest compliment I can pay her is that in fifteen years of producing various artists—her performances of 'Ball of Confusion' and 'Let's Stay Together'—were the only complete unedited 'first take' vocals I've ever had the pleasure of recording and mixing. In this world of increasingly sophisticated technology, she is still unique" (21).

The executives at EMI Records in England were thrilled with the two recordings they had done in the studio that day, and they wanted to release a twelve-inch vinyl single version of "Let's Stay Together" immediately. However, Capitol Records in America flatly didn't like it at all, and had no interest in releasing it in the States. The single was released in Europe as planned, and it became a huge hit, hitting No. 6 in the United Kingdom. Roger had booked several foreign dates for Tina when "Let's Stay Together" was first released. Here she was in concert in the Persian Gulf, while her record was scaling the British charts. When she returned to England, she was booked at a small club that Virgin Records owned, called The Venue. The record had become such a smash that the gig was extended to eleven nights to meet the sudden demand for tickets.

Tina recalls, "So I came back to London and did a tour with the hit record. Was it huge! When I sang 'Let's Stay Together' everybody sang it with me. And I looked out there and I thought, 'So this is what it feels like'" (1).

In 1983, a music writer wrote about Tina's stage show in Great Britain's newspaper *The Daily Mirror*, "When she wraps her vocal cords around a microphone, men go weak at the knees. When her hips start to gyrate, they break out in a sweat . . . the moment she walks on stage, wearing a mini-dress of leather rags, the lady becomes a vamp" (27).

To further promote "Let's Stay Together," Tina very quickly did a simple but sexy video version of the song, with her pair of female dancers—Lejeune Richardson and Ann Behringer. In the beginning of the video, Tina wore one of her mini-dresses of shredded material cut up to her thigh. With the pair of dancers groveling at Tina's feet and running their hands up and down her exposed legs in the video, it was titillating, and it looked particularly lesbian oriented. This started all kinds of speculation about Tina's own sexuality at that time. After all, if an abusive marriage wouldn't make a girl want to go gay—what would? The press wanted to know details. Tina got a big chuckle over the controversy, and purposely never made any denials. Roger agreed that publicity was publicty—whatever the rumor.

Since "Let's Stay Together" was making prominent appearances in American record stores as an "Import" single, New York City DJ Frankie Crocker started playing the song on radio station WBLS. The record was so popular that the European singles were disappearing from store shelves in the "States." Capitol Records in America, who had just turned down releasing the single, suddenly had to rush release their own version of the song to match the demand. In the United States, the song made it to No. 19 on the Pop charts, and No. 5 on the R&B charts. Suddenly Capitol wanted a whole album—immediately—in less than a month!

Davies was floored as he had just booked thirty concert appearances for Tina in England to capitalize on the success of the single. Since she was in America at the moment, Capitol wanted him to cancel the tour and get her into a recording studio instantly. Roger was insistent that since Great Britain had been the country that was the most loyal to Tina in the last couple of years, he refused to cancel the dates. The album had to be recorded in England. Capitol Records producer John Carter agreed with Davies' logic and helped persuade the company to give Roger and Tina the "green light" to record in England and to send the bills back to them. So, off Tina and Roger flew—back to London.

While Tina and her band were zigzagging their way across England, Roger Davies was in London pulling together what was to become the most important album in Ms. Turner's career.

13

PRIVATE DANCER

There was no time to take a breath or come up with a concept for Tina's first album for Capitol/EMI Records. Decisions had to be made fast. The one thing that Tina was the most insistent upon was that this album had to *rock*. This was a make-it-or-break-it kind of project. If the momentum of "Let's Stay Together" was going to be capitalized upon, it had to happen quickly and the music had to be great. There might not be another opportunity like this again.

The one song that Tina and Roger arrived in London with was the tune "Better Be Good to Me." It was a song that had been recorded by an American band, Spider. Now, they just needed the whole rest of the album. Recalling his quest for songs for Turner to sing, Davies recalls, "I hit the streets. I called everyone I knew and begged for songs" (2).

An Australian friend of his by the name of Terry Britten was currently residing in London. Roger gave him a call to see what kind of song ideas he had for Tina. Britten had once been the lead guitar player in a group called The Twilights. Terry had one song already written that he thought might be good for Tina, called "Show Some Respect." He also had another song that he had composed with his writing partner, Graham Lyle. It was a pop-oriented song called "What's Love Got to Do With It."

One of the next people Davies went to was Robert Hine, who had recently come to prominence by producing The Fixx. He thought that Hine would be the perfect producer to bring "Better Be Good to Me" to life. Hine had an idea: he wanted Tina to meet with his girlfriend, Jeannette Obstoj, with whom he was currently writing songs. Turner told her life story to Jeannette during their meeting, and, inspired by what she heard, Obstoj wrote a tailor-made song for Tina called "I Might Have Been Queen." It was all about Tina's deep belief in reincarnation. When she heard the demo for the song, Tina was so touched by it, she was in tears. It was literally tailor-made for her.

However, she had the opposite reaction when she heard the two songs that Terry Britten submitted. But Roger was persistent, and kept playing "What's Love Got to Do With It" and "Show Some Respect for Her." Tina claimed that they didn't rock enough and that they were pop songs. She claimed, "I can't sing that wimpy crap" (2).

Roger was insistent that she at least give them a try, and he booked time at Mayfair Studios. Tina wanted the songs to be rougher, and she didn't like the key in which they were written. Terry Britten obligingly started tinkering with the songs. Finally, they came up with versions that Tina could live with—however, she still didn't love them.

The next person that Davies went to was Ed Bicknell, who was the manager of Dire Straits, and a singer by the name of Paul Brady. Bicknell gave him "Steel Claw" from the Brady catalog. There was also a track left over from the latest Dire Straits album, which Mark Knopfler had written called "Private Dancer"; however, only the instrumental tracks had been recorded.

Capitol Records producer John Carter came to London to see how the album was progressing and he ended up personally producing "Steel Claw" and "Private Dancer," credited on the album simply as "Carter." Tina's guitar-playing rock star buddy from way back—Jeff Beck—was featured on both of those cuts.

After Terry Britten recorded his two cuts with Tina, he also produced her version of the Ann Peebles hit "I Can't Stand the Rain."

By adding the Martyn Ware and Greg Walsh–produced songs "1984" and "Let's Stay Together," the album was completed—in a record-fast two weeks! Adding front and back photographs by Peter Ashworth, Tina Turner's startling new album, *Private Dancer*, was complete.

As a bonus cut for the European version of the album, Tina finally nailed down The Beatles' song "Help," which was produced by Joe Sample, Wilton Felder, and Ndugu Chancler. While she was working on her album, "Help" was released in England and reached No. 40 on the British charts.

The process was very rushed, and Tina had to rely on Roger Davies' instincts a lot during this frantic process. According to her, "I can't say these are *my* type of songs. It was like our backs were against the wall to get an album out. . . . I said, 'Whatever is gonna make a hit record'" (18).

What she liked the most was the fact that it really rocked, much more so than any of her previous recordings. "It's neither rock & roll nor R&B, but it's a bit of both," she explained. "Rhythm & blues to me has always been a bit of a downer . . . in the attitude—in the moan, in the plea. Rock & roll has always been straight on. You wanna put it on to get you going" (18).

She had to admit that the album reflected the new and re-born Tina Turner. "I don't want to beg and plead and weep and moan anymore. I had enough of that. Now what I like to sing are ass kickers. I want to get crazy. That's who I am" (28).

The finished album was presented to Capitol Records in America and EMI in Europe. Now it came time to test the waters, to start releasing singles, and to promote the hell out of them. With that, Tina was off on a four-month tour as the opening act for Lionel Richie's first major solo tour.

Since Richie was hot on the charts at the time with his solo songs "All Night Long" and "Hello," there was a big demand for him in concert. Although he had been an R&B star with The Commodores for years, he was suddenly a huge star on his own with pop hits. She wanted to "rock out" and go crazy on stage, and the crowd he drew was a bit subdued for her. However, the exposure was good for her. Said Tina during this tour with Lionel, "I know I'm not at my best with Lionel" (18).

Her new album wasn't out yet, and audiences mainly knew her from the old days. "It was real hard being on stage by myself at first," she explains. "Because Lionel's crowd is not my crowd. Plus, it was brand new material, and the only things they wanted to hear were 'Nutbush City Limits,' 'Let's Stay Together,' and 'Proud Mary'" (9). That was all about to change forever.

Prior to releasing the album, the single version of "What's Love Got to Do With It" hit the marketplace. By June 1984, *Private Dancer* entered the *Billboard* charts in America at No. 101, and "What's Love Got to Do With It" was in the Top 50 and on its way up the charts.

The critical reviews of the album were ecstatic. The *New York Times* declared that *Private Dancer* was a "landmark" in the "evolution of pop-soul music" (2). The *Los Angeles Times* claimed her voice was so hot it "melts vinyl" (4).

Furthermore, MTV completely jumped on the bandwagon

by keeping her new "What's Love Got to Do With It" video in constant rotation. At the age of forty-five, she was the hottest thing with the youth-oriented MTV crowd. Tina's simple video of her singing her triumphant new signature song struck a perfect chord with MTV audiences. The video depicted her strutting in a park and on a pier, delivering the song like she was giving sage advice to lovers around the world. It didn't just become a simple hit; it became the biggest smash of the year.

In July, "What's Love Got to Do With It" hit No. 3 in the United Kingdom. The following month *Private Dancer* peaked at No. 3 in America, No. 2 in England. The only reason that the album didn't make it to the top in the United States was the fact that the No. 1 and No. 2 spots on the chart were locked in by Prince's *Purple Rain* soundtrack and Bruce Springsteen's *Born in the U.S.A.* In the United States, *Private Dancer* was to remain in the Top 10 until May 1985—eventually selling over ten million copies worldwide. On August 21, 1984, "What's Love Got to Do With It" was certified Gold in the United States. Finally, on September 1, 1984, the song officially hit No. 1 in America—her first chart-topping single ever. Tina was officially back—and bigger and better than ever!

Tina was in New York City to appear again at The Ritz and to have an autograph signing at Tower Records on Broadway in Greenwich Village. The same day, she received word that she would be starring in the third movie in Mel Gibson's *Mad Max* trilogy, *Mad Max Beyond Thunderdome.* She was ecstatic about all of this news, and reportedly ran through Tower Records shouting "My record's No. 1, my record's No. 1!" As she so succinctly put it, "Is this a happy ending or what?" (1).

Instead of being only a happy ending to a long hard struggle to the top, it was just the beginning of good things for Tina Turner. She didn't have long to rest on her laurels, however—now she really had some work to do!

On September 18, she was one of the performers at Radio City Music Hall for the *First Annual MTV Music Awards*. Hosted by Bette Midler and Dan Aykroyd, the show was to become a huge television tradition, and Tina was right there, performing at her exciting best.

Tina's tidal wave of success became an across-the-board global event. John Martin of Canada's TV video network, Much Music, claimed at the time, "Her success corresponds with a new way of looking at sexy, self-assured women. She's doing it on her own and she's a heroine because of that" (29).

On both sides of the Atlantic Ocean, Capitol and EMI continued to pull singles from this landmark album. In November 1984, "You Better Be Good to Me" peaked at No. 5 in America. And in December 1994, "Private Dancer" hit No. 26 in the United Kingdom.

In late 1984, Tina was now a regular fixture at the top of the charts and wowing rock audiences around the globe. Ironically, however, she was still fulfilling some leftover concert engagements that were set up when no one seemed to care to book her for big public events. During the pre–"What's Love Got to Do With It" days, she had signed a contract to perform at several "industrial" gigs—entertaining straight-laced corporate convention goers. Most members of the general public don't realize that hundreds of once-huge rock, pop, and soul performers exist on performing for after-dinner crowds of convention attendees. In Tina's case, she had signed a contract with the hamburger king, McDonalds, to perform at fourteen separate corporate functions. At the time she signed the contract and began the concert dates, she was happy to have the gig and the income. A performer of Tina's stature could pick up $30,000 to $50,000 in one night at such a convention. The audiences were usually stiff and unresponsive middle-aged businesspeople, but the money was always good—and guaranteed.

In Ottawa, Canada, although she had returned to rock & roll supremacy—and was all over the radio with her new material—she performed her final corporate gig that autumn, fulfilling the McDonald's contractual obligation. No more corporate gigs for hamburger salespeople or business bigwigs for Tina. After the date, she was free to move on to the much bigger hamburgers she had to fry on her rock & roll grill. She had her own mind-boggling show business comeback to focus on! Ronald McDonald would have to find someone else to entertain his corporate executives.

In 1984 when Tina staged her huge comeback, what people were most amazed about was how fabulous she looked and the kind of vitality and energy she expelled on stage. It wasn't just that she was now forty-five, it was her look, her attitude, and her inner beauty. She seemed absolutely radiant.

Keith Richards said at the time, "She's probably more energetic now than she was twenty years ago" (28). He was right—success completely became her. She was looking and sounding better than ever!

"What a lot of people don't realize about me is that I've never done drugs and I've never smoked. I became homeopathic," she explains. "So that means I didn't have any drugs in my system to tear me down. There's nothing in my body that pulls me down. I never drink when I'm working. I'm a strong, healthy person, and that comes from eating fairly well and being homeopathic and never abusing my body. I enjoy my work. I'm an unusual person. I could get onstage right now and do a show. Had I abused myself during the early days, I never would have gotten as far as I got. But I'm healthy and I'm in control" (10).

The funny thing was that the whole new MTV audience had no idea who she was. They were too young to remember The Ike & Tina Turner Revue or "A Fool in Love." To them, she was this new girl they saw on television or heard on the radio. On the Lionel Richie tour, his young fans felt their jaws drop open at the sight of her entrance. They had never seen anything like Tina Turner before. According to her, "I've built my life around performing. I give everything to my audience, and that sustains me. To the younger people I'm now drawing, I was a surprise. They'd gotten used to seeing people just sit on stage and sing. Then all of a sudden, here comes Tina Turner, flying, kicking, and jumping. And they said, 'Oh, wow! Great! Look at that!' It didn't matter that I was older. It was the energy" (11).

Her health regime helped. "I'm basically a healthy person," she explained. "My diet has changed though. When I eat less junk, I feel better, and when I have a bit too much champagne—I've never had much to drink—I don't feel good. Basically, I listen to my body" (11).

The press went crazy for Tina. During this time, you couldn't pick up a magazine in which she wasn't featured. Even the fashion bible *Vogue* was writing about her. According to their May 1985 issue, "In this life, Tina Turner looks about thirty-six, and her skin is flawless. She does not deprive herself. She sips wine at dinner, does not diet, and does not take vitamins. If she's feeling particularly stressed, she consults a homeopathic doctor in London who gives her intravenous treatments 'to cleanse the toxins from the blood" (2).

Tina got a big smile on her face reading what people were saying about her. She said at the time, "Go sing and sweat and yell, jump and dance onstage for twenty years. You'll look immortal too!" (28).

To make a fashion statement while onstage, Tina wore short leather miniskirts and punk-looking jean jackets. One of her most identifiable attributes was her shapely legs. What was her exercise regime? "You must realize I've been doing this for twenty-five years," she claimed, "so I should be in good shape.

And can you imagine all the walking I do in airports? Now, that's exercise!" (9).

Her skin looked flawlessly fabulous. What was her secret? "When I'm not performing I wear little makeup," she revealed (9).

And then there was that new hairdo, which became a trademark of hers during this era. It was full and up on her head, clipped into what looked like a rumpled and haphazard style, which was very hip, youthful, and trendsetting. She said at the time, "I washed it one day and didn't have time to blow-dry it, so it just dried naturally. I said, 'Uuuummm, this is interesting.' It works perfectly for me. It's younger, and there's a lot of freedom with it. Just wash it and wear it!" (9).

It was clearly a wig, but what did she do to it to get it in that shape? "I prepare it like a three-course meal. I wash it, let it dry, then fork it up. Then I yuk it up with this gooey stuff, let it dry, then fork it up again," she explained (30).

Beginning in this period of time, up to and including the post–year-2000 era, she never looked or acted her age. According to her, "I've never been real conscious of age because of my lifestyle—rock & roll music, traveling, always surrounded by young people" (18).

In the youth-oriented rock world, Tina Turner was clearly trailblazing. "People tell me I look great and I say, 'You're damn right!' I take care of myself," she claimed (30).

And then there was her unique look and fashion sense. She modestly said of herself, "You can't put me down there with the ugly ones, and you can't put me up there with the pretty ones. I'm in the middle lane" (18).

Now that she had paid off all of her debts and was back in the money, shopping became her new passion. "I'm going through being a girl again," she claimed (2).

Of her own personal style, Tina explained, "My taste is very European. I don't have a man to lavish me right now, so I lavish myself" (30).

One of the things she claimed was that sales girls who tried to second-guess her style were amazed to find that in her personal life, Tina never went for flashy outfits or lots of diamonds "They think sexy legs and chest out, but normally I am very conservative. I get enough attention onstage so I can dress pretty low key on the street. I buy for quality, not flash" (30).

Regarding her shopping sprees, she illuminated, "My dream is to get the American Express Gold Card. Now I borrow other people's—the chauffeur's, my manager's, anyone's. Don't worry. I always pay them back" (30). After years of bad debts caused by her split with Ike, money problems were soon to be a thing of the past.

The one thing that was missing during this era was a man in her life. She wasn't desperate to find one, but if one came along, that would be great. "After I left Ike, I had my dream to find a rich man to protect me and take care of me. I haven't found him yet," she laughed (2).

"I like to be romanced by a man," she claimed. And regarding sex: "I'm not one of those women who has to have it no matter what. When you see me on a man's arm, it means something. I am not touched easily. I don't go out with men just to have companionship" (30).

According to her, "I'm still dreaming of meeting the kind of man like the kind of woman I am, very giving, not dominating. We'll be strong enough to trust each other and give each other freedom. The type of man I'm looking for would love me as much as I love him, would accept me with all my imperfections. He'd be someone who is very honest and alive. I just want a real human being who wants comfort and happiness out of life. That's the real nitty-gritty of what living is all about" (11).

What kind of things attract her to men? "First of all, there's something about a man's hands I like. And feet. If he's got horrible feet and shoes, forget it. And I like a wide bottom. In the relationship he has to have the control—and I will give that to him—but that's only because he really has it anyway. Now that's magic. Money adds a lot, but he doesn't have to have it. I am not lonely, but I do miss giving my love. I am very affectionate," she said (30).

She noted that her on-stage image was often a cause for confusion. "The illusion I give onstage is that I'm a bitch who sleeps around. But I'm really a one-man woman. . . . The man, my soul mate—that's what's missing in my life. But if he never comes, it's all right. I'm great alone" (31).

One of the things that press interviewers kept asking her about was her relationship with Ike Turner. According to her, "Living without blame, that is the secret to life. People think I'm bitter in that I hold a grudge against my ex-husband. I'm not bitter. I had a road and I followed it" (2).

Instead of fighting his way back to the top, Ike Turner was at a very low ebb during this era. Said Tina, "I don't begrudge Ike nothing. He is a talented musician. I wish he could get something together" (30).

Ike was astounded by her success. She revealed, "I tried to help Ike mentally. The last time I saw him he said, 'I'm not going to work for nothing.' *I did!* Some nights, by the time I finished expenses and paid the band, I would end up with nothing. I told him, 'Look what I've done!' But he insisted he wasn't going to work for less money. I said, 'O.K.' I don't like to hear bad things about Ike. We were family, so it still sort of gets me here," she says motioning to her heart. "If anything good comes for him, I would be really happy to know that he finally got himself together before he was totally lost." (11) But being totally lost in drugs and depression was where he was at in the 1980s.

And then there were her children, the four boys. "We're close, but I'm not mother, mother, munchy, munchy. I'm not that father-figure thing," she revealed (18). By now, they were all old enough to have their own lives and their own responsibilities.

And her mother, Zelma Bullock, now lived in Los Angeles, where she had a job in a Beverly Hills beauty shop. She enjoyed the social interaction of having a job to go to every day. Now that Tina was back in the black financially, she could afford to support Zelma. But her mother was happy to work. "I said, 'Mom, you don't have to work anymore,' but she likes it," said Tina (31).

Tina was feeling great as 1984 came to an end. And she had a right to be. She had accomplished an incredible feat with her new album, her new look, and all of the wonderful things that were in store for her. "I'm real proud that I was able to clear up my life," she said. "I'm real proud of how I've evolved into my own shoes. I've learned to accept me. I'm proud of me" (11).

As 1984 came to a close, Tina had just turned forty-six. There weren't a lot of women in rock & roll who were in their prime at this age. Ms. Turner had broken every rule and then thrown out the rulebook. She was in uncharted territory, and she loved the rarefied air at this new peak. According to her, she would continue at this pace, at least until she was fifty years old. "I'm gonna focus on this. I think that's gonna be my message, that's why I'm here. And I think that's why I'm gonna be as powerful as I am. Because in order to get people to listen to you, you've got to be some kind of landmark, some kind of foundation. You don't listen to people that don't mean anything to you. You have to be something to make people believe you. And so I think that's what's going on now, and then when I'm ready, they'll listen. And they'll hear" (6).

Roger Davies noted that Tina especially didn't like it when the press kept calling her a "victim" of physical abuse at the hands of Ike in her former life. According to him, "She was so unhappy for so long, she can't stand it to get too dark. She hates people feeling sorry for her" (2).

As Tina herself explained, "The victim thing. . . . It's put in our heads. It's everywhere. And I don't think it does anybody any good" (8).

She was very centered in her personal life, and she continued changing and evolving. "There's a rhythm to the universe, and chanting is plugging into that rhythm," she explained. "My life is very simple. When you travel around in limousines all the time you really want to go home and do normal things" (31).

When she was interviewed in the press, reporters had the habit of asking her the same questions. One of them always seemed to be speculating as to how long she wanted to continue to live the rock & roll lifestyle. "People ask me when am I going to slow down, and I tell them, I'm just getting started," she proudly pledged (29). This was the beginning of a whole new era of success and accomplishments for Tina Turner. And, the best was still yet to come.

14

BREAK EVERY RULE

Tina Turner is living proof that nothing breeds success quite like success—especially in a show business realm. Suddenly, in 1984 and 1985 everything seemed to fall brilliantly into place in a total multimedia way. Tina was certainly the same consistent, talented person she had been for the past eight years as a solo act; however, the triumph that she was experiencing on record suddenly expanded into other areas as well. Once *Private Dancer* vaulted up the Top 10 charts, and "What's Love Got to Do With It" became a No. 1 smash, it seemed everyone wanted more of Tina. Furthermore, the videos of that song and "Let's Stay Together" were constantly playing on TV stations around the globe, letting the world know how great she looked as well.

Her appeal cut across all age-groups, nationalities, and races. Her exuberant energy and spirituality seemed to shine through and touch everyone personally. Her tough, yet somehow blasé delivery of the song "What's Love Got to Do With It" appeared to hit a chord in everyone universally. It was as though she had been hurt by love before and wasn't about to fall in that trap again. She sang it with such gutsy conviction that it was impossible not to find the song—and its singer—excitingly appealing.

According to her, she didn't just sing her songs; she acted them and brought them each uniquely to life. In fact, acting on film was a challenge she deeply wanted to tackle. She loved doing *Tommy*, but she still longed for more experiences in front of the camera.

Did she like sensitive women's kinds of films? Hell no! Not bombastic Tina. Her favorite types of movies were actually horror and action films. Speaking of the kind of horror films she liked, she claimed she enjoyed *The Exorcist* or *The Entity*. "What I like is like the dead that's really alive. People coming from outer space and how they look. I also love the Dracula movies. It excites me, the fear" (30).

She likes the mystery and the suspense: "I watch horror movies. Imagine that Frankenstein or somebody—a mummy—is coming through the door" (5).

She also liked big epics like *The Ten Commandments* or the chariot races like the ones in *Ben Hur*. "I don't want to just be prancing around in some frilly dress singing a song, you know. I want to drive one of those damn chariots. Yeow! That's excitement! That's the stuff I love," she explained (30).

Tina wanted to make that jump into doing action parts and being a movie star. She claimed that this was part of "the enormous leap I'm after" (32).

She didn't want sensitivity, she wanted action. "Right now I just want physical parts," she said at the time. "I don't want serious roles because I feel that I have another good seven to ten years of being physical and using my youth. I can do those other parts later" (9).

When the opportunity came along for her to star in *Mad*

Max Beyond Thunderdome, it was like the fulfillment of a life-long dream. When she had seen films as a child, she fantasized about one day being a movie star. "Then, after I grew up," she said, "I discovered it wasn't easy for black people to get into movies. The types of movies they were allowed to make, I didn't want to do. So I waited until now, when it doesn't make any difference what color you are" (11).

According to the film's director, George Miller, "*Mad Max* is about an apocalyptic world, and we needed someone who was powerful, but most of all, who was a wonderful survivor. That no matter what had happened after the apocalypse, this was someone who had endured and become very strong and had tremendous resources. And we were writing this character—the Queen of Bartertown—and as a writing reference we kept on saying, 'Someone like Tina Turner, someone like Tina Turner.' And then, when it came time to shooting the film, we thought, 'Let's ask Tina Turner if she really wants to do it.' Luckily, she was available, she had a gap in her concerts at that stage, and was able to do it" (21).

It was in the fall and winter of 1984–1985, while *Private Dancer* was in the Top 10, that she flew to Australia to film this exciting new role. How did she find the experience of filming such an action role as that of Aunty Entity? "Fantastic!" she claimed. "Plus, I was driving a car and wearing weird clothes. . . . Yes, yes, that was very wild" (16).

She totally enjoyed the assignment, and she had an instant rapport with her co-star and onscreen nemesis, Mel Gibson. "I won't say that when I finally got to Australia it was the easiest thing I ever did, because a lot of times there were sandstorms and it was hot and those were long days. But I learned a lot, and I loved working with Melvin. He hates that name, but that's what I call him, because he reminds me so much of one of my sons. He also reminds me of my Ikettes," she was later to laugh (30).

The director of the film, George Miller, said of Tina, "I've never seen anybody who could be on the one hand so energetic and on the other so still" (29).

The film wrapped up production in January 1985. That same month she headed to Rio de Janerio, Brazil, to appear at the huge rock festival known as *Rock in Rio*. Also on the bill were Rod Stewart, Whitesnake, Queen, and AC/DC.

That same month Tina returned to the United States. Her return was certainly not for a rest from chasing Mad Max through the hot Australian desert. Now she had real work to do, as this was just the first month of one of the most hectic and action-packed years of her entire career.

She had returned just in time to attend the international telecast of The American Music Awards, on January 28, 1985. On stage, in front of millions of viewers, Tina Turner was seen picking up awards in the categories of Favorite Female Vocalist Soul/R&B and Favorite Female Video Artist Soul/R&B of the year.

The night of the awards, dozens of singing stars were invited to A&M Recording Studios to record the song "We Are the World." The funds that the song raised were to assist relief efforts in famine-plagued Africa and especially the people in Ethiopia. "We Are the World" was written by Michael Jackson and Lionel Richie, and produced by Quincy Jones. They were able to get the participation of a virtual "Who's Who" of the concurrent recording world, primarily because it was recorded the night of the annual American Music Awards telecast. It was kind of like those old Judy Garland and Mickey Rooney movies, where someone would announce, "I've got a barn—let's put on a show." Somehow it seemed, everyone—including

Tina—wanted to be involved. In alphabetical order, the cast of singers included Dan Aykroyd, Harry Belafonte, Lindsey Buckingham, Kim Carnes, Ray Charles, Bob Dylan, Sheila E., Bob Geldof, Daryl Hall, James Ingram, Jackie Jackson, LaToya Jackson, Marlon Jackson, Michael Jackson, Randy Jackson, Tito Jackson, Al Jarreau, Billy Joel, Cyndi Lauper, Huey Lewis, Kenny Loggins, Bette Midler, Willie Nelson, John Oates, Jeffrey Osborne, Steve Perry, The Pointer Sisters, Lionel Richie, Smokey Robinson, Kenny Rogers, Diana Ross, Paul Simon, Bruce Springsteen, Tina Turner, Dionne Warwick, and Stevie Wonder. When it was released, the recording of "We Are the World" received a tidal wave of airplay and raised millions of dollars. It became a huge No. 1 hit.

So that the single version of "We Are the World" could be part of an album and raise further funds for the charity, several of the performers featured on this all-star single donated their royalties from individual songs to the cause. There were nine other cuts on the album, including "If Only for the Moment, Girl" by Steve Perry, "Just a Little Closer" by The Pointer Sisters, "Trapped" by Bruce Springsteen and the E Street Band, "4 the Tears in Your Eyes" by Prince and the Revolution, and "Good for Nothing" by Chicago. Tina Turner contributed her previously unreleased recording of "Total Control" to the project.

Several days later, Tina was busy launching a triumphant tour of Europe. In the middle of it, she took time to fly back to Los Angeles for another very special night. It was February 26, 1985, when Tina appeared on The Twenty-Seventh Annual Grammy Awards telecast as a guest and, ultimately, as a winner. Speaking of her son Craig, she recalls, "When I went to the Grammy Awards he looked at me and said, 'Mom, you're incredible! You look twenty-six!'" (31).

In 1984 Tina Turner's Private Dancer *album and the song "What's Love Got to Do with It" signaled the rebirth of her career.*

(Photo: Brian Aris / Capitol Records / MJB Photo Archives)

The Rolling Stones have been among Tina's biggest supporters throughout her career. This shot dates from the 1980s.

(Photo: Atlantic Records / MJB Photo Archives)

David Bowie helped Tina land the record deal that launched her into the stratosphere.

(Photo: RCA Records / MJB Photo Archives)

Keith Richards and David Bowie with Tina at The Ritz in 1983.
(Photo: Bob Gruen / Star File)

In the 1980s Rod Stewart helped Tina find a new audience by having her duet with him on Saturday Night Live *and his own concert special.*
(Photo: Warner Brothers Records / MJB Photo Archives)

Tina takes Paris! Throughout her career, Tina's success in Europe has been the greatest and the most consistent.

(Photo: Bob Gruen / Star File)

Tina Turner and Mick Jagger at the Live Aid Concert in 1986. Together they sang "State of Shock" and "It's Only Rock & Roll."

(Photo: Chuck Pulin / Star File)

Dressed in chain mail, warrior woman Tina Turner as Aunty Entity in the 1986 hit film Mad Max: Beyond Thunderdome.

(Photo: Warner Brothers Pictures / MJB Photo Archives)

Aunty Entity leads her Imperial Guards on an Australian desert chase in pursuit of Mad Max. Tina loved doing her own stunts in this exciting futuristic film.

(Photo: Warner Brothers Pictures / MJB Photo Archives)

Sexy and energetic in her fifties and sixties, Tina Turner has been a role model of inner strength.

(Photo: Peter Lindburgh / Virgin Records / MJB Photo Archives)

*Thanks to her conversion to Buddhism, Tina has achieved an
accomplished sense of peace. Now residing in southern France, she lives
in harmony with her surroundings.*

(Photo: Peter Lindburgh / Virgin Records / MJB Photo Archives)

Indeed, she had a youthful exuberance about her that night. Introducing her on the show, John Denver proclaimed, "Ladies and gentlemen, the woman that God put on this Earth to teach other women how to walk in spike heels" (33).

Tina was the ceremony's big winner that night. It was a triumphant and stunning reward for all that she had been through and all of the hard work and energy she had expelled on *Private Dancer*. It also felt like the audience members that night were personally cheering her on and loving her victory as much as she did.

Ultimately, she took home the prizes for Record of the Year, "What's Love Got to Do With It"; Best Pop Vocal Performance, "What's Love Got to Do With It"; and Best Rock Vocal Performance, Female, "Better Be Good to Me." Furthermore, Terry Britten and Graham Lyle won the songwriters award of Song of the Year for penning "What's Love Got to Do With It." It was an evening of sheer conquest for Tina Turner. She said that night, "We're looking forward to many more of these" (33). Well, she was officially in the winner's circle, and she was going to get very comfortable standing in it.

On March 14 Tina was in concert in London, filling massive Wembley Stadium with cheering fans. Concurrently her single version of "I Can't Stand the Rain" was on the British charts, where it peaked at No. 57. That same month, the song "Private Dancer" hit No. 7 in America, making it the third consecutive single to be pulled from her incredible hit album of the same name.

In April 1985, the "We Are the World" hit No. 1 in the United States. This became the first chart-topping album of Tina Turner's long and illustrious career—another new career milestone for her.

Amidst all of the awards and hit records, the really important thing was that Tina Turner was now performing at massive arenas around the world. She was no longer a club or a theater act. Her popularity was much too massive for that. She had graduated to becoming a stadium attraction.

According to her, "When you're talking about the guys who can pack those football stadiums, you're talking about the men that the girls love. So it's like breaking the rules for me to get a chance to be with them" (29).

She was thrilled to have had an introduction to that onstage excitement by her friends The Rolling Stones and Rod Stewart in the past. She recalled, "Then, when I was ready, I said, 'OK, I'm ready.' I knew I was ready, I knew I could do it. Working with The Stones and Rod Stewart really helped me. It wasn't hard times; it was the beginning of great times" (10).

One of the most memorable dates on the European leg of the tour came in Germany. "Playing Munich for that crowd had a special meaning to me. I still have vivid memories of the last time I played Munich with The Ike & Tina Revue. Ike kept refusing to go out because there were so few people who showed up. When we finally went on, about an hour later, there were only about 100 people in the audience. It was awful. To have thousands turn out for me this time . . . well nobody can know how much that meant to me," she claimed (30).

Then came the debut of her North American stadium tour—and it was every bit as successful as her European jaunt had been. Her first solo headlining tour took the diva to eighty-six different cities across North America, which included eleven concerts in Canadian cities. Brian D. Johnson saw Tina's first show on the 1985 cross-continent show in Newfoundland, Canada. He wrote in *McLean's* magazine, "For an hour and a half she shimmied, strutted, and slithered her way into the hearts and libidos of 5,000 Newfoundlanders who packed a St. John's hockey arena last week for the first concert of her North

American Tour. . . . At the age of forty-six, Tina Turner has never been hotter!" (29).

Speaking of her stage act, Tina claimed, "You get a little bit of everything with me—laughter, sex, sadness, and then there's energy" (29). She had it all, and her fans simply couldn't get enough.

It was exhilarating to have such massive crowds screaming and cheering her onward. "What excites me is not the lights; it's that screaming thing, like when I walk on -stage and they go crazy. That's what happens with Bowie and Jagger, the times I've worked with them when they've walked on my stage, the whole place went crazy, and I thought, 'If I'm going to be here, I want that'" (5). Well, now she was officially there.

In June 1985, her next U.S. single, "Show Some Respect," hit No. 37 on the charts. That same month, her film *Mad Max Beyond Thunderdome* premiered. Suddenly, Tina was an action heroine!

Actually, the film was the perfect vehicle for her. She didn't play the hero, she played the villain. As Aunty Entity, she portrays the ruler of Bartertown in post-apocalyptic Australia. Her nemesis is the heroic Mad Max, played by Mel Gibson. The grand finale of the film features a wild road battle between Aunty, Max, and their separate gangs. It is an exciting escapist picture, fun and fantasy filled.

One of the most outrageous aspects is Tina's futuristic costume of chain mail, and her blonde mane of hair. She was perfectly cast as the wicked and powerful leader of postwar survivors.

When Max is taken up to Aunty Entity's lair, she takes one look at him and says with a laugh, "But, he's just a raggity-man!" Analyzing him, she surmises, "How the world turns. One day cock of the walk, next a feather duster." Speaking of her own elevation to ruler of Bartertown, Tina as Aunty says, "This nobody got a chance to be somebody. So much for history." She plays the role in a cool and calculating way that is exciting to watch. She seems to take special delight in the road race sequence at the end of the film. Max is trying to escape by locomotive rail car, while Aunty and her army follow in skeletal trucks, cars, motorcycles, and cobbled-together hot rods.

In her final sequence in the film, Aunty catches up with Max. Looking down at him, Tina says, "Ain't we a pair, raggityman?" Then she laughs a hearty almost-evil laugh and strides away. Even in the post-apocalyptic world, Tina Turner is wearing her signature high heels!

According to Tina, "The part is perfect for me. She [Aunty Entity] is very strong; I like this lady because of her power. If you had asked me last year what part I would like to play, I would have said an Egyptian queen. But this part is close enough. I don't want to do sexy films, and I'm not funny, so I couldn't do comedy. I want to be dealing with some kind of war, with physical strength in a woman. It's my personality; it's how I am" (11).

Naturally, it would be silly to have Tina Turner in your movie and not have her contribute some songs. Since this was not a musical film, and Aunty Entity was an evil ruler, not a rock star, it was perfect for Tina to provide the theme song for the picture, and another tune as well. The songs she contributed to *Mad Max Beyond Thunderdome* and its resulting soundtrack album were "We Don't Need Another Hero" and "One of the Living." The film's score was handled by Maurice Jarre.

She was also thrilled with the popularity of the film, and she looked forward to it bringing many more acting offers to her. "If this movie brings a film career, I'll take it!" she claimed. "That's what I want! My singing career wasn't what I wanted. It was something I was always sort of ashamed of, because, I guess, of the lady in me. But finally, in the last ten years, I've accepted it. That is who I am now and what I offer in the music world. But I also want to act and show another side of me that isn't raunchy. I've always been very aggressive, very active, very outspoken. I just tell it like it is" (11).

Projecting ahead, she said, "I want to do really heroic woman things. I'd like to do a female version of Sylvester Stallone's *Rambo*" (29).

She was so successful in the role that another film offer came to her almost immediately. Steven Spielberg was in pre-production to bring Alice Walker's best-selling book, *The Color Purple,* to the screen. And he did not have a leading lady yet.

However, she turned it down flatly. She had no interest in playing a poor and abused woman who was labeled a "victim" of society and misogynism. "Black people can do better than that. I've lived down South in the cotton fields. I don't want to do anything I've done," she said at the time (29).

"I declined *The Color Purple*," she explains, "because it was too close to my personal life. I had just left such a life, and it was too soon to be reminded of—acting for me, I need something else. I don't need to do what I've just stepped out of. It was exciting and flattering I was asked by Mr. Spielberg, but it was the wrong movie for me at that time" (16).

The Color Purple was too big a downer for her. She wanted to be strong and exciting on screen, not beaten and looking for pity. Besides, she claimed, "The part's too old—she's been with every man in town and this man brings her into his house with his wife. No, I know this already from my past. I want to do a *Raiders [of the Lost Ark/Indiana Jones]* or a Western next. There is no way I'm a drag right now" (2).

Tina was soaring in 1985, and it seemed that there was no stopping her. On July 15, she was one of the many international star performers on the massive Live Aid global rock & roll telecast. A benefit show for the same African hunger relief that the USA for Africa/"We Are the World" project aided, Live Aid was a huge success. Tina and Mick Jagger were seen doing a rare and exciting duet in the middle of the telecast, live from Philadelphia's JFK Stadium.

In fact, this was *the* most hysterical and outlandish Tina and Mick performance ever. First, Mick did a solo set, backed up by a band featuring Daryl Hall and John Oates. In addition, former Temptations Eddie Kendricks and David Ruffin were singing background vocals. Jagger performed several songs from his recently released debut solo album, including "Just Another Night." Then, right before the final songs of his set, he shouted into the 'stage right' wings, "Where's Tina?" With that, out strides Tina—dancing to the music in a black leather top and a matching wrap-around black leather skirt. Jagger and Turner then proceeded to swing into a hot duet version of the song "State of Shock," which melded into to them singing The Stones' classic "It's Only Rock & Roll" together. ("State of Shock" was a Top 10 hit song duet between Mick Jagger and Michael Jackson, included on The Jackson's 1984 *Victory* album.)

Obviously feeling like being a little exhibitionist, mid-song, Mick stripped off his T-shirt on stage, then both he and Tina went off into the wings of separate sides of the stage while the music and singing continued. Then they both came out on stage again still singing "It's Only Rock & Roll." Shirtless, Mick now had on a new outfit of colorful spandex pants and a yellow sports jacket. Again Tina and Mick met at center stage and started cavorting with one another while singing. Then, as an obvious surprise to Tina, Mick grabbed hold of her leather skirt's fastener, and in one quick notion, he pulled it open. Her leather skit hit the stage floor, and there stood Tina—as they say in England in her *knickers*! Yes, fortunately for her, she was wearing underwear, but it was certainly more of herself than she had planned to put into her performance that evening! Like the song they had just sung together—she too looked like she was in a complete "State of Shock." Not quite knowing what to do, and laughing wildly at Mick's naughty prank, she continued singing, while grabbing onto him, and hiding her exposed crotch area behind his jacket. Finally, knowing this was a losing battle, Tina turned around—inadvertently mooning the audience—and she strode off into the wings. It was without a doubt the most outrageous Tina Turner television "exposure" that she had ever received. And in front of countless millions of viewers, no less! As the song goes, it was only rock & roll, but she liked it!

Meanwhile, for Tina, the hits just kept on coming. The single version of "We Don't Need Another Hero (Thunderdome)" became a No. 3 hit in the U.K. in August of 1985. On September 13, Tina's video of "What's Love Got to Do With It" won the Best Female Video at the Second Annual MTV Video Music Awards, held and telecast from Radio City Music Hall in New York City. That month "We Don't Need Another Hero" logged in at No. 2 on the U.S. Pop Singles chart in *Billboard*. In October, the single version of "One of the Living" peaked at No. 55 in the United Kingdom. In November a duet with Canadian rock star Bryan Adams, called "It's Only Love," hit No. 29 in Britain. It was originally released on Adams's 1984 album *Reckless*. That same month, Tina's "One of the Living" hit No. 15 in the United States. To round out the year, on December 8, 1985, Tina won the Best Actress award from the NAACP for her role in *Mad Max Beyond Thunderdome*.

In 1985, Tina projected how long she wished to continue to live the rock & roll lifestyle. According to her, "I'm not finished educating myself yet to be able to explain it totally. I figure I've got a good seven years left of being onstage with the physical thing. When it's over I'll put my attention to teaching" (2).

In January 1986 the song "It's Only Love" peaked on the American Pop chart at No. 15. On January 18, Tina won the Favorite Female Artist trophy at the Thirteenth Annual American Music Awards. Weeks later, when the Grammy Awards rolled around, Tina received another trophy, for Best Rock Vocal Performance, Female, for the song "One of the Living."

On June 20, Tina was one of the stars to participate in the *Prince's Trust Concert* in London. In the audience that evening were England's Prince Charles and Princess Diana. Ms. Turner and Joan Armatrading had the distinction of being the only ladies in a prestigious team of rock star men. Their costars for that mega-hit concert included Paul McCartney, Eric Clapton, Elton John, Bryan Adams, Dire Straits, Phil Collins, and Rod Stewart.

In Hollywood, on August 28, 1986, Tina received a star on the movie capitol's Walk of Fame. A star emblazoned with her name was dedicated just outside the headquarters of Capitol Records, on Vine Street. In September, "Typical Male," the first single off of her forthcoming new album, became a No. 33 hit in the United Kingdom. On August 15, the Tina Turner/Bryan Adams video version of "It's Only Love" won an MTV Video Music Award as the Best Stage Performance Video of the Year. Tina was also one of the performers on the show, which was simultaneously telecast from Universal Amphitheatre in Universal City, California, and the Palladium in New York City.

When Tina's album *Break Every Rule* was released, it was an instant hit. Since *Private Dancer* had been such a huge international smash, its arrival on the marketplace was much anticipated. It proved every bit as exciting as its predecessor. The majority of Tina's vocals were recorded at Studio Grande Armee in Paris, France. This was the beginning of her great-revived love affair with France. This time around, however, there were no more "cover" versions of previous rock and soul classics.

This new album was all fresh material and 100 percent rock & roll. Several of her rock star buddies either appeared on the album or delivered songs, including David Bowie, Phil Collins, Bryan Adams, and Mark Knopfler. Terry Britten, who was responsible for "What's Love Got to Do With It" continued his winning association with Tina by contributing six of the songs on the album, including "Typical Male," "What You Get Is What You See," "Two People," "'Till The Right Man Comes Along," and "Afterglow," all of which he penned with his writing partner Graham Lyle. The song "Girls" was written by Bowie and produced by Britten. "Back Where You Started" was written by Bryan Adams and Jim Vallance, and produced by Adams and Bob Clearmountain. "Break Every Rule" and "I'll Be Thunder" were written by Rupert Hine and Jeannette T. Obstoj, and produced by Hine. Mark Knopfler of Dire Straits wrote "Overnight Sensation," and Paul Brady penned "Paradise Is Here," both of which were produced by Knopfler.

The cover photos of Tina on the *Break Every Rule* album package marked the beginning of her long association with celebrity photographer Herb Ritts. Clad in a low-cut black dress with a slit up to her upper thigh, and a black leather jacket, Tina gave her trademark "rough" attitude on the cover shot. She was in her creative prime, and she looked every inch the superstar that she was. Fans around the world bought millions of copies of *Break Every Rule*. It hit No. 4 in *Billboard* magazine in the United States and No. 2 in the United Kingdom. Claimed *Rolling Stone* magazine, "She has never sung better" (34). She was every bit the "overnight sensation" that she sang of on this winning album.

In October 1986, the single "Typical Male" logged in the No. 2 slot on the U.S. Pop chart, just behind Cyndi Lauper's "True Colors." The song "Two People" hit No. 43 in the United Kingdom, and No. 30 in the United States. In November of 1986, the *Break Every Rule* album was certified Platinum by the Recording Industry Association of America.

In a year filled with more excitement, awards, and hit records, Tina was also busy conquering another creative arena as well. She was now an author who published her own story in a gutsy, frank, and forthcoming bestseller called *I, Tina*. Penned with *Rolling Stone* magazine writer Kurt Loder, *I, Tina* ripped the lid off her stormy marriage with Ike Turner. Told partially in sections of Tina's own words, partially in Loder's guiding narrative, and partially in interviews with the people in her life, the majority of the book dealt with her years with Ike. It was that material which Tina mainly wanted to communicate with the public, so that she would never have to deal with it again.

Reportedly, she was paid $400,000 for this autobiographical work. One of the underlying reasons that Tina chose to write *I, Tina*, was the fact that she was sick and tired of talking about Ike. She chose to commit her harrowing experiences to paper so she could reply to interviewers, "read my book," instead of having to go into the story all over again.

"I wrote the book because I was so tired of people being really upset that I left Ike. Like, 'How could you?' When I went out on my own, I had a hit record and people were still in my ear about Ike and 'our music.' Music? We couldn't get a hit record in those days. We didn't draw people and he was freaking out, doing more drugs," she explained (8).

According to her, "It's like going back into time, when you are trying to understand how prehistoric people lived. I am saying it one last time, and I hope people don't even think about talking to me about it anymore. If they don't understand, fine" (5).

Tina illuminated, "I'm not looking for pity about my life with Ike. It was ten years ago. I'm done with it" (31).Working on this book was a catharsis for her. She didn't really want to relive the hellish life she had at the hands of Ike Turner, but she forced herself to talk about it, knowing she would never have to detail it ever again. "I drank a lot of wine, but I did it," she said about having to speak of her most painful years (29).

People were riveted by what Tina had to say. According to her, "The world was shocked!" (8). Indeed they were! But, it made the public even more appreciative of her dramatic new-found success.

When the annual Grammy Awards were given out in early 1987, Tina was back for more. This time around she was awarded the trophy in the category of Best Rock Vocal Performance, Female, for her song "Back Where You Started."

That same year, Turner returned to the road with the *Break Every Rule* tour. A global affair, it began on March 4 in Munich, West Germany. This particular tour broke box office records in thirteen different countries. Her sponsor for this particular tour was Pepsi-Cola. As part of her deal with Pepsi, Tina also filmed a very popular and frequently broadcast commercial for the soft drink company. In April, the song "What You Get Is What You See" hit No. 13 in the United States and No. 30 in the United Kingdom. In June, the song "Break Every Rule" peaked at No. 74 in America, and the following month it made it to No. 43 in England. In September of 1987, *Private Dancer* was certified Quintuple Platinum in America for having sold over five million copies in the United States alone.

Speaking about herself and her appeal during this era, Tina claimed, "I am a fun person, and when I'm onstage I act. I like to tease to a point. I'm not teasing men. I am together and everybody gets up and they get a little cigarette and champagne and they do little things. That's the same thing I do onstage when I'm performing for the girls and then for the guys. . . . I'm not a vulgar, sexy person onstage. I think that's how people perceive me, because I have a lot of vulgar videos where they wanted me to do the garter-belt thing" (5).

How did success now suit her? According to Tina, "I'm just becoming happier. Happiness has a lot to do with the glow of life" (31).

Although she appeared to be a wild woman on stage, the off-stage version of Tina Turner is quite different. "I'm really conservative in a way, although I stay somewhat within the image," she explained (11).

She began to relish what little time she had to chill out and recharge her internal battery. Said she, "At home, I let my body relax and take the paint off my face—because soon enough I'm going to have to paint it on and get out there again" (31).

In Tina's Los Angeles home, she had a jade statue of an Egyptian queen named Hatshepsut that was prominently displayed. She had learned all about Hatshepsut, and was fascinated with her history and her forceful way of ruling Egypt. According to Tina, "She was a terror. She insisted on being treated as a pharaoh" (31). Although she might have been an Egyptian queen in the past, in this lifetime Tina Turner had truly ascended to the throne as Queen of Rock & Roll!

15

FOREIGN AFFAIR

In 1987, after three years of singing the song "What's Love Got to Do With It" Tina was ready for some love in her life. This time around, she was to find it unexpectedly. She had been living so much of her life in Europe lately that she was truly picking up a very European style to her fashion and her music—and now, even her taste in men.

The man she started a relationship with was thirty-one and from Cologne, Germany. She, at the time, was forty-eight. Erwin Bach was the managing director of her European record label, EMI, and he was assigned to deliver a complimentary Jeep to Tina for her to drive during one of her visits to Germany. Their paths crossed several times. According to Tina, "He doesn't like to be discussed, because he is a businessman. It took three years for us to get together—it wasn't one of those run-and-jump-in-bed situations" (5).

Was it a case of love at first sight? Says Tina, "Oh yeah, first sight! It's an electrical charge, really, in the body. The body responds to something. Heart boom-bama-boom. Hands are wet. But I said, 'No.' . . . Something happens to you when you're secure as a woman. I began to feel, 'Well, I'm fine. If I don't really find anybody, I'm O.K.' It's just those times when you start running the streets, and seeing couples and loving, and watching those movies where there's a lot of love, you miss being cuddled" (5).

Bach came to Los Angeles for a visit. At the time, Tina was living in a house she owned in the "valley," in Sherman Oaks. She was throwing a birthday party for a friend at the West Hollywood area in-spot restaurant, Wolfgang Puck's original Spago. After the dinner at Spago, she took the whole party home. According to her, "Afterwards, everyone came to my house, and something magic started to happen. Of course, I was attracted. By then I'm sure he knew that I was [interested in him personally]. . . . I made sure I sat next to him. Because I was also analyzing him, too. . . . After everyone left, I think we exchanged a few kisses. We started to talk, and I asked him about what his record company is like." However, his reaction was oddly cool, as he announced, "Private life is private life." So, Tina eased up (5).

However, she wasn't finished pursuing Erwin. "What I did do, to actually get him," she reveals, "was I stayed in Switzerland. I rented a house in Gstaad" (5). She decided to give a party at Christmastime in 1988. Tina invited Erwin, as well as several other mutual friends. The relationship just continued to blossom and grow from there.

When asked how Erwin's family felt about him having a relationship with an older, American rock star, Ms. Turner replied, "I believe they would prefer if Erwin had a German girl or a white woman. But when they met me, well, it's the usual 'everybody likes Tina'" (5).

While her affair with Erwin was growing and developing,

her career just continued to blossom and grow as well. During the South American leg of her incredibly popular *Break Every Rule* concert tour, on January 16, 1988, Tina Turner headlined at the Maracana Arena in Rio de Janeiro, Brazil, and attracted a massive audience of 182,000 people. It was the largest audience ever drawn for a single performer—anywhere—ever! She was added to *The Guinness Book of Records* for this incredible achievement.

On March 28, after 230 dates in twenty-five countries, Tina's *Break Every Rule* concert tour came to a conclusion. The final night of the tour was in Osaka, Japan. She not only broke rules—she broke records!

Her live version of Robert Palmer's sizzling and sexy rocker, "Addicted to Love," was released as her next European single. It made it to No. 71 in the United Kingdom in March 1988. Her new album, *Tina Live in Europe*, hit No. 8 in England, but oddly only made it to No. 86 in America. In May, a concert video, *Rio '88*, was released of her incredible show—from the same tour—in Brazil.

The *Tina Live in Europe* album captured several of the best performances from Tina's *Break Every Rule* tour. It presented songs from her past, her present, and also featured several new versions of rock classics. In addition, it even had several rare duets with some of her favorite stars that occurred during the tour. These duets included "634-5789" with Robert Cray, "Tearing Us Apart" with Eric Clapton, "It's Only Love" with Bryan Adams, and "Let's Dance" and "Tonight" with David Bowie. There were also three great versions of rock classics on this album, which Tina brilliantly made her own. They included "Land of 1,000 Dances" and "In the Midnight Hour." It was an exciting two-disc LP and CD.

On January of 1989, Tina Turner was in New York City at the fourth annual Rock & Roll Hall of Fame Celebration, held at the Waldorf-Astoria Hotel. She was there to officially induct her producer pal, the legendary and elusive Phil Spector, into the ranks of the Hall of Famers. Weeks later at the Grammy Awards, she won her seventh trophy in the category of Best Rock Vocal Performance, Female, for the album *Tina Live in Europe*.

In June, Tina reprised her role of "Acid Queen" in a special charity event, which was part of The Who's 1989 concert tour. The event, which took place in Los Angeles, further illustrated Ms. Turner's versatility as a performer.

In September 1989, Tina's next album, *Foreign Affair*, was released, blasting up to No. 1 in the United Kingdom and No. 31 in the United States. The first single from the album, "The Best," made it to No. 5 in the United Kingdom, and No. 15 in America. The song became a thematic anthem for Tina, because, according to her fans, it was she who was simply the best. "The Best" also included a searing saxophone solo by Edgar Winter.

For *Foreign Affair*, recording sessions took place in Paris and in Los Angeles. Nine of the twelve songs on the album were either produced or co-produced (with Tina) by Dan Hartman. Hartman, who is famous for his own songs like "Instant Replay" and "Relight My Fire," was a hot producer in this era and a great choice for Tina to select this time around. Other producers on the album included Tony Joe White, Roger Davies, Graham Lyle, Albert Hammond, and Rupert Hine.

The standout cuts on *Foreign Affair* included "Steamy Windows," "Undercover Agent for the Blues," "Ask Me How I Feel," and the title cut. However, the album is most famous for supplying Tina with the song "The Best." Although it wasn't her biggest chart hit, it has become one of the top five most famous songs in her entire career.

On November 26, 1989, Tina Turner celebrated her fiftieth birthday in a London nightclub called the Reform Club. Helping her with the fete were her buddies Eric Clapton, Mark Knopfler, Bryan Adams, the members of Duran Duran, and several more invited guests. She was half a century old, and her rock & roll career had never been hotter.

As the decade of the 1990s began, Tina's latest trans-Atlantic single, "Steamy Windows," was peaking on the charts—making it to No. 39 in America and No. 13 in the British Isles. On April 27, the indefatigable Turner began her *Foreign Affair* world concert tour. The 121-date tour opened in Antwerp, Belgium. On June 28 she became the first woman to give a concert at the Palace of Versailles, outside of Paris. Up until this point, there had only been one other rock concert held at this famous site, and that was Pink Floyd in 1988. It seemed most fitting that Tina was there trailblazing. Who more suited for such a task than the undisputed Queen of Rock & Roll? The spirit of Queen Marie Antoinette must surely have agreed!

In August 1990, her single "Look Me in the Heart" peaked on the U.K. charts at No. 31. She headlined Wembley Stadium in London on September 26, and the next month her next single, "Be Tender with Me Baby," hit No. 28 in the United Kingdom. On November 4, her *Foreign Affair* tour concluded in Rotterdam, Holland. Over the course of the tour, she had performed in front of more than three million people.

In December of that year, a duet of the song "It Takes Two," by Tina Turner and Rod Stewart, peaked at No. 5 in the United Kingdom. A sizzling update of the Marvin Gaye and Kim Weston single from 1967, the Tina and Rod version first appeared on Stewart's 1991 *Vagabond Heart* album. The song "It Takes Two" featured vocals that were recorded in different parts of the world, as Rod and Tina's schedules did not permit them to be in the same place at the same time. They did, however, find the time to unite to film a nightclub performance video together. The video that they did was excellently lit, and both Tina and Rod look like they are having a blast mugging with each other. The song was also used as the concurrent Pepsi TV commercial in Britain. Reportedly, Turner and Stewart split one million British pounds as a fee from Pepsi-Cola.

Suddenly, Ike Turner was back in the news. In his fourteen post-Tina years he was arrested eleven times for various violations. During this period, Ronnie, one of Tina's sons with Ike, had, on one occasion, also landed in jail in Los Angeles. He had been picked up for a series of unpaid traffic violations. Ronnie was in shock when he ended up thrown in the very same jail cell as his own father. Recalls Tina, "That made an impression. He never went to jail again" (5). Finally, in 1990, Ike was arrested and put in prison. He began serving eighteen months behind bars for cocaine possession, transporting drugs, and other various charges.

On January 4, 1991, Tina headlined a concert in Barcelona, Spain, which was entitled *The Queen of Rock Struts Her Stuff*. It was satellite broadcast globally on Pay-Per-View television. In September, the long-awaited album *Music of Quality & Distinction, Volume 2* was released by the British Electric Foundation. Tina is heard on the album singing "Change Is Gonna Come." Like its predecessor, this album was released in the United Kingdom only.

That same month, a newly recorded version of one of Tina's classics—billed as "Nutbush City Limits (The '90s Version)"— was released in the United Kingdom and made it to No. 23. There was a very cute video done of this new danceable version of the song, which features a rolling little travelogue of now-famous Nutbush, Tennessee. In the color video footage, Nutbush landmarks are featured, like the sign reading "Welcome to Nutbush, Tennessee, Population 91," the front of the Quik Stop convenience store, and the sign pointing to the Spring Hill Baptist Church. Tina wasn't in her hometown to film this footage. She was instead shown in a recording studio—looking fabulous—and in classic clips of archived footage with The Ikettes.

In October, Turner's greatest hits collection, *Simply the Best*, was released, featuring the new version of "Nutbush," as well as three brand new songs: "I Want You Near Me," "Way of the World," and "Love Thing." It also included all of her 1980s hits, starting with "Let's Stay Together," up to and including her hit Rod Stewart duet "It Takes Two."

Simply the Best soared up the charts in Britain to log in at No. 2—just behind Simply Red's *Stars* album. However, in America the album only made it to No. 113. On November 26, 1991, Tina's fifty-second birthday, she received a Quintuple Platinum award in London to commemorate 1.5 million copies of *Foreign Affair* sold in the United Kingdom. The EMI label chief, Rupert Perry, presented her with a solid silver CD in honor of the occasion.

Also that year, a great Elton John/Bernie Taupin tribute album entitled *Two Rooms* was released, featuring a sparkling new recording of "The Bitch Is Back" by Tina Turner. The album reached No. 18 in *Billboard* magazine in the United States. Also on the album are Elton hits performed by The Beach Boys, Sinead O'Connor, Eric Clapton, Sting, The Who, Joe Cocker, Kate Bush, and Hall & Oates. According to Tina, "I covered 'The Bitch Is Back' on an old album of mine in the '70s when I went solo—it used to open my shows and everyone loved it. I thought the time was perfect for an updated version. The attitude is right for me—a little bit shocking" (35).

In February 1992 the song "Love Thing" peaked on the U.K. chart at No. 29. That same month, on February 23, BBC1-TV aired a special called *The Girl from Nutbush*. It was a career-retrospective documentary. On April 11, Tina took part in the opening of the Euro Disney amusement park outside of Paris. In June, her single "I Want You Near Me" reached No. 22 in the United Kingdom.

When her U.S. recording contract with Capitol Records lapsed in July 1992, Tina signed a new deal with Virgin Records in America. This was to begin a whole new era in her recording career.

Meanwhile, in September 1991, Ike Turner was released from the California prison in which he had been residing for the previous eighteen months. Finally, after over two decades of drug abuse, jail dried out Ike. He was finally cocaine-free. For this fact alone, he was later to state, "It was the best thing that ever happened to me" (5).

Once a free man again, he decided to go back to work on the only thing that ever really meant anything to him: music. While maintaining her distance from his life, Tina was to supportively state, "What do I think of Ike? Once he was out of jail, I was happy that he was able to go back to work, because he loved to play music. I've no—I don't have a vengeance. It would be wonderful for [him]—if Ike could get a hit record and really realize his dream on his own. That's my view. I didn't feel sad for him when he was in jail because I think he needed correcting. I think he needed something very strong to actually show him what he was doing with his life" (12).

Meanwhile, Tina had permanently moved to Europe. According to her, "I have left America because my success was in another country and my boyfriend was in another country and yeah, *Private Dancer* was the beginning of my success in England, and basically Europe has been very supportive of my music. . . . I went to England for a couple of years, and then I met a man. And I lived three years with him in his country, in Germany" (16). Residing with Erwin in Cologne, she was having her own foreign affair, and Tina had never been happier.

According to her, Europe was "the start of everything for me. I had never known my real home until I came to Europe" (1).

She continued to chant and rely upon the spiritual strength that Buddhism gave her. "There are a lot of spiritual aspects of really getting in tune with yourself. You've got to have quiet. You can't get up to blasting music every day and running to a lot of parties every night," she claimed (9).

In January 1993, Tina donated $50,000 to assist in opening the Exchange Club/Tina Turner Child Abuse Center in Ripley, Tennessee. Having lived through years of debt, she was thrilled to be in a position where she was able to give back some of her success to those in need. On March 2 she was one of the stars of the huge Save the Rain Forest benefit concert at Carnegie Hall in New York City. Tina appeared on stage along with Sting, Bryan Adams, George Michael, Herb Alpert, Tom Jones, James Taylor, and Dustin Hoffman. On April 30 she was one of eight honorees at the Sixth Annual Essence Awards, held at The Paramount Theater in New York City and hosted by *Essence* magazine. That night she was a guest on *Late Night with David Letterman.*

In her personal appearances, Tina always looked so classy and composed. How did her stage preparations in the 1990s compare with those in the 1960s? Explaining her pre-show routine, Tina explained, "I start my relaxed mental state as I do my makeup. I arrive at work, get rid of whatever meetings in terms of corrections for the musicians and all. When I start makeup, it brings me right down to the place where I'm relaxed. I'm in control of that. The more time I have to just play with myself and putz around, the better. I've always done my own makeup for live shows. I don't like it too professional on-stage; sometimes it's really not you. It might work for video or something, but it's not for real life. Yes, there is something calming about putting myself together to face people on a stage. We love makeup. It's just girls playing" (7).

While all of this was going on, Tina was involved with work for her next high-profile project. Hollywood had again called upon her for the movies. However, this time they weren't tapping her to star in the movie, they wanted her to be the subject of it. Tina Turner was again to feel the lure of the cinema world.

16

WHAT'S LOVE GOT TO DO WITH IT?

In the early 1990s there was suddenly a new focus on the public's interest in the old days of Tina's career—particularly the Ike & Tina Turner era of her life. Now that Tina had established herself as one of the most popular, respected, and in-demand rock stars on the planet, people wanted to know more about her past and how it all came together.

In 1991, while Ike was still behind bars, Ike & Tina Turner were inducted into the Rock & Roll Hall of Fame, along with LaVern Baker, The Byrds, John Lee Hooker, The Impressions, Wilson Pickett, and Jimmy Reed. Ike Turner seemed to be quite unimpressed by the honor. According to him, "I don't know. A lot of people say, 'How does it feel to be in the Rock & Roll Hall of Fame?' I don't feel nothing. I was just doing something I like doing. And the next thing about it was the worst thing I've done in my life. I don't know, I am human just like everybody else, so I don't go around remembering this or that" (13).

The next major retrospective event that took place was that Disney Corporation's Touchstone Films division had purchased the rights to make a film based on Tina Turner's autobiography, *I, Tina.* Since the majority of the book dealt with her life with Ike Turner, the producers knew that one of the biggest issues was to make sure that they were legally in the clear to depict Ike in the fashion in which Tina had portrayed him in her book. In order to do this, they paid Ike a sizeable sum of money for the rights to depict him in the film and to keep him from suing the company if he was unhappy with what transpired on screen. He certainly knew how he treated Tina in reality. And, he must certainly have known that he was depicted as a physically abusive habitual drug user in her book. To say that he was an unsympathetic character in the book was a vast understatement.

As Ike was later to defensively explain it, "See, what happened, back during my 'druggie days,' I signed a contract with Walt Disney, giving them permission. This lawyer lied to me. I thought I was giving them permission for somebody to play me in the movie, and that I wouldn't sue them for somebody else being Ike Turner in the movie. I didn't care. If Tina didn't want to do it with me, that's okay. I didn't find out until I got sober and clean, coming out of jail, when I was trying to find out how I was going to start back with my career. Only then did I find out that I had signed away my rights to sue them, and they could portray me any way that they wanted to" (13).

As the deal took shape, Tina was brought in as a creative consultant, as well as a major contributor to the film. The decision was made that whomever it was who was to play her on screen would have to lip-sync to Tina's singing. Furthermore, in the very last scene of the movie, the real Tina—the soul survivor herself—was to be shown as herself on the screen. According to her, the scriptwriters took some liberties with the material. A decision was made that the bulk of the film should be centered on Tina's meeting, singing with, marrying, fighting with, and ultimately escaping from Ike Turner. To fit all of the events of her life into a two-hour movie, things had to be truncated somewhat. Every twist and turn in her life couldn't make it into the script. To simplify things, actual events were used to bring the story to life, but many of the facts had to be scripted differently to fit into the film.

Said Tina, "I felt like they took the idea of my life and sort of wrote around it. I've got to say that the script that I read was far—quite far—from reality" (8). However, the essence of her story was there, and the larger facts were in place. A decision was also made to entitle the film *What's Love Got to Do With It?*, to capitalize on the biggest international hit of her career.

One of the most crucial aspects of the pre-production process was finding the perfect actress to portray Tina on screen. The final list of possible actresses included Robin Givens and Angela Bassett. As Tina explains, "There was a lot of talk that she should look like me, have great legs, a body. I said, 'Hey, we're talking about acting.' That's why I had a lot to do with the decision between Robin Givens and Angela Bassett" (8). Ultimately, it was decided that Laurence Fishburne would play Ike. Laurence wasn't skinny and trim like the real-life Ike, but he was a great choice for showing both the suave side and the volatile side of Ike's personality.

During the filming of *What's Love Got to Do With It?*, Ike Turner found out where they were shooting it, and showed up one day in a chauffeured white Lincoln Continental. From his car he distributed autographed photos of himself. The producers were so frightened by his presence that bodyguards were assigned to escort Angela from the set to her makeup trailer. They wouldn't let him anywhere near her, for fear he would do or say something to upset her. "By the time I figured out how to sneak out, he'd gone," remarked Bassett (5).

However, Laurence Fishburne did meet Ike on the set that day. Fishburne asked Ike what name he called Tina in real life. Said Ike, "I called her Ann" (5).

To make sure that the music used in the movie had a uniform sound, and to remove any musical contribution from Ike Turner, the songs from Tina's early career had to be rerecorded for the soundtrack album. According to Tina, "When Disney company bought the film rights to my autobiography, *I, Tina*, seven years ago, I never really believed it would make it to the screen. Then when filming finally started late last year [1992] I soon realized I would be asked to rerecord some of the old Ike & Tina hits to suit modern sound systems. To be honest, the thought did not thrill me. I hadn't sung some of these songs for a couple of decades and that was fine by me. But my band had fun working on the arrangements, and from the very first day of rehearsals their enthusiasm rubbed off on me. It was surprising to hear how well most of those songs have withstood the test of time. We also recorded three wonderful new songs for the soundtrack. I am grateful to Sade Adu for finding 'I Don't Wanna Fight,' a song which I feel perfectly summarizes a large part of my life it seemed like the ideal theme for the film" (36). Indeed, "Smooth Operator" Sade had discovered the perfect tune for Tina to sing! "I Don't Wanna Fight" was a song cowritten by pop star Lulu and her writing partners Steve DuBerry and Billy Lawrey.

"A Fool in Love" and "It's Gonna Work Out Fine" were two of the Ike & Tina songs that she had refused to sing since she left Ike in 1976. To put it in the context of this film, Fishburne vocalized the spoken part that Ike had in the original "It's Gonna Work Out Fine."

In the spring of 1993, Tina began to publicly preview some

of the new songs from the upcoming film of her life, *What's Love Got to Do With It?* On May 12, she was in Monaco where she was honored at the World Music Awards with a trophy for Outstanding Contribution to the Music Industry. At the awards ceremony, held at the Sporting Club in Monte Carlo, she sang her first single for Virgin Records, the movie's theme song, "I Don't Wanna Fight."

Suddenly Tina was all over the media again. On May 14 she was a guest on *The Tonight Show* in America. On May 27 she was back in London to sing "I Don't Wanna Fight" on BBC1-TV's hot music show *Top of the Pops.*

On June 6, 1993, Tina kicked off her first North American concert tour in six years in Reno, Nevada. Her opening act was Fleetwood Mac star Lindsey Buckingham. On the second leg of the tour, her show was opened by Chris Isaak.

What's Love Got to Do With It? debuted as a huge box-office success. Ultimately, both Angela Bassett and Laurence Fishburne were nominated for Academy Awards the following year for their strong and very believable roles as Tina and Ike Turner.

Said Angela Bassett of Tina, "Portraying her life as an artist was the most gratifying creative experience. What a source of inspiration her survival has been and can be to others" (21).

It was another triumphant time for Tina Turner. The film's success and across-the-board appeal with movie audiences once again put the spotlight on her past and her present life. Making the rounds of talk shows, everyone of course wanted her to talk about her life with Ike, since that era was 90 percent of the plot of the film *What's Love Got to Do With It?*

While promoting the film, Tina proclaimed, "You know, I wonder when the day will come that I don't have to talk about Ike Turner anymore. I wonder. Will that day come? A totally Ike-less future. 'Lord, what decade?'" (8). Well, the bad news was that while the whole movie media blitz was on, she would have to do a lot more talking about Ike Turner. But the good news was that after she was done publicizing the film, she could finally put the subject of Ike to rest—once and for all.

Tina certainly had some criticisms with how she was portrayed in *What's Love Got to Do With It?* In her opinion, the script had a few too many tears in it. And she wasn't happy with the fact that her home life was glazed over a bit. According to her, "There was a mother there. To Ike, to the children. Not this sniveling, crying, little weak woman. They had me crying in the film script, and I said, 'I never cried that much in my life.' Maybe from anger, sometimes" (8).

She was also a little upset that the reviews—in sympathy for her in real life and on the screen—often used the word "victim" to describe her. Did she see herself as a helpless victim? "Never!" she claimed. "Some people want that title. It's an excuse. I never needed it and I didn't want it, would never use it to describe me. . . . 'Enabler?' What is that, anyhow? 'Dysfunction?' You'll never hear that come out this mouth. Maybe it's because I was brought up a country girl—I didn't get into all that. . . . Someone tells me I was a victim, I become angry! I was not a victim. I want to talk about that. Because, okay, yes, if you tell my story to somebody who knows nothing about Tina Turner, they would label me as a 'victim.' But I was in control of everything I was doing" (8).

She had wanted to make sure that the film had the right tone to it. "I tried to explain it to Disney," says Tina of the way she was depicted in the film *What's Love Got To Do With It?* She was worried that she would just be portrayed as a helpless victim. She didn't want to be seen as someone with a "deep need— a woman who was a victim to a con man. How weak! How shallow! How dare you think that was what I was? I was in control every minute there. I was there because I wanted to be, because I had promised" (5).

Was it a difficult decision for her see her life story filmed? "Yes," she claimed. "Because I had had a lot of violence, houses burnt, cars shot into, the lowest that you can think of in terms of violence, and I didn't know what would happen at that point because it had kind of died down and the divorce was final and my life was kind of getting back on the road, and I didn't know what would happen. I didn't know what kind of mess it would stir, so I—I had to really take a deep breath and make a decision. I felt somehow like getting it out—I guess it was instinct. But I felt that getting it out would be not suppressing it anymore, letting the world really know, because they were constantly talking to me about why I cannot separate. I could never tell the truth; nobody really understood, and they still don't understand, but I think slowly now they're beginning to" (16).

Analyzing the demise of her real-life marriage to Ike, Tina said, "What ruined it was Ike had his way of feeling that he controlled people through sex, you know, and that wasn't what held me there. I was very loyal and that's why I stayed. And then, after about seven years of it, I decided that I couldn't help the situation, that it wasn't—it was irreparable—and that I must get on with my life and my children, etc. So, you see, I was thinking the whole time. It wasn't as if I was just being battered, and that's what the movie [*What's Love Got to Do With It?*] didn't show" (12).

With all of that being said, in her opinion, did Disney do her life justice in the film? "Yes, I think in way," says Tina. "I would have liked for them to have had more truth, but according to Disney, they said, 'It's impossible, the people would not have believed the truth.' And I understand that" (16).

Since Ike Turner is presented as the film's bullying villain, whenever he got the opportunity to complain about how he was portrayed, the unhappy star took full advantage of it. Consistently, he tried to downplay the physical abuse issue. He also expressed an underlying belief that Tina was to blame for everything bad that happened. According to him, "Whatever happened with Ike and Tina—if we fought every day—it's just as much her fault as it was mine. Because she stayed there and took it for whatever reason she was taking it. Why would she stay there for eighteen years? You know, I feel like I've been used. . . . Didn't nobody else grab her and put her where I put her. . . . I blame Tina as much for that as I blame myself. Because she always acted like it didn't bother her for me being with women, unless she seen me with *this* woman every night, or something like this . . . and this is what be wrong with her. She'd be pissed off about some girl or something, and she would lie and say she wasn't. . . . We had fights, but we was together twenty-four hours a day, and so, in other words, she feels more like an employee than a wife, because I would tell her what words to say, what dress to wear, how to act onstage, what songs to sing. You know, it all came from me. . . . There is no Tina in reality. It's just like the story that she's written. The movie's not about her. The movie's about me!" (5).

His attitude was that since she had not complained about his womanizing while they were married, why complain now? "Tina was my buddy," says Ike. "I never touched her as a woman. She was just my buddy. I would send her to go get this girl for me, go get that girl for me. And if I bought my old lady a mink coat, I would buy her one. And that's the way we were—just hope-to-die buddies. And that's why it was never no contract between us. Because I felt we had a bond, you understand, and I never did think that nobody, white or black, could come up and brainwash her. Like, right now I feel she's totally brainwashed" (5).

And then there was the film's depiction of the physical beatings. "I've got a hell of a temper," says Ike. "Sure I slapped Tina. We had fights and there have been times when I punched her without thinking. But I never beat her" (17). According to Tina, she was beaten with everything from telephones to wire coat hangers to Ike's own shoes.

Ike said in *Vanity Fair* magazine, "Did I hit her all the time? That's the biggest lie ever been told by her or by anybody that say that. I didn't hit her any more than you been hit by your guy. . . . I'm not going to sit here and lie and say because I was doing dope I slapped her. If the same thing occurred again, I'd do the same thing. It's nothing that I'm proud of, because I just didn't stop and think" (5).

But the most controversial scene in the film involved Ike raping Tina up against one of the giant aquariums of the house. He claimed it didn't happen. The scene itself might have been fictionalized for the film, but according to Tina, "Sex had become rape as far as I was concerned" (5). The exact scene may have been different, but the facts seemed to remain true.

Ike complained, "The only thing I have to say on that is that I made a mistake by signing a contract that said I wouldn't sue if somebody played me in the movie. I didn't know that meant they could treat me any way they wanted to, and that I couldn't do anything about it. So they got away with it, and it's been seven years of hell. They sabotaged my career, man. . . . You know, I got dirt in my closet just like everybody. But if I had to live my life over, I can't say I wouldn't do everything the same" (15).

Ike said of the film, "It dogged me and all that kind of crap. Man, and you know I'm not saying that I've been a good father either, I've done a lot of wrong things, right. But you can't undo things. Everybody's done wrong. I'm not talking about anybody, I'm talking about Ike right now. I've done a lot of wrong things, real right. You know? All I can do is apologize to the people that I may have done wrong. But I'm not the dude that you see in that movie. Nowhere close. Not at all" (13). That's obviously not what Tina thought—since she had a creative hand in the film.

Undeniably, the best thing that happened during his stint in jail was the fact that it forced him to give up drugs. "I've been clean since 1989," says Ike. "In that year, I went to jail, and I haven't touched drugs since then" (13).

At the time he was projecting where he thought his own career should be. "When I was with Tina, we would open up for Bill Cosby, like, in Vegas. I'm going to start by doing stuff like that. Going on tour with Elton John. Going on tour with The Stones. Going on tour with people like that. I got a lot of friends out there. I have no shame; it took it all to make me what I am today, and I love me today" (5). None of these dreams were fulfilled.

For Tina the whole *What's Love Got to Do With It?* experience signified the last time that she had to look back over this era of her past. She pondered, "I know what I've done. Sometimes I'm a little blown away by it, but I am what I am and I don't relate to what other people are saying. So when they come to me and say 'How did you? How could you?' I say, 'What else was I supposed to do? I had to work. One must work on this planet. So, what is this that I've done?' I've worked. I can sing and dance better than I can do anything else. I care about myself, my health, how I look. I never did drugs, drank alcohol. I never abused myself. There's nothing I did that's so extraordinary. But people don't expect rock & roll people to care about themselves" (8).

The multimedia *What's Love Got to Do With It?* blitz pai[d] in a big way. The movie was a huge success, with the *Los A[nge]les Times*, *Entertainment Weekly*, and the *Chicago Sun-Time[s]* calling it "One of the Year's Top 10 Movies." In his review o[f the] film, the *Sun-Times* writer Roger Ebert claimed, "*What's [Love] Got to Do With It?* ranks as one of the most harrowing, unc[om]promising showbiz biographies I've ever seen. . . . *What's [Love] Got to Do With It?* has a lot of terrific music in it (includi[ng a] closing glimpse of the real Tina Turner), but this is not the [typ]ical showbiz musical. It's a story of pain and courage, unc[om]monly honest and unflinching, and the next time I hear [Tina] Turner singing I will listen to the song in a whole new w[ay]" (37). In the *Washington Post* Rita Kempley wrote, "*What's L[ove] Got to Do With It?* Not much, I'm afraid. . . . An exploratio[n of] Tina Turner's life with the abusive Ike, it's a sketchy but bru[tal] bio-pic with a weft of beatings and a warp of rhythm & blu[es.] One minute she's belting out 'Proud Mary,' the next Ike's belti[ng] her. The film, like the couple's co-dependent relationship, [is] fiercely acted out and ablaze with flashy production numbe[rs]" (38).

In addition to having *What's Love Got to Do With It?* in t[he] theaters, Tina also appeared in another film in 1993. She w[as] one of the many stars to have cameo roles in the latest Arno[ld] Schwarzenegger film, *Last Action Hero*. Always one to make [a] great and forceful leader, in this film Tina was seen in a br[ief] role as the mayor. Other stars who made a brief appearance [in] *Last Action Hero* were Joan Plowright, Anthony Quinn, Che[vy] Chase, Little Richard, and Sharon Stone.

Tina's one scene in *Last Action Hero* comes in the very begi[n]ning of the film. A gunman has a class full of children he[ld] hostage on a Los Angeles rooftop, and police officer Jack Slat[er] (Schwarzenegger) appears on the scene to remedy the situa[a]tion. As he is heading toward the scene of the crime, out fro[m]

between the police cars pops Tina as the mayor, accompanied by a well-dressed gentleman. She pleads with him, "Jack, I know as mayor of this great metropolis, you and I have had our little tiffs, but this is the Lieutenant Governor." With that, Arnold slugs the man in the face and says, "When the governor gets here, call me." It's a fast sequence, but there stood Tina, looking great in a classy beige skirt suit, her hair elegantly coiffed for the role.

When the soundtrack album from *What's Love Got to Do With It?* was released, it debuted on the charts at No. 1 in England. It made it to No. 17 in the United States. The movie's theme song and lead single was "I Don't Wanna Fight," which peaked at No. 9 in America. It topped the singles charts in Germany, France, Holland, Denmark, and Switzerland. In the United Kingdom, the next single was Tina's recording of "Disco Inferno," which hit No. 12. On both sides of the Atlantic, "Why Must We Wait Until Tonight?" was the next single released, which made it to No. 16 in the United Kingdom and No. 97 in the United States.

On August 22, 1993, Tina played the final date of her *What's Love* U.S. concert tour, in Miami, Florida. She then moved on to Australia where she sang at the Australian Rugby League Championship game in Sydney, New South Wales.

On December 14, a star with Tina Turner's name on it was unveiled in the sidewalk in front of New York City's Radio City Music Hall, as part of its "Sidewalk of the Stars." And, December 28, Fox-TV aired a special from Tina's recent American concert tour entitled *Tina, What's Love? Live.* The show that had been filmed was the one she had done in September in San Bernardino, California.

The year 1993 had been a very high-profile and triumphant one. She had two movies in the theaters, a hit album, a new No. 1 international hit, a TV special, and cover stories in *Newsweek*

and *Vanity Fair*. What did love have to do with it? A hell of a lot. Tina Turner had cemented her position as one of the most beloved singing stars in the world, and she was at a new peak in her long creative career. Thanks to the success of the film *What's Love Got to Do With It?*, whenever anyone heard a Tina Turner song from this point forward, they instantly knew that they were listening to a remarkable singer who was truly a triumphant "survivor."

17

WILDEST DREAMS

For Tina, the last ten years had been a nonstop whirlwind of activities. She finally decided that the time had come for something that had never occurred in her life: a vacation. From 1993 to 1996, she explained, "I took off three years for the first time in my life. It's always been year after year album following into album, touring, having about a good year off and then starting an album again. And then after the last tour two—three years ago, I took off three years for the first time in my life" (16).

What did she do with her time off? "A lot of nothing, really. I just experienced what it feels like to do nothing, to just get up and think—'What do I want to do today?' And maybe sometimes do a lot of nothing, just get back into decorating my own house," she proclaimed (16).

In March 1994 she and Erwin moved from Cologne, Germany, to Zurich, Switzerland. Why Zurich? "Because my boyfriend was moved there to run the company, I always wanted to go to Switzerland, and I was very happy" (16).

Then, she unexpectedly continued her European quest even further south, to the Mediterranean Sea, and the famed Côte d'Azur. As she explained it, "Then I bought a house, in the meantime, in the South of France, and I started to rebuild that" (16).

In a way, it had been a gradual progression. When Tina's career became so hot in Europe, before the United States fully embraced her return to prominence, she spent much more time in England and mainland Europe. Then, when her relationship with Erwin blossomed, she was in Cologne. Then from Cologne to Zurich, and now to Nice, France. According to her, "I lived the first half of my life in America. The second half, I'll live in Europe. I don't believe I'll ever go back to America to live. It's fine to go back to show my fans that I didn't just die out, but what I don't like in America is having the press down my throat about the old stuff. It's the part that upsets me a little bit—maybe it's too much of the past. I don't dwell. I visit my mother and sister, but I don't go back to Tennessee. That's me—I don't go back" (39).

While she was taking her self-imposed sabbatical from the public eye, her music continued to sell briskly. Her *Simply the Best* album stayed in the U.K. Top 50 album charts for an astonishing 154 consecutive weeks. In November 1994, in America, the RIAA certified *Simply the Best* and the movie soundtrack *What's Love Got to Do With It?* both as Platinum million-selling albums.

In 1994, Capitol Records in the United States issued an impressive and excellently conceived Tina Turner boxed set of three CDs entitled *Tina Turner: The Collected Recordings—Sixties to Nineties*. With an eighty-four-page color booklet with liner notes by music expert Paul Grein, it was truly the ultimate Tina package. The first disc encompassed the Ike & Tina years, from "A Fool in Love" to "It Ain't Right (Lovin' to Be Lovin')" and sixteen impressive cuts in between. The second disc traced Tina's solo career, from "Acid Queen" into her 1980s and 1990s rarities—including "Johnny and Mary," "Games," "Let's Pretend We're Married," and her duets like "It Takes Two" with Rod Stewart. The third disc represented her chart-topping new era of international smashes, from "Let's Stay Together" to "I Don't Wanna Fight."

In September of 1995, Tina went into a recording studio with Bono and The Edge of the Irish group U2 to sing the theme song for the James Bond film *Goldeneye*. When it was released in November, the solo song that Bono and The Edge wrote for Tina, "Goldeneye," became an instant No. 10 hit in the United Kingdom.

In October, Tina started recording sessions for her first all-new studio album in five years. At the helm of this one was famed English producer Trevor Horn. Hit-making duo the Pet Shop Boys, along with Sheryl Crow were among the list of songwriters who contributed tunes for her to record on her exciting new album, titled *Wildest Dreams*.

With regard to choosing material for her albums, Tina revealed, "That usually comes through my manager, and then after he goes through everything, then he and I sit down and listen to things, songs, and choose what we feel that's—is the right song. It's very difficult to listen for the world [audience], to listen for the media and what's happening out there today. Choosing good songs and choosing trend songs is the problem these days" (16).

She chose several more artsy songs for the *Wildest Dreams* album. However, she was insistent that she couldn't get too mellow, that the overall tone had to truly rock & roll. "That's my style," she insists. "I take great songs and turn them into rock & roll songs on stage. I don't really actually get rock & roll material because there's not that much good music out there. Because my performance is an energy on stage, I need that kind of music, so I just transform the music. . . . I like really good ballads, melodic songs. And of course, I like uptempo rock & roll songs. Energy and fun, naughtiness a little bit" (16).

In November 1995, Tina announced her plans for a massive European tour of stadiums in the summer of 1996. It was to be her first European tour in six years. That same month she attended the Royal premiere of *Goldeneye* alongside the handsome actor who portrayed the new 1990s James Bond, Pierce Brosnan.

On December 3, 1995, VH-1 in America broadcast their first *Fashion & Music Awards*, which featured Tina Turner singing "Goldeneye," as well as a duet with Elton John. December 6 found her performing at the Billboard Music Awards, which were telecast live from New York's Coliseum. In February 1996, in England, Tina presented Annie Lennox with the award for Best Female Solo Artist at the Fifteenth Annual BRIT Awards.

On March 8, 1996, Tina announced that Hanes nylons would be sponsoring her upcoming tour of America. Since she has one of the most famous pairs of legs in all of show business, it was a perfect union of product and spokesperson. Tina was also featured in a heavy advertising campaign for the famed nylons, showing off her sexy gams. According to her, "They're sponsoring us. They also are furnishing me with hosiery for the show, me and the girls. . . . It's wonderful working with them" (16).

In April 1996, Tina's *Wildest Dreams* album was released— everywhere in the world *except* the United States. Since the States had proven such a fickle record-buying marketplace for Tina, the strategy was that the album would be released in Europe and the rest of the world first, where it was guaranteed that it would be a hit; then it could come into the United States as an established hit. That way, if snobby American rock critics didn't like it for some reason, it really didn't matter.

Tina's albums were no longer sure-fire sellers in her home country. It was not a desirable outcome—but in the long run, who cared? She had the rest of the world eating out of the palm of her hand. As predicted, the *Wildest Dreams* album became a huge smash in the United Kingdom and the rest of the world, and received a lukewarm reception when it came out in the United States.

When *Wildest Dreams* was released in the United Kingdom in April, it hit No. 4 on the album chart. The single that followed "Goldeneye," "Whatever You Want," hit No. 23 in the United Kingdom, and its successor, "On Silent Wings," hit No. 13. Tina was on tour in England from July 12 to 24 when the fourth single from the album, "Missing You," hit No. 12 in the United Kingdom. She then continued her tour of mainland Europe. Her next single, "Something Beautiful Remains," peaked at No. 27 on the U.K. charts.

In September 1996, *Wildest Dreams* was released in America and peaked in *Billboard* at No. 61. The album included a seductive duet with crooner Barry White on the song "In Your Wildest Dreams," and Sting is heard as a special guest vocalist on "On Silent Wings." With U2 and the Pet Shop Boys each contributing cuts, it was a fitting all-star event. The first American single to be pulled from it was Tina's hot version of John Waite's "Missing You," which made it to No. 84.

From December 11 to 14, Tina headlined at Birmingham, England's National Exhibition Centre. It was the final European date for her that year, and a tour that had encompassed more than 150 concerts throughout that continent.

On February 22, 1998, Tina Turner was the musical guest star on NBC-TV's *Saturday Night Live*. And, on February 28, she kicked off the Australian leg of her *Wildest Dreams* tour by headlining the Indoor Stadium in Canberra. On March 25, Tina's longtime keyboard player, Kenneth L. Moore, suddenly died from apoplexy while on tour, in Sydney, Australia. Tina was saddened to lose him as a musician and a friend. He was replaced in the band, and the tour moved onward.

Tina kicked off the U.S. leg of her world tour with a guest spot on the late night TV program, the *Tonight Show with Jay Leno*. The tour opened with a two-day engagement at the Cynthia Woods Mitchell Pavilion at Woodlands, Texas, May 1–2. Her opening act for this tour was Cyndi Lauper. The tour continued across America until August 10, where it concluded at the Meadows Music Theatre in Hartford, Connecticut.

Speaking admirably of Tina, Cyndi Lauper exclaimed, "Tina always looks stunning!" (40). According to the beautiful Ms. Turner, "It's always been a priority for me to look as good as I can. Even when Ike was totally in control, telling me what I could and could not wear, I did my best. I knew that I was always capable of making myself look better. I'd look back at photographs, and I wasn't pleased. And I wanted to be. Now that I'm in control, I'm still working on myself. I don't think I'll ever stop. I'm crazy when it comes to this" (7).

At the end of August 1997, the entire world was stunned when Diana, Princess of Wales, was suddenly killed in a horrifying car crash in the streets of Paris. All activity on the globe seemed to come to a stop in its unity of sorrow. Late in the year, an all-star double album of songs was released to raise money for the Diana, Princess of Wales Memorial Fund. Several stars recorded new material, and others contributed their songs for the cause. Among the celebrities featured on the album entitled *Diana, Princess of Wales—Tribute* included Aretha Franklin, Queen, Annie Lennox, Paul McCartney, Whitney Houston, Simply Red, Placido Domingo, Lesley Garrett, Luciano

Pavarotti, Brian Ferry, Eric Clapton, Rod Stewart, and several others. Tina Turner donated her version of the song "Love Is a Beautiful Thing." It was a new recording, only available on this album.

On the *Wildest Dreams* tour, she was still expelling an incredible amount of onstage energy. "I don't believe that I can go and stand and sing for the people," she claimed. "I can't stand the idea of just standing there like Barbra Streisand or Ella Fitzgerald or Diana Ross. I have never been that kind of performer. I have been in rock & roll all my life. You can't be a rock & roll old woman. You can be a rock & roll old man" (5). Her fans begged to differ. If she looked as sexy as she did, she simply could do no wrong!

What amazed many of her fans the most was her ability to dance and whirl like a dervish—in high-heeled shoes! Explaining her ability to do such strenuous choreography in pumps, Tina claimed, "Well, you know, it's because you're on your toes. I'm never standing on my feet with all the weight on both of them. I'm always either on the right leg or the left. And it's basically with the weight on the ball of the foot. The only time it's full on is when I'm doing a heavy dance step, because you need to balance. But it's not about the high heel at all—it's the lift for me. It keeps me up where I can have the spring, the ability to move fast, to leap" (7).

How did she continue to be so utterly youthful? She, however, doesn't always believe that she does look entirely youthful. "Sometimes I feel like I'm Mother Teresa," she laughs with regard to her age. "Fortunately, I did not have an easy life. I've experienced a lot, and I can share it in terms that might help people. Let's just say, I've offered good advice; I've been fortunate to give that. But it's all the time. I think people put a bit too much on me sometimes. People want to know, of course, how I got through my life. They ask about relationships with men, but it's mostly to do with changes in life. A lot of people can't deal with the changes" (7).

At the age of fifty-eight, she still had the same lean body that she had when she was in her twenties. Can she eat anything that she wants? "Yes, anything I want!" she confirms. "I'm really fortunate I have that privilege to eat mostly everything I want, because I can say it's how I am, it's my stage work. But I never really get overweight" (16).

When people try to get her to admit to liposuction and plastic surgery, she scoffs. "They don't take into consideration that I've been singing and dancing—and that's exercise," she explains. "It's got to do something. I have muscle. From control" (5).

It is impossible not to notice that everything about Tina Turner exudes class and refinement. She saw what she wanted her own life to be like, and she simply went after her dreams— not stopping until she attained them. According to her, "I patterned myself from classy ladies. I take as much from them as I can, but I take it naturally, because I'm not going to be phony about it. I'm not going to walk around in Chanel suits or Gucci suits—that's a little bit too much, because that's not my nature. But watching my manners, caring about not being overdressed at the wrong time—it matters how I carry myself—that's what I'm concerned about as far as being a lady. Nobody would ever think that Tina Turner is a lady. I am" (5).

Speaking of class, the renovation of her house in the hills of Nice, France, was finally completed during this era. It was her retreat from the hectic world of show business—and what a luxurious retreat it had blossomed to become. Her manager, Roger Davies, first introduced Tina to the wondrous and beautiful south of France. She fell in love with the area and its lively but tranquil ambiance. For a while, she rented a "little pink house" near the same summit upon which she now lives.

The whole city of Nice lies below. The western part of the crescent-shaped bay is known as Cap Ferrat—the most exclusive part of the city. "The Cap is Beverly Hills, and that's what I fled," explains Tina. "When we heard that this property was for sale, we were told that 'angels live here,' and we laughed about it. But in fact it's a very spiritual place—between two mountains, surrounded by woods that are full of wildlife—and that's essential to me. I was raised in the country, come from a Bible-reading family and grew up on church music. My mother's Indian side has given me a different kind of religious heritage. Up here the wind and clouds breeze through the house, and the sky makes mesmerizing pictures. I can watch them for hours" (41).

According to Tina, her home's interior has to be harmonious with her fantastic new life. "A great interior has to coalesce. When I see something I love—a suite of furniture, a piece of art—I never measure, I never hesitate, I just buy it. Eventually I'll find a place for it. I have strong tastes—and big storerooms. I've always wanted and needed to transform my surroundings, because decorating is my first response to loss and upheaval; settle, collect—create a private universe. I was a little girl when my parents separated, and I moved in with relatives, claiming a back room in their house. I brought a bedspread from home and a few treasures. Even thought it was freezing in the winter and broiling in the summer—and no bigger than a closet—I made it a place of my own. And that's what I've always done on tour—rearrange the hotel furniture, sheet the ugly paintings. But getting things perfect in a house this scale was taking me too long. Eventually I saw that I needed professional help—the right kind for me" (41).

The way in which she found the interior designers she employed came about in a roundabout way. She vacationed in Aspen, Colorado, and she was the guest of Jim and Betsy Fifield.

Tina immediately loved the baroque manor that her friends lived in, and she inquired of her hosts as to who had decorated their home. Through the Fifield's, Tina was put in touch with their interior designers, Stephen Stills and James Huniford.

They jumped at the opportunity to work with Turner. Huniford recalls, "Having always loved her music, immediately adored her" (41).

The three of them hit it off together, and agreed to try some interesting combinations of design influences. According to Tina, "I let them try things. They never push. I'll say to them 'Yes, let's do it; [or] no thanks—I've been there.' We work from feelings. It's like mixing a CD" (41).

Recalling their working relationship with Turner, Stills explains, "Designing involves culture, intuition, artisanship, and an ideal of transparency, which I can best compare to the art of literary translation. Your sensibility functions like a prism. In working with Tina, who's a natural-born decorator, it was really a matter of helping her to find her own voice—to express her own style—rather than to impose ours. We toured museums together, went shopping on the Quai Voltaire in Paris, exchanged books and ideas—which Tina accepted or rejected, as it suited her—and we helped to edit her collections. But she was the mastermind of this house. It's her own invention" (41).

Tina fell in love with an outrageously expensive bedroom suite that had once belonged to Emperor Louis Philippe, including fauteuils and canopés—twenty-two fabulous gold finished pieces. There was, however, one piece missing from the suite: the king's bed. It is currently owned by and displayed at the Louvre in Paris. According to her, "I wasn't intimidated by the fact that it was palace furniture. It's beautiful, it's comfortable, and it set the tone for the whole house" (41). She might have been queen in a former life, but now she is literally living like one! You go, Miss Tina!

The *pièce de résistance,* of course, is the Louis-Philippe bed-room suite, circa 1830. According to designer Sills, "I thought it was too grand and very expensive. But Tina just pointed at it and said, 'Sorry, boys, that's it!' She said, 'I don't care what it is or who it's by, I'm just having it!'" (39).

Says Tina of the sumptuous court furniture that she now owns, "When I leave the planet, I plan to donate it to the Lou-vre so it can go back to its bed!" (12).

She is very happy and comfortable in her house on the hill overlooking the port city of Nice down below. According to her, she rarely leaves the grounds "except maybe to walk down the hill to a local restaurant" (41).

Off of the master bedroom is a terrace decorated in a decid-edly ancient Egyptian motif, with hanging silk ropes, and a bronze bed. "This is my refuge," claims Tina, "my favorite spot in the house. I call it Cleopatra's barge" (41).

According to her, she doesn't play a lot of rock music when she is at home with Erwin. "I love quiet. If I want to have mu-sic, I make it—but who wants music when they can hear this?" she says (39).

The house in Nice was so grand that Tina felt overwhelmed when it came time to decorate it properly. According to her, "A lot of times, what interior decorators do looks pretty when you walk in, but there's nothing there that's personal. And I don't want it too polished" (39).The house is very classic in design and decor, yet very rock & roll at the same time. She had her builder reproduce a pond from a painting that is hung in her bedroom. The painting depicts the ruin of a Roman temple. In another room, which is the video screening room, the walls are lined with Gold and Platinum records, plus her Grammy, American Music Awards, and MTV Awards are also on display. The room has a karaoke machine, so that guests can sing for the diva at her parties. And she has a huge television set that swivels 360 degrees, so it can be viewed from the kitchen, the drawing room, or the terrace.

In the garage at the Nice house of Ms. Turner is a navy blue Mercedes Benz sports car from the 1960s, totally refurbished, with soft beige upholstery. It was a tenth anniversary present from Erwin.

Says Tina, "We were at a friend's house, and it was parked outside when we came out. I was looking at it, thinking, 'This is a snazzy number,' and Erwin just said, 'By the way, it's yours!'" (39).

Tina claims that her house in Nice thrills her. "When I look around, I need to like every single thing I see—and where it is" (39).

According to Huniford, "Tina loves to decorate. She has the most incredible eye for detail. At the end [of the design assignment], we joked with her that she could come work for us if she ever retired" (39).

Not only was her new house making her happy, so was her life with Erwin. "When I had no money and was experiencing freedom for the first time, I made a few mistakes with men," she admits. "I didn't mind making those mistakes, because I was searching and playing, but the ones that were bad were *awful*. I ran into a few of them! But it never would have been about involvement. I have common sense. I have a *lot* of it!" (39).

Then came Erwin. "I finally got involved with a man who cared about me," says Tina. "I had a problem even getting a relationship out of him, because he didn't want a high profile [life]. . . . I like the way Erwin handled it. We lock in somewhere. I receive comfort from him. Erwin's not here for the money. He's beginning to accept this lifestyle now, but he wasn't even interested in that for a long time" (39).

Even when Tina is on one of her global concert tours, they

find time to get together. "When I am working he comes to me, because I can't come to him. But no, my relationship with Erwin has nothing to do with my work, in the sense of where I go and what I do," she explains (16).

Since Erwin is also in the music business, would she ever consider making him her manager? "No, no, no!" replies Tina. "That was understood in the beginning; I didn't want a boyfriend or a husband as a manager. No, I wouldn't do that again. That would have been bad news. That would have been a very bad mistake" (16).

In interviews, Tina was consistently asked if she ever thought of retirement. According to her in 1997, "I think of it often. I did actually make an attempt. It wasn't actually retiring. I wanted to get more into movies and travel less. Continue to record, very little road traveling and acting, and I was still—I will never stop recording. Acting is still—if something comes that I can" (16).

Still, that big "rush" of energy she gets from performing live is very addicting. "Yes, it's at the moment when I walk on stage," she explains, "there's such a feeling of faces looking back at me with love and admiration. And it turns into a togetherness. It really is about a desire from the people. And the last tour I actually announced to my audience that I would be back. It was only because of that feeling, because that's the kind of audience I have" (16).

She was able to utilize the rush that she got from performing when she was on stage. And the calmness and sense of serenity and purpose that she got from Buddhist chanting helped. "It's not about spirituality in God. Chanting is about contacting the subconscious mind. The subconscious mind helps us out in life, and when you find the right words to connect with that, it's stronger than anything you can get from man. One must do it for oneself. That is my philosophy of Buddhism," she explains (39).

In 1998, Tina was heard on a popular duet with European singing star Eros Ramazzotti, called "Cose Della Vita." She was also busy recording her next album, which was due for release the following year.

Ensconced in her fairy tale dream house in the south of France, she had again succeeded in making more of her wildest dreams come true, but she wasn't finished yet. After more than forty years as a recording and singing star, for Tina Turner, more of the best was still yet to come.

18

TWENTY FOUR SEVEN AND THE FINAL TOUR

According to the dictionary, a "diva" is a "goddess," a "prima donna," and a "divine" creature. In the opera world, the word has long been used to describe the most demanding, exciting, temperamental, and talented of female singing stars. In a rock & roll realm, few are more goddess-like and worshiped than Tina Turner.

Taking that into consideration, it was most fitting indeed when VH1 invited Turner to star on its second annual *Divas Live* TV special, on April 13, 1999. In fact, it was Tina who was asked to open the whole show. The popular music divas who were invited to share the stage with Turner were Cher, Faith Hill, Whitney Houston, Mary J. Blige, and Chaka Khan. As the young divas-in-the-making, Brandy and Leann Rimes rounded out the list. And, as a special tribute to *his* own unique diva-ness, Elton John was the honorary male diva of the evening.

Elton was very well involved professionally with several of

the ladies on the show. Elton had known Cher since the mid-1970s when he was a guest on the TV special that kicked off the Sonny-less weekly *Cher* show on CBS-TV. On March 23, 1999, Polygram Records had just released his latest musical venture, the concept album *Elton John and Tim Rice's* Aida. The album was based on the famed opera *Aida*, and on it Tina Turner had recorded the song "Easy as Life." In addition, Leann Rimes recorded a duet with Elton on the album, called "Written on the Stars."

Tina and Elton were further associated because they were in the middle of making plans for a new joint venture. They were supposed to go on tour together later that year. It seemed like a good idea to have them usher in their working together with an appearance together on this *Diva* show.

The afternoon of the live telecast, all of the performers had access to New York City's majestic Beacon Theater for musical and staging rehearsals. While rehearsing together, Elton and Tina had a huge argument about something that they differed upon. Elton reportedly stormed off to his dressing room trailer. Tina followed him out, and the two of them had a heated conversation together while the bewildered musicians remained on stage.

When Elton and Tina returned to the stage, Elton apologized to Tina in front of the other musicians. Tina forgave him, and the rehearsal went on as scheduled. That night Elton and Tina performed together, but their projected concert tour together was officially "off." The question still remains who was guilty of the most "diva-like" behavior: Elton or Tina? No one was talking.

The *Divas Live '99* show was a *tour de force* TV event. It opened with Tina stepping out of a limousine that had pulled up to the front of the Beacon Theater on Broadway. She stepped out, strutted through the lobby, down the stage right aisle, and through the seated audience on her way up to the stage. Along the way she was singing one of her signature songs, "The Best." As she strode onto the stage, Elton was there playing a grand piano with the house band. It was a brilliant way to open the show, and it left no question in everyone's mind who was the "divaest" of them all that night—it was the lovely Miss Tina.

As a duet, Elton and Tina sang his hit song "The Bitch Is Back." It was rather an amusing choice of songs, in light of the argument they had gotten into that afternoon. After the song, Tina laughed to the star-studded audience, "Wow, divas and bitches, my goodness!" For their next number together, Tina and Elton launched into a song that was about—says Tina—"the oldest diva of all, Proud Mary." Midsong they were to be joined on stage by another stratospheric diva, Cher. It was a wonderful moment in the show to see Tina singing her hit song with her long-time buddies, Cher and Elton.

After Tina and Elton left the stage, Cher launched into her own solo song, "If I Could Turn Back Time." The show progressed along with the other stars—including duets between Faith Hill and Brandy, and Elton with Leann Rimes. Whitney Houston dominated the last segment of the show. At the grand finale it was anticipated that the whole cast would be present for an all-star version of "I'm Every Woman." However, Tina and Cher were conspicuously missing from the finale.

Were Tina and Cher distancing themselves from Whitney's well-publicized drug scandals? Did the argument between Tina and Elton make it uncomfortable for Turner to be there any longer? No one in diva-land was talking, but everyone was speculating. What's a show of dueling divas without some backstage bitching and intrigue anyway?

In any case, it was a triumphant evening for Tina and all of the divas who followed her to the stage. It also yielded a hit al-

bum and video/DVD package, capturing Tina's live performance of those three star-studded songs.

For Tina, 1999 was a year filled with major events concern-
ing her past, her present, and her future. One of the saddest
things to occur was the death of her mother in October of that
year. For years there were many unresolved issues between
Tina and Zelma Bullock.

"She ended up living in a very nice house, being very respected and recognized as 'Tina Turner's mother.' I think her
last days were her best," says Tina. However, she was to lament
of their strained relationship, "My mother never really knew
me—and my success she always attributed to Ike. She never
thought it was me, so there was always a gap between us" (42).

Tina had the underlying suspicion that her mother never
loved her. She suspected that she was an unwanted pregnancy.
Then there were the lingering emotional issues that she felt
from Zelma having abandoned her when she was a child. According to Tina, "I confronted her years later, when a European
psychic explained to me that I had been an unwanted child
while still inside her. I said, 'Ma, I want to talk to you because
we never got along.' And she cried and told me the story. My
mother never looked at me. When I was with Ike, she thought
he did everything, because he was a star when I met him. It was
as if Ike was the connection I made for them. It was very hard
for my mother and sister to respect me for my talent. We were
two people, but [Ike] took the credit. They weren't even smart
enough to see that I mattered. Eventually, I brought Ma to
Paris, London, Switzerland, and New York to show her what
the world was like, and she still didn't believe that I had done
everything for myself. When we got to my house in the south
of France, she believed that my boyfriend had decorated it,
even though he told her, 'Tina is the interior decorator.' Ma

said, 'I don't think she did it.' Finally, I proved it to her. At my house in Switzerland, everything was lying around—we were building—and in thirty minutes I put the house all together. She walked upstairs and she said, 'You did all this?' I said, 'Ma, I told you! This is what I can do.' And she was quiet. She realized, finally, in her own way, at her age, who I was" (3).

Tina claims that Zelma was not an easy woman to get along with. "She gave everybody a hard time. During her illness we went through twenty nurses. No matter how much pleasure I tried to give her, she couldn't find her peace. She really suffered those eight months. Whatever her karma was, it reached in and squeezed the life out of her" (3).

At the age of eighty-one, Zelma died in the United States. Where was Tina at the time? "In Europe on a promotional tour for the new album [*Twenty Four Seven*]. But I called daily. One afternoon I was preparing for a bath when Rhonda came in and said, 'Tina, Ma died.' And I just went, 'Ahhhhhhhhhhh!'" (3).

Tina chose not to attend her mother's funeral. She sensed that it was going to end up a media three-ring circus, so she stayed away. However, Ike Turner went to Zelma's funeral. According to Tina, "He and Ma had kept in touch, and he showed up and was very upset that I wasn't there. So he went to the newspapers, and all over Europe the press said, 'Tina shuns her mother's funeral!' I wanted to give my mother her moment. Everyone called asking, 'Is Tina going to be there?' We said, 'Don't come just because of Tina.' I wasn't in the frame of mind to be stared at. I didn't need it, nor did Ma need it from me. So I felt 'let her have that day'" (3).

She let her mother be the star of her funeral. Then Tina went to the cremation. Her premonitions about the press getting involved proved correct. Tina recalls, "Somebody took pictures of me that appeared in the European papers, which said, 'Tina is here after all.' People saw Ike using my dead mother to get press. That's when I really cried, when they put the casket into the crematorium, I could see the flames leaping, saw the fire catch her hair and clothes and suddenly thought, 'I'm burning my mother,' even though she wanted it. I thought, 'She's really gone now'" (3).

Throughout 1999, Tina had been at work on her next studio album, ultimately to be entitled *Twenty Four Seven*. The musical recipe for this album involved going to some tried and true song sources and delving into some fresh territory as well.

The songs that Tina chose for this recording have more of an overall upbeat pop feeling to them than her latest recordings. A well-crafted and exciting album, *Twenty Four Seven* showed Tina off as a fresh pop diva with rock & roll flourishes. There are no hard-core rockers with wailing guitars on this album, but eleven catchy songs about finding love, losing love, and being devoted to someone around the clock.

The album opens with "When the Heartache Is Over," which was co-written by John Reid of The Nightcrawlers. It was produced by Metro, the London production team behind Cher's multimillion-selling hit song "Believe," and it features the same danceable beat and some of the same vocal sound effects.

From her long-time writer and producer, Terry Britten, came the crackling productions of "Absolutely Nothing's Changed," "Falling," and the more traditionally rock & rolling cut, "Twenty Four Seven." Graham Lyle, the cowriter of "What's Love Got to Do With It" contributed the song "Talk to My Heart," which he wrote with Johnny Douglas.

The album also includes a previously unrecorded song that was written by The Bee Gees' Barry, Robin, and Maurice Gibb. It is the ballad about devotion titled "I Will Be There." In addition, three tracks were produced by The Spice Girls/Geri Halliwell collaborators who call themselves Absolute.

To bring in some more familiar collaborators, the song

"Without You" includes a "cameo" vocal by Bryan Adams. To give a couple of the songs a truly "grand" sound, "Go Ahead" and "Whatever You Need" feature The Royal Philharmonic Orchestra, conducted by David Arnold.

According to Jane Stevenson of the *Toronto Sun*, "*Twenty Four Seven* finds Turner in an upbeat, adult contemporary kind of mood on such songs as the strings-accompanied 'Whatever You Need,' 'All the Woman,' 'Talk to My Heart' (complete with a gospel choir), 'Don't Leave Me This Way' and the Bee Gees-penned 'I Will Be There.' . . . Interestingly, too, this collection came together after Turner and Cher's knockout performances at last year's VH-1 *Divas* show, in which they both wiped the floor with Elton John, Brandy, and Whitney Houston" (43).

Reviewing *Twenty Four Seven*, Paul Elliot in *Q Magazine* wrote, "Gone is the grit of the music she made with former husband Ike. . . . Tina Turner remains a genuine superstar fifteen years after effecting the most unlikely comeback of the '80s. . . . The first single, 'When the Heartache Is Over,' is a dance tune from the producers of Cher's 'Believe.' These eleven tracks of grown-up pop should keep business ticking over smoothly" (44).

The next major event of the year occurred on November 26, 1999, when Tina Turner turned sixty years old. To celebrate her birthday, the hardest-working woman in rock & roll marked the occasion by doing one of the things that she did best—she performed a gala concert in London. It was a truly exciting event. In addition, Britain's ITV broadcast a special to commemorate her birthday and celebrate her life. Tina's birthday concert was captured on film, and it became the exciting DVD release *The Best of Tina Turner—Celebrate!* The triumphant concert found Tina performing several of her classics—from "River Deep-Mountain High" to "What's Love Got to Do With It" to "The Best." She also sang several of the tracks from her brand-new *Twenty Four Seven* album, like "When the Heartache Is Over" and an incredibly moving version of "Whatever You Need," which found her backed up by The London Community Gospel Choir and The Royal Philharmonic Concert Orchestra. When she came to the song "Talk to My Heart," she dedicated it to her late mother.

She looked truly stunning that night, and expelled an indefatigable amount of energy. It was hard to believe that she was actually sixty years old! Her dancers, girls in their twenties and thirties, looked like they were really struggling to keep up with the incomparable Tina Turner.

How did she feel about this milestone birthday? "Well . . . it's just mental," she claimed. "I think I look all right. I think I've done pretty good, because I take care of myself. So I look OK. And I'm just about ready to sit down and sing, and not perform. In the really big arenas, you can't always absorb the music. It's almost like . . . eating without seasoning" (45).

She was in remarkable shape, appearing as sexy and energetic as ever. Did she feel any older? According to her, "Oh, it's very real for me. Spiritually, I'm very much more aware. I'm not wise, but the beginning of wisdom is there; it's like relaxing into—and an acceptance of—things. First of all, I'm happy that I'm healthy. I know a lot of people who reach this age and the body starts to break down. So I'm very pleased that I'm just able to enjoy it. It's like you look out at youth, and you say, 'I'm happy where I am. I don't need to move further up or further down.' That's where I am" (45).

When New Year's Eve 1999 rolled around, instead of going to a party or celebrating quietly, Tina presented a huge millennium concert show. "I was in Las Vegas when the century changed," she explained, "and it was a little bit quiet, let's say. I would have preferred to have been celebrating with everyone else. But then I decided to work, and it's been a hard year, a very strenuous year of working one-nighters on the road. It's tough. Coming to an end, I feel that it was a long trip, of course, and very successful. . . . It seemed like it was inspirational, and a lot of people got a charge just out of the vitality that's in the show. There's five women up there, working hard but having a good time, and it seems like it really gave a lot of people something. It lifted them. Somehow I feel like I did a little bit more than entertain this year" (45).

In the year-end issue of *Billboard* magazine, in the "Hits of the World" international charts, *Twenty Four Seven* was No. 5 on the Eurochart, No. 8 in Germany, No. 10 in Belgium, and No. 2 in Switzerland. It was certified Platinum in the United Kingdom.

In January 2000, *Twenty Four Seven* was released in the United States. The first American single released off of the album was the song "When the Heartache Is Over." According to the ARC Weekly Top 40 radio charts, the song made it up to No. 40 in the United States.

On January 30, 2000, Tina Turner was seen singing "Proud Mary" and "When the Heartache Is Over" on the mega-American TV event, the Super Bowl pre-game show live from Atlanta, Georgia.

With her *Twenty Four Seven* album in stores around the globe, Tina set about to promote it with her most dramatic and exciting arena stage show yet. The American leg of the concert tour opened in Minneapolis, Minnesota, on March 23, encompassed 116 concert dates, and was set to end in Anaheim, California, on December 6, 2000. During the tour, she announced that it would be her *last* such tour. Her fans were stunned by the news, and tickets sold like hotcakes. According to her, "I'm still in good shape, I still have the energy, but when you work at a job for so long, you start to feel the need to make a change. I don't know what I'm going to do. I'm not even thinking about it. I'm just enjoying the fact that I won't have a calendar for a few years" (42).

She explained how she arrived at this decision by stating, "I decided I would work myself to a place where I can retire, and be financially secure and live nicely and enjoy knowing that I don't have to work ever again unless it's something I want to do. I feel really fortunate to have arrived at that. I'm rock & roll, and I'm a woman, and at a certain age you stop looking the part" (42). Well, for Tina, that age certainly hadn't come yet!

The May 8, 2000, issue of America's *People* magazine featured their annual list of "The 50 Most Beautiful People." Fittingly, Tina was one of the fifty they chose that year. According to makeup artist to the stars, Kevin Aucoin, "She has a beautiful nose, great cheekbones, an amazing head and a gorgeous sexy body. She's pushing the limits for everyone" (40). Indeed she was!

That same year, Tina appeared on the top-rated TV show *Ally McBeal.* One of her final *Twenty Four Seven* shows was taped and made into a CBS-TV special, which was broadcast on December 4. Between her TV exposure and the massive U.S. concert tour that she was in the middle of, *Twenty Four Seven* was certified Gold by the RIAA.

Wherever she appeared in 2000, she was met with cheering sold-out crowds, dying to see the last official Tina tour. How on earth was she able to perform two-and-one-half-hour shows night after night? According to her, "I've always been a tomboy kind of girl. I'm always doing something. So I don't get caught gaining weight. I've never worked out at all. I started to run when I went into a change of life because I was told that I needed to. But when I haven't run, it hasn't bothered me. I'm a country girl, and I lived a full country life, and it made me strong, I think" (7).

Touring year after year, she had to admit, was beginning to

wear on her. "When I travel, I am absolutely miserable," she was to confide. "I talked to an astrologist about it, 'cause I was really suffering. And he said that, astrologically, I am a home person. I try to make the hotels homey. I immediately walk into a room and get security to change the room the way I want it. Some places it's impossible and you can do nothing but sit there. I miss being at home very much" (7).

As much as she loved performing, she was starting to look forward to an open-ended rest. "I enjoy it once I'm right there onstage. But every night, for over 200 days, to think that you've got to go onstage and have a party . . . well, since I'm not a party person, I see it as a party without a drink for me. It's having a party with the people. And, I don't crave it—no! I'm fine when I'm there, I'm on a mission—to give the people a good time, because that's what it's about. It's not about a message or anything. It's about laughter and a little bit of dancing. And all kinds of intrigue. That's basically it. But I don't miss it when I'm not onstage. At all. It's a job out there and people always think it's fun. It's fun to a point, yes. I remember when it was more fun to put on those dresses and do the makeup and all that stuff. But, when you've had nearly forty years of it, it ceases to be that kind of fun and magic. It's a job that you've got to go out there and do. And be successful at it. That's the mission," she claimed (7).

For the last leg of the last tour, the sponsor of the concerts—and the CBS-TV special—was the popular American department store chain, Target. As part of the deal, Tina filmed a series of TV commercials for Target. She was seen singing and dancing to a new and exclusive song on the ads, her version of the Prince composition "Baby, I'm a Star." It was a fitting song for her to cover, and she did an exciting version of it. In 2000, Target marketed a special limited-edition CD that was available in their stores only, featuring live and studio versions of six of her hits, plus "Baby, I'm a Star." That special disc that Target released, entitled *All That Glitters*, was the only place her version of "Baby, I'm a Star" could be purchased.

On December 6, 2000, Tina Turner played the final show of her farewell tour in front of a sold-out audience of 18,000 fans who were packed into the massive Arrowhead Pond auditorium in Anaheim, California, thirty miles south of downtown Los Angeles. It was an incredibly exciting evening, and the last night of the final stadium rock concert of her career. Looking and sounding amazing that evening, Tina had finished off at the top!

The show business industry publication *The Hollywood Reporter* stated, "Turner, 61, took in $80.2 million in ticket sales for 95 concerts. Her success surprised experts because it has been several years since she has had a hit record. 'She had announced it was going to be her farewell tour, and people took her at her word,' *Pollster* [magazine] editor Gary Bongiovanni said" (46). Her tour was ranked as *the* highest-grossing concert attraction of the entire year 2000.

According to Tina, "I have looked forward to retiring for a long time, because this is something that doesn't run in my culture—most people work all their lives. Like Ella Fitzgerald, I think she might have been seventy-five when she left. I don't want to get that far. And fortunately I've gotten to the point where I can do it, and I'm going to celebrate it. I like the idea of waking up and not having a single thing in terms of meetings or anything to do. I love the freedom to choose to do whatever I decide to do with my day. That's my ideal" (45).

After her final concert in Anaheim, Tina left the public eye for her much-deserved break from the business. However, in her absence there have been several new packages reprising her greatest and most recent material. In 2000, one of Tina's final tour dates, at Wembley Stadium in London, was captured on film and turned into a wonderful concert video and DVD entitled *One Last Time in Concert*. Her sixtieth birthday celebration concert made another great DVD package that year, called *The Best of Tina Turner—Celebrate!* In 2002 all of her greatest videos—from "Let's Stay Together" up to "It Takes Two" with Rod Stewart and "Love Thing"—were gathered together on *Simply the Best—The Video Collection*. The collection also includes a never-before-seen, black-and-white version of "What's Love Got to Do With It" with scenes of several couples arguing with each other, while Tina sang the song as relationship advice. To date, she has sold over sixty million copies of her albums, singles, and CDs around the world.

Meanwhile, in her personal life, Tina is very happy with her relationship with Erwin. "It's wonderful, yes. It was the first, actually, man I have lived with after my separation. It was—yes, it's been—it's a very good relationship. Not like any that I have ever had." But does she feel that she wants or needs to get married? The answer is a definite negative. "It's good like it is," she smiles (16).

One of the things that she is slightly at odds with in her past was her overtly sexual image in the late 1960s and early 1970s. As she explains it, "The raunchy, the wild, sexy—it was uncomplimentary. But I understood it. I still see photographs, and my stance and my body form is very much like that. I have to stand like that to hit high notes, and high-heeled shoes will give you a certain body form. So I never liked [being viewed that way], but I thought, 'Well, that's what you've done, Tina. I mean, you have stood there with crotch open, ripped at the seams'" (7).

According to her, "It was only after I started chanting that I realized, 'Well, that's what you've put out there. That's what people see. They have no way of knowing anything else.' So that's what I accepted. As soon as I got around to accepting it, that's when it all started to change—where the knowledge of who and how I am became public and people accepted me differently" (7).

In an event-filled life, Tina finds that she has very few things that she would go back and change. However, she admits, "I regret not having had more time with my kids when they were growing up" (47).

One of the biggest misconceptions that Tina became aware of was the fact that her public image, as this wild rock & roll entity, was believed to be what she was like in real life. Since she was such a hugely popular star, and because of the controversy that *I, Tina* and *What's Love Got to Do With It?* caused, the public was curious to find out what her personal life was really like. Tina explained, "What got me here was from the life that I live, that I went public with. Before it was raunchy Tina, legs open, her red lips, her long hair. Wild! They just thought that I was just another of those raunchy singers, 'cause no one knew the other side. Only people very close to me knew. I've always been very spiritual, but my image—in terms of my work—was very far from that. And then when the book came out, and [TV news show] *60 Minutes* filmed me chanting and being into meditation, everybody went, 'What?' Everyone started to take a different view" (7).

In fact, she claims there is not a single sequin in her own personal closet. "I'm not that person. I don't even wear colors. My work is noisy, but my life is quiet. I need nature and solitude—they nurture me. My idea of a vacation is reading a book on the terrace while my boyfriend cooks us dinner" (41).

In 1999, Ike Turner published his own autobiography with writer Nigel Cawthorne, entitled *Takin' Back My Name*. Instead of publicly apologizing to Tina for his treatment of her, he took the stance that she should share the blame. "If I beat Tina every day, if I did what they say I did, if I fought her every day and she stayed there for eighteen years and she took it, it's as much her fault as it is mine," he defiantly proclaimed (17). He also seems amazed that the stars he once appeared on stage with, like The Rolling Stones, won't even acknowledge his existence. He is astounded that they could have sided with Tina. In 2001, Ike Turner recorded an album called *Now and Then*, which reprised his hit "Rocket 88." It received great reviews, and was nominated for a Grammy Award under the category Best Traditional Blues Recording, but failed to win. However, if Tina has worked through all of her "karma," clearly Ike has never dealt with any of his.

Tina is finally able to clearly look back at her years with Ike and see them for what they were. "I was a victim," she admits. "I don't dwell on it. I was hurt. I'm not proud of being hurt; I don't need sympathy for it. Really, I'm very forgiving. I'm very analytical. I'm very patient. My endurance is very good. I learned a lot being there with that very sick man" (5).

She is not one to dwell on her problems or her past. According to her, "I don't really have any bad times. It looked like bad times from the orthodox way of thinking, but the times without a record have been great for me" (32).

Explaining her spiritual beliefs, she says, "I'm a Buddhist-Baptist. My training is Baptist. And I can still relate to the Ten Commandments and to the Ten Worlds. It's all very close, as long as you contact the subconscious mind. That's where the coin of the Almighty is" (5).

Tina would rather look forward than to look back. She loves astrology, reading about Ancient Egypt, and fortune tellers. "Psychics are my drug," she admits. "It is like looking into the past and seeing a wonderful movie of your life that can guide you. My real ultimate goal in life is to open that third eye" (30).

She feels that it is everyone's personal quest to work toward bettering themselves. "It's a strong belief that we cause an effect," she says. "The cause you make this lifetime could be the effect of a better life the next lifetime. It speaks of chanting this lifetime can help your life to be better the next time, because now you're clearing up, you're making your life better, you're making better causes this lifetime time. So then the next lifetime it will be better, and gets better and better" (16).

Ms. Turner has very definite ideas about the things she has in her life. With regard to her striking fashion sense and her ability to always look absolutely fabulous, she says, "I am vain. When I look in the mirror, I want to look good to myself" (40).

With a catalog of hits like hers, what is Tina's favorite of her own songs? She claims it's "The Best." She is also very fond of the video for the song. In the context of the video, she is seen prancing around in the night on the dry, cracked soil of the desert. Shots of her long legs dancing to the song are juxtapositioned with shots of an equally sleek prize race horse. Finally, Tina is seen on horseback—riding this magnificent animal. Of the song's success, she explains, "It's very special because at the time when I got it, no one believed in it but me. I organized riding the horse. It was really a struggle with Roger, my manager, and the record company. And they said, 'What are you going to do with the horse?' It was a freedom I felt. I felt just riding and that music in the back, and I felt it was would be great for sport, and it ended up in many different countries for sport. I mean—my dream came true with that particular song" (16).

She had worked hard to get her house in France together, now it was time to enjoy it. Tina is so fond of the home that she has named it "Anna Fleur." She explains, "I furnished my homes. I got myself organized, so I'm not moving anymore. I've gotten to the stage where I don't want to own a lot in my life. And my families are organized in their places. The house that I own is in the south of France, and the house that I've leased for many years is in Switzerland, but they're all decorated, and I don't want to move anywhere else, and I look forward to no more workers and no more decorators" (45).

Tina is perfectly at home in Europe. "If I'm in America for work," she says, "I find myself hankering to return. I may be an American in a foreign country, but I am very happy, very comfortable, and very contented here. Europe offers me security. It is a place where I have found more success, more appreciation, and that makes me feel comfortable. And of course I am fortunate to have two lovely homes here and this is where my relationship is based" (48).

One of the most opulent features of Tina's house in Nice is the Greek amphitheater she had constructed in the backyard. She has hosted some grand parties in this sumptuous setting. The house also has a kitchen with every convenience. She says, "Nowadays, I find extravagant cooking for large groups of people less and less interesting and the preparation involved too much work. Erwin is a very good cook and he does a lot of it. In general, we eat pasta galore, a lot of Thai food, chicken, prawns, and loads of salads" (48).

One of her favorite things to do is to sit on her patio in Nice and watch rain storms over the Mediterranean. "I know this sounds loony, but this come from my stomach, this love of looking at that type of thing," she laughs (8).

Tina is not only loved by her fans and the general public, but she is also one of the most admired and revered celebrities around—according to her peers. "River Deep-Mountain High" producer Phil Spector claims, "She's the closest thing to a gem—a diamond—I've ever seen. She has the roughness, the rawness, she has the beauty. She shines—she's bright, and most of all, she's priceless. She is just a gem of a person. Always has been. Always will be. Did not receive the recognition due her until much too late in life. But it is certainly due her in every extent one can possibly have managed. She meant everything, she can do anything, she was like the perfect instrument" (21).

According to Ann-Margret, "She's a quadruple threat. She sings, she dances, she acts, she writes music. I mean she does everything! I think she's one of the most talented people in this world of entertainment. She can do anything." Al Green glows, "I think Tina Turner is a legend, a personification of a survivor. Tina Turner—unforgettable!" Cher claims, "Ten! I mean you know she's great. I mean, it's like there's only one Tina Turner." David Bowie extols, "She is great! People go see her for what she represents. She is a phoenix that has risen from the ashes. She has been through far worse than any of us and has been able to survive it. It is the element of resoluteness and discipline that people respect. I think she has an enormous amount of dignity." Bryan Adams says, "She's just a rocker, man. She's just a rock & roll chick, and she loves rock and I think that's what drives her." And, Elton John insists she is "the first real woman rock & roll singer!" (21).

What's next for Tina? That's what everyone wants to know. She may have retired from huge arena tours, but a talent as vast as hers cannot rest for long. Whatever new incarnation she chooses to appear in can only be attention-getting, dramatic, and enthusiastically received. More great music is assuredly in the cards for her.

In August of 2003 it was announced that Tina would return to the big screen in a new film called *The Goddess,* to be produced by Ismail Merchant and James Ivory for their famed Merchant Ivory company. She is slated to play the role of Kali. Explains Ivory, Kali is "one of the main Hindu goddesses, sort of a recycler of souls, a destroyer as well as a creator, who wears a necklace of men's skulls" (49). The role will reportedly find the goddess-like Turner singing and dancing while riding on the back of a tiger. It sounds tailor-made for the ageless Tina!

Looking at her life so far, Tina feels that it has been one long learning process that has only made her stronger in the transition. "I am happy that I'm not like anybody else," she proclaims. "Because I really do believe that if I was different I might not be where I am today. If you asked me if I ever stood up for anything—yeah, I stood up for my life" (5).

Tina Turner is a rare entity in the world of show business. She is a unique singer, a talented actress, an inspiration, a legend, a diva, and one of the most beloved women in rock & roll. The songs she has created have a life all of their own. One cannot think of "River Deep-Mountain High," "Proud Mary," "Let's Stay Together," "Private Dancer," "What's Love Got to Do With It," or "The Best," and not think instantly of Tina. Her short skirts, her incredible legs, her wild mane of hair, her unbridled raw energy, and her incredible grace—when all else is said and done, one fact remains: Tina Turner *is* simply the best.

Quote Sources

(1) www.TinaTurner.com (accessed May 2003).

(2) Maureen Orth, "Tina: It Took a Grown-Up Woman to Save Rock and Roll . . . and Soul to Save Herself," *Vogue* (May 1985).

(3) "Tina Turner: Interview with *US Magazine*," *US* (March 2000).

(4) Tina Turner with Kurt Loder, *I, Tina* (New York: William Morrow & Company, 1986).

(5) Maureen Orth, "The Lady Has Legs!" *Vanity Fair* (July 1993).

(6) Kurt Loder, "Tina Turner: She's Got Legs! / "Soul Survivor," *Rolling Stone* (October 11, 1984).

(7) Gerri Hershey, "Tina Turner" (as part of the "Women of Rock" cover story), *Rolling Stone* (November 13, 1997).

(8) Gerri Hirshey, "Woman Warrior at 53, the Amazing Tina Turner Just Keeps on Rollin'," *Gentleman's Quarterly* (June 1993).

(9) Lynn Norment, "Tina Turner Sizzling at 45/What's Age Got to Do with It?" *Ebony* (May 1985).

(10) Joe Smith, ed. Mitchell Fink, *Off the Record* (New York: Warner Books, 1988).

(11) David Wallace, "Tina Turner: A Success Story You Won't Forget," *McCall's* (August 1985).

(12) Interview with Tina Turner, *The Oprah Winfrey Show* (February 21, 1997).

(13) Dominick A. Miserandino, "Ike Turner: Rock and Roll Hall of Famer," www.CelebrityCafe.com (2000).

(14) Margaret Moser, "Spotlight: Ike Turner," *The Austin Chronicle* (March 16, 2001).

(15) Rod Harmon, "Ike Turner's Star Is Rising, Despite Scars of Infamy," *The Miami Herald* (April 24, 2002).

(16) Interview with Tina Turner, *Larry King* (February 21, 1997).

(17) Ike Turner, with Nigel Cawthorne, *Takin' Back My Name* (London: Virgin Books, 1999).

(18) Debby Miller, "Tina Turner Returns to the Top of the Charts," *Rolling Stone* (August 30, 1984).

(19) *The Best of Tina Turner: Celebrate!* Image Entertainment DVD (2000).

(20) Ike & Tina Turner / *River Deep-Mountain High*, album liner notes of the 1990s German CD reissue, A&M Records, by Tony Hall.

Tina Turner: The Collected Recordings—Sixties to Nineties, 1994, Capitol EMI Records, eighty-four-page booklet written by Paul Grien.

(22) "Letter From The Editor," by Jann S. Wenner, quoting a performance review from the November 25, 1967 issue of *Rolling Stone*, "Tina Turner" by Jann S. Wenner, *Rolling Stone* (November 13, 1997).

(23) Ben Fong-Torres, "Ike & Tina Turner," *Rolling Stone* (October 14, 1971).

(24) Ann-Margret, with Todd Gold, *Ann-Margret My Story* (New York: G.P. Putnam's Sons, 1994).

(25) *Time*, 1975, as quoted on the DVD packaging of the film *Tommy*.

(26) Leonard Maltin, *TV Movies 1985–86* (New York: Signet/New American Library Books, 1984).

(27) *Jet*, January 9, 1984, "At 45, Sexy Tina Turner Still Makes London Men 'Break Out in a Sweat.'"

(28) Cathleen McGuigan, "The Second Coming of Tina," *Newsweek* (September 10, 1984).

(29) Brian D. Johnson, "The Comeback Queen of Rock & Roll," *McLean's* (July 22, 1985).

(30) Carl Arrington, "Mad Max's Tina Turner/Thunder Dame," *People* (July 15, 1985).

(31) "An Exclusive Visit at Home with Tina Turner,"*Life* (August 1985).

(32) David Van Biema, "Tina Turner," *People* (December 21–31, 1984).

(33) *The Grammy Awards*, 1985, CBS-TV.

(34) Davitt Sigerson, "Tina Repeats a Winning Formula," *Rolling Stone* (November 6, 1986).

(35) *Two Rooms*, liner notes (Polydor Records, 1991).

(36) *What's Love Got to Do With It?* (Original Soundtrack), liner notes (Virgin Records 1993).

(37) Roger Ebert review of *What's Love Got to Do With It?*, *Chicago Sun Times* (June 11, 1993).

(38) Rita Kempley review of *What's Love Got to Do With It?*, *Washington Post* (June 11, 1993).

(39) Sarah Mower, "Private Tina," *Harper's Bazaar* (December 1996).

(40) "50 Most Beautiful People: Tina Turner,"*People* (May 8, 2000).

(41) Judith Truman, "*Architectural Digest* Visits Tina Turner," *Architectural Digest* (March 2000).

(42) Galina Espinoza and Fannie Weinstein, "Stage Flight," *People* (December 4, 2000).

(43) Jane Stevenson, "Tina Turns It On: Upbeat, Edgy and a Beat You Can Groove To," *Toronto Sun* (January 30, 2000).

(44) Paul Elliott review of *Twenty Four Seven* album, *Q Magazine*.

(45) Mim Udovitch, "Tina Turner: The Hardest Working Legs in Showbiz Finally Get a Rest," *Rolling Stone* (December 14–21, 2000).

(46) "Still Rollin': Turner Leads Concert Acts with $80 Mil." *Hollywood Reporter* (December 29–31, 2000).

(47) "Proust Questionnaire: Tina Turner,"*Vanity Fair* (Februrary 2000). "Tina @ Home: A Visit at Her Mansion in the Mediterranean," *Hello!* (November 1999).

(48) Gregory Kirschling and William Keck, "The Dead Report," *Entertainment Weekly* (August 15, 2003).

Bibliography

BOOKS

Ann-Margret with Todd Gold. *Ann-Margret: My Story*. New York: G.P. Putnam's Sons, 1994.

Maltin, Leonard. *TV Movies 1985–86*. New York: Signet/New American Library Books, 1984.

McAleer, Dave. *The Book of Hit Singles*. San Francisco: Miller Freeman Books, 1999.

Shore, Michael, with Dick Clark. *The History of American Bandstand*. New York: Ballantine Books, 1985.

Smith, Joe, edited by Mitchell Fink. *Off the Record*. New York: Warner Books, 1988.

Terrace, Vincent. *Encyclopedia of Television Series, Pilots and Specials 1974–1984*. New York: Zeotrophe Books, 1985.

Turner, Ike, with Nigel Cawthorne. *Takin' Back My Name*. London: Virgin Books, 1999.

Turner, Tina, with Kurt Loder. *I, Tina*. New York: William Morrow & Company, 1986.

Whitburn, Joel. *The Billobard Book of Top 40 Albums*. Menomonee Falls, Wisc.: Record Research Inc., 1995.

———. *Top 10 Charts*. Menomonee Falls, Wisc.: Record Research Inc., 2001.

———. *Top Pop 1955–1982*. Menomonee Falls, Wisc.: Record Research Inc., 1983.

————. *Top Pop Albums 1955–1985*, Menomonee Falls, Wisc.: Record Research Inc., 1985.

MAGAZINE ARTICLES

Ali, Loraine. "Ike's Peak." *Gentleman's Quarterly*, June 2001.

Arrington, Carl. "Tina Turner: *US* Interview." *US*, November 13, 1989.

Dougherty, Steve, and Lorenzo Benet. "Soul Star On Ice: Divorced by Tina, Ike Turner Pays for His Romance with Cocaine in a California Prison." *People*, September 30, 1990.

Loder, Kurt. "The Heroes of Thunderdome." *Rolling Stone*, August 29, 1985.

McGuigan, Cathleen, and Tony Clifton. "Rock's New Women/The Sexy Godmother of Rock." *Newsweek*, March 4, 1985.

Newman, Judith. "Tina's Turn." *Target the Family*, December 2000.

Windeler, Robert. "Tina Turner, the New Acid Queen, Turns Down the Voltage for a Solo Career Sans Ike." *People*, May 5, 1975.

Discography

Author's Note: Having written more than forty books on music stars, I have never seen such a complicated discography as this one. The solo Tina Turner material (starting with *Tina Turner Turns the Country On*) was very simple to list and pretty straightforward. However, the Ike & Tina discography was quite a jumble. Ike had the habit of changing record labels several times during the duo's recording career in the 1960s and 1970s. Originally signed to Sue Records in 1960, Ike would accept overlapping advances from other labels, which yielded releases on Warner Brothers, Blue Thumb, Liberty, Teena, Kent, Tangerine, Modern, Loma, Minit, and Fantasy Records. For instance, in 1964, both Warner Brothers and Kent Records released albums entitled *The Ike & Tina Turner Show Live*, which were completely different material. Also, after Tina Turner left Ike in 1976, Ike continued to sell and release "Ike & Tina" songs from previously recorded sessions. In addition, during their time together, several songs were rerecorded several times by Ike & Tina. For instance, there are at least five different versions of "Fool in Love" that I can find—none of which are the same recording. Likewise, there is the original Phil Spector–produced version of "River Deep-Mountain High" and a clearly different version of the song later produced by Ike Turner. Since few of the original Ike & Tina albums are available—on CD or vinyl—in their original format, what does exist are dozens of compilation albums culled from all of these labels. The most accurate source seemed to come from Ike's autobiography, which no less than seven different people worked on compiling. There were also several websites that were helpful in rounding out this exhaustive list of Tina's history on record.

IKE & TINA TURNER: ALBUMS

- *The Soul of Ike and Tina Turner* (Sue Records / 1961)
  PRODUCER: IKE TURNER
  I'm Jealous
  I Idolize You
  If
  Letter from Tina
  You Can't Love Two
  I Had a Notion
  A Fool in Love
  Sleepless
  Chances Are
  You Can't Blame Me
  You're My Baby
  The Way You Love Me

- *Dynamite* (Sue Records / 1963)
  PRODUCER: IKE TURNER
  You Should'a Treated Me Right
  It's Gonna Work Out Fine
  A Fool in Love
  Poor Fool
  I Idolize You
  Tra la la la La
  Sleepless
  I'm Jealous
  Won't You Forgive Me
  The Way You Love Me
  I Dig You
  Letter from Tina

- *Don't Play Me Cheap* (Sue Records / 1963)
  PRODUCER: IKE TURNER
  Wake Up
  I Made a Promise Up Above

Desire
Those Ways
Mamma Tell Him
Pretend
Don't Play Me Cheap
The Real Me
Forever Mine
No Amending
Love Letters
My Everything to Me

■ *It's Gonna Work Out Fine* (Sue Records / 1963)
PRODUCER: IKE TURNER
Gonna Find Me a Substitute
Mojo Queen
Kinda' Strange
Why Should I
Tinaroo
It's Gonna Work Out Fine
I'm Gonna Cut You Loose
Poor Fool
I'm Fallin' in Love
Foolish
This Man's Crazy
Good Good Lovin'

■ *Get It* (Cenco Records / 1964)
also released as *Her Man, His Woman* (Capitol Records / 1969)
PRODUCER: IKE TURNER
Get It
You Weren't Ready
I Believe
I Can't Believe
My Babe
Strange
That's Alright
Rooster
Five Long Years
Things I Used to Do

- *The Ike and Tina Turner Revue, Live* (Kent Records / 1964)
  PRODUCER: IKE TURNER
  Please, Please, Please
  Feelin' So Good
  The Love of My Man
  Think
  Drown in My Own Tears
  I Love the Way You Love
  Your Precious Love
  All in My Mind
  I Can't Believe What You Say

- *The Ike and Tina Turner Show, Live, Volume 2* (LOMA Records / 1964)
  PRODUCER: IKE TURNER
  You're No Good
  It's All Over
  All I Can Do Is Cry
  A Fool for You
  Shake a Tail Feather
  Ooh-Poo-Pah-Doo
  Keep On a Pushin'
  You Must Believe in Me
  Early in the Morning

- *The Ike and Tina Turner Show, Live* (Warner Brothers Records / 1965)
  [No. 126 / *Billboard*]
  PRODUCER: IKE TURNER
  Finger Poppin'
  Down in the Valley
  Good Times
  You Are My Sunshine
  Havin' a Good Time
  Twist and Shout
  I Know (You Don't Want Me No More)
  Tight Pants
  My Man, He's a Lovin' Man

I Can't Stop Loving You
To Tell the Truth

- *Ike & Tina Turner Greatest Hits* (Sue Records / 1965)
  PRODUCER: IKE TURNER
  A Fool in Love
  Poor Fool
  Tra la la la La
  I'm Jealous
  Mojo Queen
  Sleepless
  I'm Jealous
  Won't You Forgive
  Way You Love Me
  I Dig You
  Letter from Tina

- *River Deep-Mountain High* (A&M Records / 1966)
  PRODUCER: PHIL SPECTOR +
  PRODUCER: IKE TURNER
  River Deep-Mountain High +
  I Idolize You
  A Love Like Yours (Don't Come Knocking) +
  A Fool in Love
  Make 'Em Wait
  Hold on Baby +
  I'll Never Need More Than This +
  Save the Last Dance for Me +
  Oh Baby! +
  Every Day I Have to Cry +
  Such a Fool for You
  It's Gonna Work Out Fine

- *The Soul of Ike & Tina Turner* (Kent Records / 1966)
  PRODUCER: IKE TURNER
  Am I a Fool in Love
  Chicken Shack
  If I Can't Be First
  Goodbye, So Long

Hurt Is All You Gave Me
I Don't Need
Gonna Have Fun
I Wish My Dream Would Come True
Flee Flee Fla
It's Crazy Baby
Something Came Over Me
Don't Blame It on Me

- *Festival of Live Performances* (Kent Records / 1967)
  PRODUCER: IKE TURNER
  A Fool in Love
  He's Mine
  Stop the Wedding
  Please Please Please
  If I Can't Be the First
  My Man
  You Don't Love Me No More
  It's Gonna Work Out Fine
  If I Only Had You
  I Can't Stop Loving You
  Treat Me Right

- *So Fine* (Pompeii Records / 1968)
  PRODUCER: IKE TURNER
  My Babe
  I Better Get Ta Steppin'
  Shake a Tail Feather
  We Need An Understanding
  You're So Fine
  Here's Your Heart
  Please Love Me
  Freedom Sound
  Crazy 'Bout You Baby

- *Ike & Tina Turner* (London Records / 1968)
  PRODUCER: IKE TURNER
  River Deep-Mountain High
  I Idolize You

A Love Like Yours
A Fool in Love
Make 'Em Wait
Hold On Baby
Poor Fool
I'm Jealous
Save the Last Dance for Me
Oh Baby!
Every Day I Have to Cry
A Fool for a Fool
It's Gonna Work Out Fine
You're So Fine
Mojo Queen
Good Good Lovin'

- *Cussin', Cryin' and Carryin' On* (Pompeii Records / 1969)
  PRODUCER: IKE TURNER
  Black Angel
  Getting Nasty
  It Sho' Ain't Me
  A Fool in Love
  Nothing You Can Do, Boy
  I Better Get Ta Steppin'
  Shake a Tail Feather
  We Need an Understanding
  You're So Fine
  Too Hot to Hold
  I'm Fed Up
  You Got What You Wanted
  Betcha Can't Kiss Me (Just One Time)
  Cussin', Cryin' and Carryin' On
  Ain't Nobody's Business
  Funky Mule
  Thinking Black
  Black Beauty
  Ghetto Funk
  Black's Alley

- *Get It Together* (Pompeii Records / 1969)
  PRODUCER: IKE TURNER
  Betcha Can't Kiss Me (Just One Time)
  T'aint Nobody's Business
  Too Hot to Hold
  You Got What You Wanted
  I'm Fed Up
  Beauty's Just Skin Deep
  What You Got
  Cussin', Cryin', and Carryin' On
  Make 'Em Wait
  Funky Mule
  Freedom Sound
  Poor Little Fool
  So Blue Over You

- *Get It, Get It* (Cenco Records / 1969)
  PRODUCER: IKE TURNER
  Get It, Get It
  I Believe
  I Can't Believe (What You Say)
  My Babe
  Strange
  You Weren't Ready
  That's Right
  Rooster
  Five Long Years
  Things That I Used to Do

- *Her Man, His Woman* (Capitol Records / 1969)
  PRODUCER: IKE TURNER
  Get It, Get It
  I Believe
  I Can't Believe (What You Say)
  My Babe
  Strange
  You Weren't Ready
  That's Right
  Rooster

Five Long Years
Things That I Used to Do

■ *Outta Season* (Blue Thumb Records / 1969)
  [No. 91 / *Billboard*]
  PRODUCER: IKE TURNER
  I've Been Loving You Too Long
  Grumbling
  Crazy 'Bout You Baby
  Reconsider Baby
  Mean Old World
  Honest I Do
  Three O'Clock in the Morning
  Five Long Years
  Dust My Broom
  I Am a Motherless Child
  Please Love Me
  My Babe
  Rock Me Baby

■ *The Hunter* (Blue Thumb Records / 1969)
  [No. 176 / *Billboard*]
  PRODUCER: IKE TURNER
  The Hunter
  I Know
  Bold Soul Sister
  You Don't Love Me (Yes I Know)
  You Got Me Running
  I Smell Trouble
  The Things I Used to Do
  Early in the Morning
  You're Still My Baby

■ *Ike & Tina Turner & The Ikettes in Person* (Minit Records / 1969)
  [No. 142 / *Billboard*]
  PRODUCER: IKE TURNER
  Everyday People (by the Ikettes)
  Gimme Some Lovin'
  Sweet Soul Music

Son of a Preacher Man
I Heard It through the Grapevine
Respect
Medley: There Was a Time / African Boo's (by the Ikettes)
Funky Street / A Fool in Love (by the Ikettes)
MEDLEY: The Summit / All I Could Do Was Cry / Please Please
    Please / Baby I Love You Goodbye, So Long

■ *Come Together* (Liberty Records / 1970)
    [No. 130 / *Billboard*]
    PRODUCER: IKE TURNER
    It Ain't Right (Lovin' to Be Lovin')
    Too Much Woman (for a Henpecked Man)
    Unlucky Creature
    Young and Dumb
    Honky Tonk Women
    Come Together
    Why Can't We Be Happy
    Contact High
    Keep on Walkin' (Don't Look Back)
    I Want to Take You Higher
    Evil Man
    Doin' It

■ *Workin' Together* (Liberty Records / 1971)
    [No. 25 / *Billboard*]
    PRODUCER: IKE TURNER
    Workin' Together
    (As Long as I Can) Get You When I Want You
    Get Back
    The Way You Love Me
    You Can Have It
    Game of Love
    Funkier Than a Mosquita's Tweeter
    Ooh Poo Pah Doo
    Proud Mary
    Goodbye, So Long
    Let It Be

- *Live In Paris* (Liberty Records / 1971)
  PRODUCER: IKE TURNER
  Grumbling (Instrumental)
  You Got Me Hummin' (The Ikettes)
  Every Day People (The Ikettes)
  Shake a Tail Feather (The Ikettes)
  Gimme Some Loving
  Sweet Soul Music
  Son of a Preacher Man
  Come Together
  Proud Mary
  A Love Like Yours
  I Smell Trouble
  Respect
  Honky Tonk Women
  I've Been Loving You Too Long
  I Want to Take You Higher
  Land of 1,000 Dances

- *Live at Carnegie Hall: What You Hear Is What You Get* (United
  Artists Records / 1971)
  [No. 25 / *Billboard*]
  ["Gold" Record]
  PRODUCER: IKE TURNER
  Introductions (by DJ Frankie Crocker and MC Eddie Burkes)
  Piece of My Heart (the Ikettes)
  Everyday People (The Ikettes)
  Introduction to Tina (by MC Eddie Burkes)
  Doin' the Tina Turner
  Sweet Soul Music
  Ooh Poo Pah Doo
  Honky Tonk Women
  A Love Like Yours (Don't Come Knockin' Every Day)
  Proud Mary
  Proud Mary (Encore version)
  I Smell Trouble
  Ike's Tuner
  I Want to Take You Higher

I've Been Loving You Too Long
Respect

- *'Nuff Said* (United Artists Records / 1972)
  [No. 108 / *Billboard*]
  PRODUCER: IKE TURNER
  I Love What You Do to Me
  Baby What You Want Me to Do
  Sweet Frustrations
  What You Don't See (Is Better Yet)
  'Nuff Said
  Tell the Truth
  Pick Me Up
  Moving into Hip Style—A Trip Child
  I Love Baby
  Can't You Hear Me Calling
  'Nuff Said, Pt. 2
  River Deep-Mountain High

- *Feel Good* (United Artists Records / 1972)
  [No. 160 / *Billboard*]
  PRODUCER: IKE TURNER
  Feel Good
  Chopper
  Kay Got Laid (Joe Got Paid)
  I Like It
  If You Can Hully Gully (I Can Hully Gully Too)
  Black Coffee
  She Came in through the Bathroom Window
  If I Knew Then What I Know Now
  You Better Think of Something
  Bolic

- *Let Me Touch Your Mind* (United Artists Records / 1973)
  PRODUCER: IKE TURNER
  Let Me Touch Your Mind
  Annie Had a Baby
  Don't Believe in Her
  I Had a Notion

Popcorn
Early One Morning
Help Him
Up on the Roof
Born Free
Heaven Help Us All

■ *Ike & Tina Turner's Greatest Hits* (United Artists Records / 1973)
  PRODUCER: IKE TURNER
  Proud Mary
  Come Together
  Ooh Poo Pah Doo
  Nutbush City Limits
  Sexy Ida, Pt. 2
  I Want to Take You Higher
  It's Gonna Work Out Fine
  A Fool in Love
  Baby Get It On
  I've Been Loving You Too Long

■ *Live in the World of Ike and Tina Turner* (United Artists Records / 1973)
  PRODUCER: IKE TURNER
  Theme from Shaft
  I Gotcha
  She Came in through the Bathroom Window
  You're Still My Baby
  Don't Fight It
  Annie Had a Baby
  With a Little Help from My Friends
  Get Back
  Games People Play
  Honky Tonk Women
  If You Love Me Like You Say
  I Can't Turn You Loose
  I Wish It Would Rain
  Just One More Day
  Stand by Me
  Dust My Broom

River Deep-Mountain High
Let Me Touch Your Mind
Chopper
1-2-3

■ *Nutbush City Limits* (United Artists Records / 1973)
[No. 163 / *Billboard*]
PRODUCER: IKE TURNER
Nutbush City Limits
Make Me Over
Drift Away
That's My Purpose
Fancy Annie
River Deep-Mountain High
Get It Out of Your Mind
Daily Bread
You Are My Sunshine
Club Manhattan

■ *The Best of Ike & Tina Turner* (Blue Thumb Records / 1973)
PRODUCER: IKE TURNER
Bold Soul Sister
I've Been Loving You Too Long
The Hunter
I Know (You Don't Love Me No More)
I Am a Motherless Child
I Smell Trouble
Crazy 'Bout You Baby
Rock Me Baby
Early in the Morning
You're Still My Baby
You Got Me Running
Dust My Broom

■ *The Gospel According to Ike & Tina Turner* (United Artists Records
/ 1974)
PRODUCER: IKE TURNER
Farther Along
Walk with Me (I Need You Lord to Be My Friend)

Glory, Glory
Just a Closer Walk with Thee
What a Friend We Have in Jesus
Amazing Grace
Take My Hand Precious Lord
Nearer the Cross
Our Lord Will Make a Way
When the Saints Go Marching In

■ *Sweet Rhode Island Red* (United Artists Records / 1974)
PRODUCER: IKE TURNER
Let Me Be There
Living for the City
I Know
Mississippi Rolling Stone
Sugar Hill
Sweet Rhode Island Red
Ready for You Baby
Smooth Out the Wrinkles
Doozie
Higher Ground

■ *Delilah's Power* (United Artists Records / 1977)
PRODUCER: IKE TURNER
Delilah's Power
Never Been to Spain
Unhappy Birthday
(You've Got To) Put Something Into It
Nothing Comes to You When You're Asleep But a Dream
Stormy Weather (Keeps Rainin' All the Time)
Sugar, Sugar
Too Much for One Woman
Trying to Find My Mind
Pick Me Up (Take Me Where Your Home Is)
Too Many Women
I Want Take You Higher

- *Soul Sellers* (United Artists Records / 1979)
  PRODUCER: IKE TURNER
  Nutbush City Limits
  I Want to Take You Higher
  It's Gonna Work Out Fine
  Workin' Together
  Honky Tonk Women
  Baby—Get It On
  Come Together
  I've Been Loving You Too Long
  Sexy Ida, Pt. 2
  Proud Mary
  Crazy 'Bout You Baby
  Sweet Rhode Island Red
  A Fool in Love
  Ooh Poo Pah Doo
  I Idolize You
  Let It Be
  Get Back
  River Deep-Mountain High

- *Mississippi Rolling Stone* (Spartan Records / 1979)
  PRODUCER: IKE TURNER
  Mississippi Rolling Stone
  Living for the City
  Golden Empire
  I'm Looking for My Mind
  Shake a Hand
  Bootsie Whitelaw
  Too Much for One Woman
  I Know (You Don't Love Me No More)
  Rockin' and Rollin'
  Never Been to Spain
  Sugar Sugar
  Push
  Raise Your Hand
  Tina's Prayer
  Chicken
  If You Want It

Let's Get It On
You're Up to Something
You're Still My Baby
Jesus

- *The Edge* (Fantasy Records / 1980)
  PRODUCER: IKE TURNER
  Shame Shame Shame
  Lean on Me
  Philadelphia Freedom
  Use Me
  Only Women Bleed
  Party Vibes
  Lum Dum
  No Other Woman
  I Can't Believe
  I Don't Want Nobody

IKE & TINA TURNER: COMPILATION ALBUMS

Author's Note: Since 1980, there have been countless repackaged albums of the above music, and more. Some of the most notable packages include albums on the following list, including U.S., British, and other foreign releases. The majority of these titles were taken from www.tinaturner.com.

Star Collection
16 Great Performances
Soul Sellers
Juke Box Giants
Too Hot to Hold
Rock Me Baby
Sixteen Peaches
Sue Sessions
Nice and Rough
The Soul of Ike and Tina
River Deep-Mountain High: 24 Soul Hits
Tough Enough
Souled from the Vaults

Get Back
Working Together the Best of the Rest
40 Rare Recordings
Tina Turner Favorites
Tina Turner Best Rarities Collection
Goodbye So Long
Tina Turner The Ike and Tina Turner Sessions
Twice as Much
Mississippi Rolling Stone
Movin' On
Ike & Tina Turner Ultimate Collection (four CD set)
Forever Gold
Absolutely the Best
Every Hit Single 1962–1974

IKE & TINA TURNER: SINGLES

A Fool in Love / The Way You Love Me
I Idolize You / Letter from Tina
I'm Jealous / You're My Baby
It's Gonna Work Out Fine / Won't You Forgive Me
Poor Fool / You Can't Blame Me
I Can't Believe What You Say / My Baby Now
Finger Poppin' / Ooh Pop A Doo
Please Please Please / (Am I) A Fool in Love
River Deep-Mountain High / I'll Keep You Happy
Tell Her I'm Not at Home / Finger Poppin'
Anything You Wan't Born With / Beauty Is Just Skin Deep
A Love Like Yours / Hold On Baby
Goodbye So Long / Hurt Is All You Gave Me
Somebody (Somewhere) Needs You / Just to Be with You
I'm Hooked / Dust My Broom
I'll Never Need More Than This / Save the Last Dance for Me
So Fine / So Blue Over You
We Need an Understanding / It Sho' Ain't Me
River Deep-Mountain High / Save the Last Dance for Me
I'm Gonna Do All I Can / You've Got Too Many Ties That Bind
I'll Never Need More Than This / A Love Like Yours
Crazy 'Bout You Baby / I've Been Loving You Too Long

Come Together / Honky Tonk Woman
Make 'Em Wait / Everyday I Have to Cry
The Hunter / Bold Soul Sister
I Want To Take You Higher / Contact High
Proud Mary / Funkier than a Mosquita's Tweeter
River Deep-Mountain High / Oh Baby
Ooh Poo Pah Doo / I Wanna Jump
I'm Your's / Doin' It
Feel Good / Outrageous
Let Me Touch Your Mind / Chopper
River Deep-Mountain High / A Love Like Yours / Save the Last
    Dance for Me
Born Free / Work on Me
Nutbush City Limits / Help Him
Fancy Annie / River Deep-Mountain High
Sweet Rhode Island Red / Get It Out of Your Mind
Sexy Ida, Pt. 1 / Sexy Ida, Pt. 2
Baby Get It On / Baby Get It On (disco version)
Delila's Power / That's My Purpose

TINA TURNER: SOLO ALBUMS

- *Tina Turns the Country On!* (United Artists Records / 1974)
  PRODUCER: TOM THACKER
  Bayou Song
  Help Me Make It through the Night
  Tonight I'll Be Staying Here with You
  If You Love Me (Let Me Know)
  He Belongs to Me
  Don't Talk Now
  Long Long Time
  I'm Moving On
  There'll Always Be Music
  The Love That Lights Our Way

- *Acid Queen* (United Artists Records / 1975)
  [No. 158 / *Billboard*]
  Note: 1975—original version; 1991—remastered extended version

CD on Razor and Tie Records. The additional tracks that appear
on this version of compact disk *only* are denoted with an "+".
PRODUCERS: DENNY DIANTE AND SPENCER PROFFER *
DENNY DIANTE, SPENCER PROFFER, AND IKE TURNER **
IKE TUNNER ***
Under My Thumb *
Let's Spend the Night Together *
Acid Queen *
I Can See for Miles *
Whole Lotta Love *
Baby—Get It On **
Bootsy Whitelaw **
Pick Me Tonight **
Rockin' and Rollin' **
I Know *** +
Crazy 'Bout You Baby *** +
I've Been Loving You Too Long *** +

■ *Rough* (Liberty Records / 1978)
  PRODUCER: BOB MONACO
  Fruits of the Night
  The Bitch Is Back
  The Woman I'm Supposed to Be
  Viva la Money
  Funny How Time Slips Away
  Earthquake & Hurricane
  Root Toot Undisputable Rock & Roller
  Fire Down Below
  Sometimes When We Touch
  A Woman in a Man's World
  Night Time Is the Right Time

■ *Love Explosion* (Liberty Records / 1979)
  PRODUCER: ALEC R. CONSTANDINOS
  Love Explosion
  A Fool for Your Love
  Sunset on Sunset
  Music Keeps Me Dancin'

I See Home
Backstabbers
Just a Little Lovin' (Early in the Morning)
You Get What I'm Gonna Get
On the Radio

- *Private Dancer* (Capitol Records / 1984)
  [No. 3 / *Billboard* U.S. and No. 45 U.K.]
  Note: 1984—original version; 2000—remastered extended version
  CD. The additional tracks that appear on this version of compact
  disk ONLY are denoted with an "+".
  PRODUCERS: RUPERT HINE *
  TERRY BRITTEN **
  [JOHN] CARTER ***
  MARTYN WARE AND GREG WALSH ****
  JOE SAMPLE, WILTON FELDER, AND
        NDUGU CHANCLER *****
  I Might Have Been Queen *
  What's Love Got to Do With It **
  Show Some Respect **
  I Can't Stand the Rain **
  Private Dancer ***
  Let's Stay Together ****
  Better Be Good to Me *
  Steel Claw ***
  Help! ***** (originally on Europe LP only)
  1984 ****
  I Wrote a Letter +
  Rock & Roll Widow +
  Don't Rush the Good Things +
  When I Was Young +
  What's Love Got to Do With It (Extended Version) ** +
  Better Be Good to Me (Extended Version) * +
  I Can't Stand the Rain (Extended Version) ** +

- *Break Every Rule* (Capitol Records / 1986)
  [No. 4 / *Billboard* U.S. and No. 2 U.K.]
  PRODUCERS: TERRY BRITTEN *
  BRYAN ADAMS AND BOB CLEARMOUNTAIN **
  RUPERT HINE ***

MARK KNOPFLER AND NEIL DORFSMAN ****
Typical Male *
What You Get Is What You See *
Two People *
Till the Right Man Comes Along *
Afterglow *
Girls *
Back Where You Started **
Break Every Rule ***
Overnight Sensation ****
Paradise Is Here ****
I'll Be Thunder ***

■ *Tina Live In Europe* (EMI / Capitol Records / 1988)
  [No. 86 / *Billboard* U.S. and No. 8 U.K.]
  PRODUCER: JOHN HUDSON *
  TERRY BRITTEN **
  Disc 1
  What You Get Is What You See *
  Break Every Rule *
  I Can't Stand the Rain **
  Two People *
  Girls *
  Typical Male *
  Back Where You Started *
  Better Be Good to Me **
  Addicted to Love *
  Private Dancer **
  We Don't Need Another Hero *
  What's Love Got to Do With It *
  Let's Stay Together **
  Show Some Respect **
  Disc 2
  Land of 1,000 Dances *
  In the Midnight Hour *
  634-5789 (Soulsville U.S.A.) (with Robert Cray) *
  Change Is Gonna Come (Robert Cray on guitar) *
  River Deep-Mountain High **
  Tearing Us Apart (with Eric Clapton) *
  Proud Mary *

Help! **
Tonight (with David Bowie) **
Let's Dance (with David Bowie) **
Overnight Sensation *
It's Only Love (with Bryan Adams) **
Nutbush City Limits *
Paradise Is Here *

■ *Foreign Affair* (EMI / Capitol Records / 1989)
    [No. 31 / *Billboard* U.S. and No. 1 U.K.]
    PRODUCER: DAN HARTMAN *
    DAN HARTMAN AND TINA TURNER **
    RUPERT HINE ***
    ROGER DAVIES, GRAHAM LYLE AND
        ALBERT HAMMOND ****
    ROGER DAVIES AND TONY JOE WHITE *****
    Steamy Windows *
    The Best **
    You Know Who (Is Doing You Know What) *
    Undercover Agent for the Blues *
    Look Me in the Heart *
    Be Tender with Me Baby *
    You Can't Stop Me Loving You *
    Ask Me How I Feel **
    Falling Like Rain ***
    I Don't Wanna Lose You ****
    Not Enough Romance *
    Foreign Affair *****

■ *Simply the Best* (Capitol / EMI Records / 1991)
    [No. 113 / *Billboard* U.S. and No. 2 U.K.]
    PRODUCERS: VARIOUS
    The Best
    Better Be Good to Me
    I Can't Stand the Rain
    What's Love Got to Do With It
    I Don't Wanna Lose You
    Nutbush City Limits
    What You Get Is What You See
    Let's Stay Together

River Deep-Mountain High
Steamy Windows
Typical Male
We Don't Need Another Hero (Thunderdome)
Private Dancer
Look Me in the Heart
It Takes Two (with Rod Stewart)
I Want You Near Me
Way of the World
Love Thing

■ *What's Love Got to Do With It* [Original Soundtrack]
(Virgin Records / 1993)
[No. 17 *Billboard* U.S. and No. 1 U.K.]
PRODUCERS: CHRIS LORD-ALGE AND ROGER DAVIES *
CHRIS LORD-ALGE, TINA TURNER, AND ROGER DAVIES **
BRYAN ADAMS AND ROBERT JOHN "MUTT" LANGE ***
RUPERT HINE ****
TERRY BRITTEN *****
I Don't Wanna Fight*
Rock Me Baby**
Disco Inferno**
Why Must We Wait Until Tonight***
Nutbush City Limits**
(Darlin') You Know I Love You**
Proud Mary**
A Fool in Love**
It's Gonna Work Out Fine**
I Might Have Been Queen****
Stay Awhile**
What's Love Got to Do With It *****
Tina's Wish (only in Europe)

■ *Tina Turner: The Collected Works* [Boxed Set]
(EMI / Capitol Records / 1994)
PRODUCERS: VARIOUS
Disc 1
A Fool in Love
It's Gonna Work Out Fine
I Idolize You

Poor Fool
A Letter from Tina
Finer Poppin'
River Deep-Mountain High
Crazy 'Bout You Baby
I've Been Loving You Too Long
Bold Soul Sister
I Wanna Take You Higher
Come Together
Honky Tonk Woman
Proud Mary
Nutbush City Limits
Sexy Ida, Pt. 1
Sexy Ida, Pt. 2
It Ain't Right (Lovin' to Be Lovin')

Disc 2
Acid Queen
Whole Lotta Love
Ball of Confusion (That's What the World Is Today)
Change Is Gonna Come
Johnny and Mary
Games
When I Was Young
Total Control
Let's Pretend We're Married (Live)
It's Only Love (with Bryan Adams)
Don't Turn Around
Legs (Live)
Addicted to Love (Live)
Tearing Us Apart (with Eric Clapton)
It Takes Two (with Rod Stewart)

Disc 3
Let's Stay Together
What's Love Got to Do With It
Better Be Good to Me
Private Dancer
I Can't Stand the Rain
Help!
We Don't Need Another Hero (*Thunderdome*)
Typical Male

What You Get Is What You See
Paradise Is Here
Back Where You Started
The Best
Steamy Windows
Foreign Affair
I Don't Wanna Fight

■ *Wildest Dreams* (Virgin Records / 1996)
 [No. 61 / *Billboard* U.S. and No. 4 U.K.]
 PRODUCERS: TREVOR HORN *
 TERRY BRITTEN **
 PET SHOP BOYS AND CHRIS PORTER ***
 ANDRE LEVIN AND CAMUS MARE CELLI ****
 GARY HUGHES *****
 NELLE HOOPER ******
 Missing You *
 In Your Wildest Dreams (with Barry White) *
 Whatever You Want *
 Do What You Do **
 Thief of Hearts *
 On Silent Wings (with Sting) *
 Something Beautiful Remains **
 Confidential ***
 The Difference between Us****
 All Kinds of People *
 Unfinished Sympathy *****
 Goldeneye ******
 Dancing in My Dreams *

■ *Twenty Four Seven* (Virgin Records / 1999)
 PRODUCERS: JOHNNY DOUGLAS *
 ABSOLUTE **
 BRIAN RAWLING AND MARK TAYLOR ***
 TERRY BRITTEN ****
 Whatever You Need *
 All the Woman **
 When the Heartache Is Over ***
 Absolutely Nothing's Changed ****

Talk to My Heart
Don't Leave Me This Way ***
Go Ahead *
Without You **
Falling ****
I Will Be There **
Twenty Four Seven ****

UNIQUE TINA TURNER COMPACT DISC COMPILATIONS

■ *Soul Deep* (Slam Records / 1999)
> *Note*: This is also a British album called *Simply Tina*, which contains the first ten tracks only. These songs are previously unreleased cuts from the same era as the sessions that yielded Tina's country & western album, *Tina Turns the Country On.*

Lay It Down
Lovin' Him Was Easier
Good Hearted Woman
If This Is Our Last Time
Stand by Your Man
Freedom to Stay
We Had It All
Soul Deep
If It's Alright with You
You Ain't Woman Enough to Take My Man
Raise Your Hand
Golden Empire

■ *Tina Turner Dues Paid,* Volume One (Frank Music Records / 1999)
> *Note:* This is a compilation album from 1970s sessions.

You Took a Trip
Put Some Time Into It
I Had a Notion
Lean on Me
Stay with Me
Pick Me Up
Never Been to Spain
Stormy Weather

Trying to Find My Mind
It's Too Late
What's on a Woman's Mind
Woke Up This Morning
I Don't Want Nobody Why I Sing the Blues

■ *All That Glitters* (Virgin Records / 2000)
Note: This album is a seven-track disc that was only available at Target stores in the United States. It is the only place that Tina's solo recording of Prince's "Baby I'm a Star" appears. The disc also includes some unique live performances.
Baby I'm a Star
Let's Stay Together
Private Dancer
What's Love Got to Do With It
When the Heartache Is Over (Live)
Hold on I'm Coming (Live)
The Best (edit)

TINA TURNER: APPEARANCES ON OTHER ALBUMS

All This and World War II, Various Artists (Twentieth Century Records / 1976)
"Come Together" by Tina Turner
Tommy [Original Soundtrack] (Polydor Records / 1975)
"The Acid Queen" by Tina Turner
Summer Lovers [Original Soundtrack] (Warner Brothers Records / 1982)
"Johnny & Mary" by Tina Turner
"Crazy in the Night" by Tina Turner
The Tom Jones Show—Live in Vancouver by Tom Jones (Koch Records 1981)
"Hot Legs" by Tom Jones & Tina Turner
Rod Stewart Absolutely Live by Rod Stewart (Warner Brothers Records / 1982)
"Stay with Me" by Rod Stewart, Kim Carnes, and Tina Turner
Music of Quality and Distinction by BEF (Virgin Records / 1982)
"Ball of Confusion" by Tina Turner
Miami Vice [TV Soundtrack] by Various Artists (MCA Records / 1985)
"Better Be Good to Me" by Tina Turner

We Are the World for Africa (Columbia Records / 1986)
> "We Are the World" by Tina Turner, Michael Jackson, The Pointer Sisters, Bruce Springsteen, Lionel Richie, etc.
> "Total Control" by Tina Turner

Mad Max Beyond Thunderdome [Original Soundtrack] (EMI Capitol Records / 1986)
> "We Don't Need Another Hero" by Tina Turner
> "One of the Living" by Tina Turner

The Best of Cool Yule by Various Artists (Rhino Records / 1988)
> "Merry Christmas Baby" by Ike & Tina Turner

Vagabond Heart by Rod Stewart (Warner Brothers Records / 1991)
> "It Takes Two" by Rod Stewart and Tina Turner

Two Rooms, Various Artists (Polydor Records / 1991)
> "The Bitch Is Back" by Tina Turner

Goldeneye [Original Soundtrack] (Capitol / EMI Records / 1996)
> "Goldeneye" by Tina Turner

Diana Princess of Wales Tribute (Columbia Records / 1997)
> "Love Is a Beautiful Thing" by Tina Turner

Carnival! Various Artists (RCA Records / 1997)
> "Row, Row, Row Your Boat" by Tina Turner

Eros by Eros Ramazzotti (BMG Records / 1998)
> "Cose Della Vita" by Tina Turner and Eros Ramazzotti [Europe only]

Ultimate Divas (Arista Records / 1999)
> "What's Love Got to Do With It" by Tina Turner

Elton John and Tim Rice's Aida (Polygram Records / 1999)
> "Easy as Life" by Tina Turner

Divas Live '99, Various Artists (Arista Records / 1999)
> "The Best" by Tina Turner
> "The Bitch Is Back" by Tina Turner and Elton John
> "Proud Mary" by Tina Turner, Elton John, and Cher

The Best of Bond . . . James Bond 007 by Various Artists (Capitol / EMI Records / 2000)
> "Goldeneye" by Tina Turner

TINA TURNER: SOLO SINGLES

> River Deep-Mountain High / I'll Keep You
> May 1966 (London HLU 10046)

The Acid Queen / Rockin' & Rollin'
January 1976 (UA UP 36043)

Root Toot Undisputable Rock & Roller / Fire Down Below
February 1979 (UA UP 36485)

Sometimes When We Touch / Earthquake and Hurricane
April 1979 (UA UP 36513)

I See Home / Backstabbers / Just a Little Lovin' (Early in the Morning) / You Got What I'm Gonna Get / On the Radio
September 1979 (UA UAG 30267)

Backstabbers / Sunset on Sunset
November 1979 (UA BP 322)

Tina Turner with BEF
Ball of Confusion / Ball of Confusion (Instrumental)
May 1982 (Virgin VS 500)

Let's Stay Together / I Wrote a Letter
November 1983 (EMI/Capitol CL 316)

Help! / Rock & Roll Widow
February 1984 (EMI/Capitol CL 325)

What's Love Got to Do With It / Don't Rush the Good Things
June 1984 (EMI/Capitol CL 334)

Better Be Good to Me / When I Was Young
September 1984 (EMI/Capitol CL 338)

Private Dancer / Nutbush City Limits (Live)
December 1984 (EMI/Capitol CL 343)

I Can't Stand the Rain / Let's Pretend We're Married
February 1985 (EMI/Capitol CL 352)

We Don't Need Another Hero (*Thunderdome*) / We Don't Need Another Hero (Instrumental)
July 1985 (EMI/Capitol CL 364)

One of the Living / One of the Living (Dub version)
September 1985 (EMI/Capitol CL 364)

Typical Male / Don't Turn Around
1986 (EMI Capitol Records)

Two People
1986 (EMI/Capitol Records)

Addicted to Love
March 1988 (EMI/Capitol CDCL 484)

Tonight (live, with David Bowie) / River Deep-Mountain High (live)
June 1988 (EMI/Capitol Records)

The Best / Undercover Agent for the Blues
August 1989 (EMI/Capitol CDCL 543)

Steamy Windows / Ask Me How I Feel
October 1989 (EMI/Capitol)

I Don't Wanna Lose You
December 1989 (Capitol CDCL 553)

Look Me in the Heart
August 1990 (EMI CDCLX 584)

Be Tender with Me Baby
October 1990 (Capitol CDCL 593)

It Takes Two (with Rod Stewart) / Hot Legs (with Rod Stewart)
November 1990 (WEA ROD 1CD)

Nutbush City Limits (1990s version) / Nutbush City Limits (studio version) / Nutbush City Limits (live)
August 1991 (Capitol CDCL 630)

Way of the World
October 1991 (Capitol CDCL 637)

Love Thing / Nutbush City Limits (studio version) / I'm a Lady
January 1992 (Capitol CDCL 644)

I Want You Near Me
June 1992 (Capitol CDCLS 659)

I Don't Wanna Fight
May 1993 (Virgin/EMI CDRS 6346)

Why Must We Wait Until Tonight
July 1993 (Virgin/EMI CDRS 6366)

Disco Inferno
October 1993 (Virgin/EMI)

Proud Mary (U.S. version) / Proud Mary (Live) / We Don't Need Another Hero (Live) / The Best (Live)
November 1993 (Virgin) from the soundtrack album

Golden Eye (Single Edit) / Golden Eye (A/C Mix) / Golden Eye (Urban A/C Mix) / Golden Eye (Club Edit)
October 1995 (EMI/Virgin)

Whatever You Want / Unfinished Sympathy / Golden Eye (Single Edit)
February 1996 (EMI Parlophone) [European single]

On Silent Wings / Private Dancer / Do Something / I Don't Wanna Lose You
May 1996 (EMI Parlophone) [European single]

Missing You / Something Beautiful Remains
July 1996 (EMI Parlophone) [Eurpean single]

Missing You
August 1996 (Virgin) [U.S. and Canada single]

Something Beautiful Remains
September 1996 (EMI/Virgin)

Tom Jones and Tina Turner
Hot Legs (Tom Jones and Tina Turner) / All by Myse (Tom Jones)
October 1996 (Koch Records) [European single]

In Your Wildest Dreams (with Barry White) / In Your Wildest
    Dreams (with Antonio Banderas)
November 1996 (EMI/Virgin)

When I Was Young / What's Love Got to Do With It (Extended
    Version) / Better Be Good to Me (Extended Version) / I Can't
    Stand the Rain (Extended Version)
March 1997 (EMI / Capitol Records)

Cose della Vita (Can't Stop Thinking of You) (Tina Turner and
    Eros Ramazzotti) / Taxi Story (Eros Ramazotti)
March 1998 (BMG) [Europe and South America]

When the Heartache Is Over
October 1999 (EMI/Parlophone) [European single]

Whatever You Need / The Best (Live in London '99) / River Deep-
    Mountain High (Live in London '99) / Whatever You Need
    (Quicktime video)
January 2000 (Parlophone) [European single]

When the Heartache Is Over
February 2000 (Virgin) (vinyl single, U.S. release)

Don't Leave Me This Way / The Best (Live in London '99) / River
    Deep-Mountain High (Live in London '99)
February 2000 (EMI Electrola) [German single]

filmography

Gimme Shelter (1970)
  Tina Turner: Herself
Taking Off (1971)
  Tina Turner: Cameo Role
That Was Rock (1984)
  Tina Turner: Herself
Tommy (1975)
  Tina Turner: The Acid Queen
Sgt. Pepper's Lonely Heart's Club Band (1978)
  Tina Turner: Guest Star at the Finale
Mad Max Beyond Thunderdome (1985)
  Tina Turner: Aunty Entity
What's Love Got to Do With It? (1993)
  Tina Turner: Herself in final sequence
Last Action Hero (1993)
  Tina Turner: The Mayor

TINA TURNER: VIDEOS, CONCERT VIDEOS, AND DVDS

Tina Turner Live: Nice 'n' Rough
MC 2014
1982 EMI Records Ltd.

Private Dancer: The Videos
1984 EMI Records Ltd.

Tina Live: Private Dancer Tour
Picture Music International 7243 4 91308 3 8
1985/1994 EMI Records Ltd.

What You See Is What You Get
MVR 99 0069 2

Break Every Rule: The Videos
1986 EMI Records Ltd.

Break Every Rule (Live)
Castle Music Video 1091
1987 Zenith Productions LTD.

Foreign Affair: The Videos
MVR 99 0087 3
1989 EMI Records Ltd.

Do You Want Some Action . . . ? / Foreign Affair Live Barcelona 1990
1991 EMI Records Ltd.

Simply the Best
1991 Capitol Records Inc. / EMI

The Girl from Nutbush
Interviews and Videos
1991 EMI Records Ltd.

Tina: What's Love Got to Do With It?
Starring Angela Bassett and Laurence Fishburne
Based upon *I, Tina* by Tina Turner and Kurt Loder
1993 Touchstone Home Video

"What's Love" Live 1993
Taped in San Bernardino

"Wildest Dreams" Live 1996
Taped in Amsterdam

Celebrate!: 60th Birthday Special
Taped in London
1999 Image Entertainment

Tina: One Last Time Live
Taped in London
2000 Image Entertainment

Tina Turner: Simply the Best—The Video Collection
2002 Capitol Records

Twenty Four Seven Concert Tour Set List
    (Debuting on stage March 23, 2000)

    I Want to Take You Higher
    Absolutely Nothing's Changed
    A Fool in Love
    Acid Queen
    River Deep-Mountain High
    We Don't Need Another Hero
    Get Back
    Better Be Good to Me
    I Heard It through the Grapevine
    Private Dancer
    Let's Stay Together
    What's Love Got to Do With It
    When the Heartache Is Over
    Baby I'm a Star (performed by Tina's back-up girls)
    Help!
    Whatever You Need
    Try a Little Tenderness (with John Miles)
    Hold On, I'm Coming
    The Best
  (Intro to the band)
    Proud Mary
    Nutbush City Limits
    Twenty Four Seven

GRAMMY AWARDS

1971 Best Rhythm & Blues Performance by a Duo or a Group: "Proud Mary"

1984 Record of the Year: *What's Love Got to Do With It*

1984 Best Pop Vocal Performance: "What's Love Got to Do With It"

1984 Best Rock Vocal Performance, Female: "Better Be Good to Me"

1985 Best Rock Vocal Performance, Female: "One of the Living"

1986 Best Rock Vocal Performance, Female: "Back Where You Started"

1988 Best Rock Vocal Performance, Female: *Tina Live in Europe* (album)

index

About the Author

Mark Bego is the author of several best-selling books on rock & roll and show business. With forty-five books published and more than ten million books in print, he is acknowledged as the best-selling biographer in the rock and pop music field. His biographies have included the life stories of some of the biggest stars of rock, soul, pop, and country. His first Top 10 *New York Times* best-seller was *Michael!* about Michael Jackson (1984). Since that time he has written about the lives of *Cher!* (2001), *Rock Hudson: Public & Private* (1986), *Aretha Franklin: Queen of Soul* (1989), *Jewel* (1998), *Madonna: Blonde Ambition* (2000), *Bette Midler: Still Divine* (2002), and *Bonnie Raitt Still In The Nick of Time* (2003).

In the 1990s Bego has branched out into country music books, writing *Country Hunks* (1994), *Country Gals* (1995), *I Fall to Pieces: The Music and the Life of Patsy Cline* (1995), *Alan Jackson: Gone Country* (1996), *George Strait: The Story of Country's Living Legend* (1997), *LeAnn Rimes* (1998), and *Vince Gill* (2000).

Bego has coauthored books with several rock stars including Martha Reeves *Dancing in the Street, Confessions of a Motown Diva,* which spent five weeks on the *Chicago Tribune* Best Seller list in

1994. He worked with Micky Dolenz of the Monkees (*I'm a Believer*, 1993), Jimmy Greenspoon of Three Dog Night (*One Is the Loneliest Number*, 1991), and Mary Wilson (*Dreamgirl: My Life as a Supreme*, 2000 edition).

His writing has also been featured in several record albums and compact disks. In 1982 he wrote the interior notes to the Columbia House five-record boxed set, The Motown Collection. His liner notes can also be found in the Mary Wilson CD *Walk the Line* (1992).

In 1998 Mark wrote books about three of the hottest leading men in late 1990s cinema. His *Leonardo DiCaprio: Romantic Hero* spent six weeks on the *New York Times* Best Seller list. He followed it up with *Matt Damon: Chasing a Dream* and *Will Smith: The Freshest Prince*. He has also written about the lives of actresses in *The Linda Gray Story* (1988) and *Julia Roberts: America's Sweetheart* (2003).

In 1998 Melitta Coffee launched *Mark Bego: Romantic Hero* blend coffee as part of their Celebrity Series. He is currently developing his book *Rock & Roll Almanac* (1995) into a television series. Mark divides his time between New York City, Los Angeles, and Tucson, Arizona.

Visit his website at www.markbego.com.